W9-CAM-422

Is There Hope for Uncle Sam?

*For Cathy & Eric,
thanks. Jan NP*

Is There Hope for Uncle Sam?

Beyond the American Bubble

JAN NEDERVEEN PIETERSE

ZED BOOKS
London & New York

Is There Hope for Uncle Sam? Beyond the American Bubble was first published in 2008 by Zed Books Ltd, 7 Cynthia Street, London N1 9JF, UK and Room 400, 175 Fifth Avenue, New York, NY 10010, USA

www.zedbooks.co.uk

Copyright © Jan Nederveen Pieterse 2008

The right of Jan Nederveen Pieterse to be identified as the author of this work has been asserted by him in accordance with the Copyright, Designs and Patents Act, 1988

Designed and typeset in Monotype Jansen by illuminati, www.illuminatibooks.co.uk

Cover designed by Andrew Corbett

Printed and bound in Malta by Gutenberg Press Ltd

Distributed in the USA exclusively by Palgrave Macmillan, 175 Fifth Avenue, New York, NY 10010, USA

All rights reserved. No part of this publication may be reproduced, stored in a retrieval system or transmitted in any form or by any means, electronic, mechanical, photocopying or otherwise, without the prior permission of Zed Books Ltd.

A catalogue record for this book is available from the British Library
Library of Congress Cataloging in Publication Data available

ISBN 978 1 84813 022 7 Hb
ISBN 978 1 84813 023 4 Pb

Contents

Acknowledgements

EARLIER VERSIONS of Chapters 4–7 have been published in journals and presented at universities in Australia, Britain, China, Germany, India, Japan, Pakistan, South Africa, Sweden, Thailand, and the United States. All the material has been rewritten and rearranged. An early version of Chapter 4 appeared in *Asian Review* (16, 2003), Bangkok; Chapter 5 appeared in *Third World Quarterly* (27(6), 2006) and a short version in *Historically Speaking, Bulletin of the Historical Society*; and Chapter 6 in *Review of International Political Economy* (14(3), 2007). Amit Prasad encouraged me to put my reflections together on whether the United States can correct itself in an article that appeared in *Cultural Studies – Critical Methodologies* (4(2), 2004) and *World Affairs*.

The cartoon that appears as a frontispiece on p. ii is by Elliott Banfield, and originally appeared in the *Claremont Review of Books* in fall 2003 (as an illustration alongside Thomas S. Hibbs, 'Angst, American Style,' a review of George Cotkin's *Existential America*). I thank Elliott Banfield for permission to reproduce his drawing. The cartoon that appears on page 93 is by Mike Luckovich and originally appeared in the *Atlanta Journal–Constitution* and *New York Times* on February 15, 2004. I thank Creators Syndicate for permission to reproduce this cartoon.

A book like this arises out of many conversations. Over the years I have benefitted from inspiring conversations with Nezar AlSayyad, Luciano d'Andrea, Patrick Brantlinger, Steve Brechin, Sharron Coeurvie, Kathy Cox, Norman Denzin, Jan Ekecrantz, Hadi Esfahani, Carl Estabrook, Richard Falk, Jaap van Ginneken, Peter Gowan, Amit Gupta, Frank Hirtz, Habib Khondker, Niamh King, Ed Kolodziej, Anand Kumar, Bruce Lambert, Lauren Langman, Ronald Lipschutz, Siddharth Mallavarapu, Arthur Mitzman, Bhikhu Parekh, Michael Pollock, Doug Rokke, Mark Rupert, Dan Schiller, Hermann Schwengel, David Slater, Manfred Steger, Clinton Stockwell, Howard Wachtel, Michael Watts, Philip Wheaton, David Wilson, and many other colleagues and seminar participants. My special thanks go to those who also commented on earlier versions of the text: Lisa Chason, Amit Prasad, Fazal Rizvi, Kim Scipes and referees of journal articles. I particularly thank Ellen McKinlay of Zed Books for her helpful comments. I also thank graduate students at the University of Illinois Urbana–Champaign, the University of Freiburg and the Global Studies Program, and Chulalongkorn University in Bangkok, among others Ravi Ghadge, Jae Kim, Jongtae Kim, and Erik Taylor. The usual disclaimer applies. For the title I thank Manfred Steger and Italian colleagues who convinced me that people relate better to the personification of a nation than to a state as an abstract entity.

A Study in Decline

SURELY IT IS POSSIBLE to be magnanimous about countries. It means viewing a country in its most generous expressions, highlighting its attractive features, valuing its idiosyncrasies as appealing eccentricities, viewing its constraints in light of its ideals and aspirations, and giving it the benefit of the doubt when it comes to its dark pages and the dilemmas it faces. Of course this is possible in the case of the United States. Indeed, admiring America has a much longer lineage than anti-Americanism. It goes back to the sixteenth-century idea of the 'new Golden Land,' includes French thinkers from Tocqueville to Sartre and Baudrillard, Soviet leaders from Lenin to Khrushchev who admired American industrial and technological prowess, and Gramsci, who admired high American wages in manufacturing, hence the theme of Fordism. Many, from Fidel Castro to Hugo Chávez, point out that they have no problem with the United States but only with American policies.

A generous perspective on the United States avoids predictable anti-Americanism. For progressives the world over the American Revolution, American social movements, and Wilsonian ideals have served as beacons, and for elites as threats – if we bracket the other United States of slavery, manifest destiny and hegemony. Gradually, particularly since the Reagan administration, this relationship has reversed and the United States has become an ogre for progressives and a guiding light for corporate elites and governments.

Introducing his book *After the Empire*, the French demographer Emmanuel Todd gives an extensive account of his sympathies for the United States before launching his critiques of American empire. American critics don't need such qualifications; they can look at the US from a people's point of view rather than government, corporate or technocratic viewpoints. Thus Howard Zinn's *People's History of America* and Benjamin Barber's work are part of the tradition of American active democracy, at times populist, radical or reform minded. And at times reform has prevailed, as in the New Deal and civil rights legislation.

No matter the qualifications, talking about a nation is inevitably essentializing and generalizing. The main justification for doing so in this case is that American discourse so often essentializes the United States and presents it as a beacon to the world (as in the 'freedom agenda').

This is not a book in the 'rogue nation' mould; nor is it a variation on the 'why people hate America' theme. I doubt people hate America; people have better things to do. Across the world many enjoy American music, movies and popular culture, use American technology and admire American democracy, at any rate the ideal if not the practice. Yet I don't follow the magnanimous approach to the United States. First, it is simply unnecessary. There is enough America boosterism to go around – self-congratulations in a country that organizes 'World Series' without international participation and claims world leadership while it translates fewer foreign books than any advanced country. American power is often overestimated also internationally. Second, the United States has not typically been magnanimous, particularly in its relations with weaker countries, as in its everlasting embargo of Cuba.

There are two more specific reasons why I don't opt for this approach. One is that social inequality in the US has been growing steadily and produces social pathologies such as growing child poverty, 37 million below the poverty line and many more near poverty, 47 million without health insurance, and 2.4 million incarcerated. Hurricane Katrina showed the world this face of America. The second problem is American hegemony. The two are related; if the United States can't get its own house in order, its claims to world leadership are shaky. Even if one leaves social inequality as a problem for Americans to sort out (and bid goodbye to the American Dream) the problem of hegemony remains. Entrenched as it is in American power structures, the American claim to world power will not easily go away. It has become an American habitus that comes with path dependence on the security apparatus, including high-risk operations with limited electoral penalty.

This is not another book about the neoconservatives. Take the neoconservatives out of the equation and dismiss them from public office and the problems remain. It makes more sense to focus on the trends that *enable* the neoconservatives, such as the American bubble (discussed in Chapter 1) and thirty-five years of backlash politics and backlash culture (Chapter 3). Focusing on the neoconservatives exaggerates how distinctive their positions are. In fact the differences between realists, liberal hawks, and neoconservatives are negligible; their positions all turn on muscular moralism. The spotlight on the neoconservatives diverts the attention from the liberals and liberal hawks that represent the mainstream of Washington and American public opinion. The real problem is that American liberalism has become a liberalism of power in which democracy is reified and liberal values and human rights are used as tools of intervention, which is taken up in Chapter 6.

The United States is an intriguing case study of contemporary power. With Europe and Japan it shares the chauvinism of prosperity. It differs in greater cultural diversity (as an immigrant society) and a level of social inequality that rather parallels Latin America.

It is the last of the great powers to display nationalist bombast and it stands apart in its posture and pathos of global leadership.

In recent years the idea of American decline is gradually becoming commonplace. It poses two questions: what form will decline take and what does decline mean? This study focuses on how key American problems – social inequality and hegemony – and the American economy interact and precipitate American decline. It poses decline as a script that needs unpacking. Will decline be just that or will it be a source of hope and regeneration, in particular the hope that it will make the US a 'normal country'?

I don't think the classic image of economic crisis in the sense of Marx applies any longer. There are regional and sectoral crises but the nineteenth-century image of crisis as total breakdown has become unlikely. Constant adjustments make system crash less likely. Capitalism survives due to the biodiversity and interaction of *capitalisms*. Reserves in different parts of the world are marshaled to forestall a total breakdown and the interweaving of economies is both an incentive and a resource to forestall the total collapse of a leading economy. Crisis, then, should be disaggregated: whose crisis, which crisis?

A plausible option is the continuing social decline of the United States – with more home foreclosures, more financial family crises due to lack of health insurance, more homeless, more incarcerated, fewer entering college, and more bridges collapsing. All this can take place while corporate profits and Wall Street stocks rise and the Pentagon budget continues to expand. This would mean that decline takes the form of the normalization of the multi-speed economy that is already in place. Indeed these trends are correlated. When corporations downsize and workers are sacked, stocks rise and CEO remuneration soars. The power structure of the gilded age is being reproduced with stepped-up policing to guard the boundaries between the spheres of the economy.

But the health of the economy is at risk. Like all advanced economies the US has become a service economy, but, unlike other advanced societies, the US has undergone this transition without a national economic strategy, even though managing this transition needs active government that promotes education, inward investment, innovation, and productivity rather than simply rewarding offshoring. Instead, laissez-faire government driven by a borrower–service complex and an oil–military complex pushes the nation to war and the economy to the brink. Leading banks, defense contractors, and multinationals may prosper, but can American consumer purchasing power survive and, without consumer power driving the economy, how long will American power last?

The literature on the US is huge, particularly now, so let me indicate how this book differs from others. As a sociologist and originally an anthropologist, I adopt a kaleidoscopic perspective. I'm not only interested in politics and geopolitics but as much in culture and society, political economy and finance, and in viewing ongoing trends in the context of long-term changes and how oscillating trends form a cultural ensemble. 'Uncle Sam' represents such a moving assemblage. As a European living in the US I seek to understand the American political and cultural ambience. I came to the US from Amsterdam, the Netherlands, to take up a professorship in global sociology at an American university a week after September 11, 2001. I lived in the US as a graduate student during the early Reagan years in 1981 to 1984. The years since September 11 have been tense and exasperating for Americans and for the world. The jest of citizens of other nations seeking a vote in the American presidential elections, because American futures shape theirs, applies more than ever, unless they would rather give up on American futures altogether.

A vital question is whether the United States is able to correct its course or whether correction will come from outside. The key problems are social inequality, hegemony, and the economy, which, in turn, are embedded in the American bubble, the collective cocoon of the American public sphere and the cultural continuum of American common sense. Chapter 1 reviews the American public

sphere and argues that the American bubble and the national entertainment state media dim and flatten American self-awareness. By
problematizing American clichés the book seeks to open a window
'beyond the American bubble.'

Chapter 2 deals with social inequality, including the cultural
politics and economic explanations of inequality. Since the economic explanations of growing social inequality are insufficient,
Chapter 3 explores a political explanation. This chapter considers
the American right-wing turn since about 1980, including the shift
of Southern Democrats to the Republican Party, the break-up of
the liberal coalition, conservative campaigns, the deregulation of
corporations and the consolidation of 'Permanent Washington.'
Another source of growing inequality is the financialization of the
American economy.

In a previous study, *Globalization or Empire?*, I argue that the
Reagan administration built on the 'Southern strategy' of corporations moving from the northeast to the low-wage, low-tax, anti-
union American South and Southwest and turned Dixie capitalism
into the national norm. IMF and World Bank structural adjustment
policies, accompanying American multinationals moving to low-
wage countries from Mexico to Asia, made it the international
norm. Here I take the thesis of Dixie capitalism further to Dixie
politics. Driving forces of this period were a cultural backlash
against the rebelliousness of the 1960s and a political backlash
against Democrats, which converged in a politics of disciplining
society by unleashing market forces in tandem with strong law
and order. By 'governing through the market,' not merely Dixie
capitalism but Dixie politics became the norm during thirty-five
years of Republican sway. The key problem, then, is not the neoliberal doctrines of the Chicago School but the cultural and political revanchism of conservatives who sought to use market forces
for political ends, except that in the process market forces gave
society an extreme makeover and walked off with the winnings.
The main problem is not the neoconservatives but the conservatives

and their economic and demographic power base in the South, which over time has culminated in an alliance of conservatives and neoconservatives; this has run its course, as the elections of 2006 and 2008 show.

Chapters 4–6 discuss the problems of hegemony; each chapter zeroes in on a specific problem. Chapter 4 takes up the idea of benevolent hegemony that is upheld by advocates of American power. The claim that hegemony stabilizes world order and the world economy has already been examined in hegemonic stability theory. This chapter resumes these debates to see whether the major justifications of hegemony apply now.

Chapter 5 examines the two main hypotheses that seek to explain hegemony – is it an expression of capitalism or a demonstration of power? From the viewpoint of flexible and increasingly deterritorialized capitalism, does empire matter or is it a costly liability? Are the new wars an expression of American capitalism or do they reflect a superpower syndrome and path dependence on the national security state? In a previous book I discussed *neoliberal empire* or the merger of neoliberalism and hegemony and argued that it is an unstable, contradictory project. War is business but can a lean state run an empire by using marketing ploys? A dark side of the new wars is the extraordinarily high civilian casualty rates in Iraq and Afghanistan, which occur at the confluence of the United States seeking land power on a distant continent, the tendency to view countries as strategic real estate, and the lack of cultural savvy that comes with the American bubble.

Chapter 6 poses American liberals, rather than neoconservatives, as a problem and examines the liberalism of power. The reality test of liberal views is how political aims are interpreted and implemented by security professionals. Hegemony is layered and its hidden transcripts are profoundly different from the public declarations of freedom and democracy. Inner circles of the security apparatus may promote instability and chaos as levers in politics of tension and strategies of brinkmanship. A different question is whether American laissez-faire economic policies, too, can be viewed as brinkmanship at a time when exports become imports, the trade deficit deepens, income inequality widens, and external deficits rise to unsustainable levels.

Chapter 7 turns to the central question: is the balance of forces such that the United States, short of undergoing a major economic and political crisis, can chart a significantly different course? Domestically this would mean reinventing New Deal politics and internationally a return to genuine constructive multilateralism. We come back to the main problems facing Uncle Sam – growing inequality, hegemony, and the economy – and consider three scenarios of American decline: crash-landing, the Phoenix, and a new New Deal. Meanwhile, as the closing chapter argues, a new global balance is already taking shape. In 2006 I visited six Asian countries to gain a sense of the contours of the new globalization that is taking shape and how it is experienced in emerging societies. Together with earlier visits to South Africa, Brazil and other countries, this gives a sense of dynamics that are unfolding far from and far beyond the American bubble. It is not the worries of a waning hegemon that shape times to come but the dynamics unfolding among the rising forces. The closing chapter turns another page.

ONE

The American Bubble

JUST AS POETS AND PHILOSOPHERS fashion themselves a 'metaphorical body,' a metaphorical expression of their chosen selves,[1] so do nations through the narratives of identity that media, plays, novels, musicals, educators, and politicians tell. Nations as 'imagined communities' are sustained and re-created through narratives that tune legacies to novel conditions. We relate to nations not directly but through the aura of their collective attitudes. Before the Second World War this used to be assiduously studied as 'national character,' but in our fleeting postmodern times this consistency no longer exists, to the extent that it ever did, and with multiculturalism and globalization national boundaries and identities have blurred at the edges.

We relate to the United States through Uncle Sam's metaphorical body, the narratives that Americans tell each other and the world about the United States. Since American history is based on multiple ruptures of intercontinental migration, settler colonialism, and anti-colonial revolution, these narratives claim American exceptionalism. The US is larger than most countries and geographically insular so its social field takes the form of a self-referential cocoon. These factors (rupture, remoteness, size) produce an American bubble.

The American bubble is a discursive comfort zone, a cultural continuum that constructs American identities as it reflects them. Because the bubble is an echo chamber it tends to be self-reinforcing, and as a hall of mirrors it reflects images back to Americans. The bubble, of course, is not seamless or static. There are bubbles within the bubble, from the Washington press corps to sports enthusiasts, yet most subcultures share the cultural continuum except minority and bohemian subcultures, which exist in part outside the bubble. Native American and African-American subcultures exist in part in friction with the bubble; rap and hip-hop play on these frictions. In middle America the bubble may feel comfortable like air conditioning, whereas at America's peripheries it may feel alienating. Because of these frictions and external influences the bubble is continually changing. The bubble is layered with high narratives of national purpose and flows of popular culture; to several themes there is both a high articulation and a lowbrow version. The bubble is movable; Americans can travel abroad without leaving the bubble just as they can hop between Sheraton or Hilton hotels in different countries while remaining tuned to CNN or MSNBC. Exporting the bubble, however, is extremely difficult. The claim to exceptionalism is both the foundation for the American sense of mission to transform the world and its limit, for the historical conditions that generated American projects don't exist elsewhere. The combination of the island effect of the bubble, narcissistic media, and the claim to world leadership creates a peculiar friction. A central American paradox is that the United States, wired to yet cut off from globalization, undertakes the mission impossible to guide and 'control' globalization.

This chapter gives an overview of themes in the American public sphere to set the stage for the discussions that follow. I devote vignettes to components of the American bubble such as the relative absence of the social, the influence of corporations, hegemony talk, the Israel lobby, the iconization of the military, and the inward-looking character of debate. The second part turns to the frictions that arise when the American bubble is exported and viewed from the outside.

In the Bubble

What happened to society?

Tocqueville praised the civic voluntarism of American society, yet what is striking now is the relative absence of the social in the American public sphere. Communities are abundantly present, such as civic groups and victims of hurricanes or floods, and individuals are amply represented, such as celebrities, CEOs, contestants in competitions or natural disaster victims, but many representations of social and civic life that are commonplace in most countries are rare in the US. This first shows in the relative absence of the voices of labor and trade unions. In European countries when there are major labor disputes the voices represented in media typically include trade unions, employers, and government. Often workers are interviewed directly. This reflects the nature of European social contracts. In American media often only the employers' point of view is reported. American newspapers let go of their labor reporters decades ago and many labor disputes go unreported and remain local, with groups of workers picketing on the pavement. Union membership has shrunk to 7.4 percent of workers in the private sector and 12 percent overall (compare Italy with a union membership of 53 percent and France with 33 percent). The demobilization of labor has come in stages, from the gilded age dominance of business and the postwar Taft–Hartley Act that restricted the right to strike, to the Reagan administration's firing of striking air-traffic controllers. Unions in the US are more fragmented than in Europe and union federations are weaker. A major failure of the union movement has been to neglect organizing workers in the service sector, which are now the largest segment of the workforce.[2]

Another feature of the American public sphere is the marginality of social movements and activists. In many countries social movements are a visible, vocal and vibrant part of civil society, articulating social demands and occupying significant space on the public stage. In the US this was the case during the 1960s, but is now no longer, with occasional exceptions. When social organizations organize major festivals or concerts they may be cursorily mentioned in news reports. Thus the nationwide movement against the Iraq war has gone virtually unreported. Major demonstrations in Washington have been cursorily covered and Cindy Sheehan's protest actions near President Bush's ranch in Crawford, Texas, were reported, but otherwise Americans would hardly know that there is an anti-war movement, a movement that holds monthly demonstrations (weekly at an earlier stage of the war) in many cities and towns, a movement that is regionally and nationally coordinated, but is not given a public platform and hence isn't part of American collective awareness. Because of lack of recognition on the public platform, movements and citizens in the US don't find resonance and thus barely know themselves. This absence of recognition has itself become routinized, as has the wonderment of activists upon finding out their massive numbers at the occasional Washington demo.

The social ambience was quite different in the 1960s when civil rights, student, anti-war, women's, and environmental movements were a vibrant part of America that shaped the image of the US abroad. Since then social movements have become more single-issue and more preoccupied with identity politics. To some extent this has been a worldwide trend, but what is notable in the US is the way social movements are shut out of the public sphere. Media marginalize them and government ignores them as beyond the pale of polite society. The 1999 WTO meeting that joined Teamsters and Turtles in the 'battle of Seattle' was startling and unexpected, so activism momentarily landed on the front pages. But the default mode of American media is to ignore or marginalize civic activism. Heckling in public meetings leads to instant security intervention; wearing a T-shirt with a political message may lead to one's removal from a mall or public space. Public events usually take place in private spaces with private security details. Public space itself has been privatized and regimented.

The contrast with most other countries is so stark that one suspects that ignoring or suppressing popular sentiment has been a deliberate policy, which, over time, has become a public habitus. Throughout the world there has been a backlash against the protests and cultural effervescence of the 1960s. In Europe a keynote was the 'crisis of authority'; in the US the backlash against the 1960s has been far more incisive.

Commercial media represent acquisitive individualism as the default mode of social life, an image of the world in which individuals have problems (health, economic, emotional), so individual problems matter and social problems (crime, violence, drugs) matter as they impinge on the well-being of individuals, families, communities. The representation of civil rights organizations has dwindled to ceremonial occasions on Martin Luther King Day or commencement speeches; in media they have been reduced to and routinized as media personalities (such as the reverends Al Sharpton and Jesse Jackson). Consumerism, of course, looms much larger in media than in everyday life. Many ordinary Americans don't match the stereotype of possessive individualism and local community ties are often strong. But Norman Rockwell America is no more, and the social consciousness of Americans is not being nourished, replenished, or affirmed in the commercialized public sphere.

Self-censorship is routine in media culture, but in the face of new events the script occasionally surfaces. In the first month of the war in Afghanistan the chairman of CNN, Walter Isaacson, sent a memo to correspondents urging them not to pay undue attention to civilian casualties and to mention at every occasion why the war was being fought: 'it seems perverse to focus too much on the casualties or hardship in Afghanistan.'[3] In a similar vein the White House instructed federal employees and military personnel to refer to the invasion of Iraq as a 'war of liberation' and to Iraqi paramilitaries as 'death squads'[4] (until they became allies following the surge of 2006). Scripting the public sphere is an ordinary occurrence in the US.

During the Vietnam years, Noam Chomsky referred to the mandarins, the intellectuals of the state. Decades later and deep into other wars, American media are even more conservative because mistakes of the past have been corrected – body bags are no longer on display, reporters are pooled or embedded, and news events meet with 24/7 official response. Conservatism has been entrenched, honed through focus groups, fine-tuned through marketing techniques and is on the offensive with think-tank talking points and Doberman talk-show hosts. The new wars come with the voice-over of retired generals and think-tank experts. The networks are packed with experts who paraphrase official perspectives. PR techniques snugly wrap the status quo.

Media in the United States are both extraordinarily important (a large country, thinly populated, suburbanized) and extraordinarily inane. The cliché that the media are part of the problem is an understatement. Since the American media are largely commercial a public sphere in a European sense barely exists. 'The US does not just display a tendency toward private ownership of media and unregulated political content; it is likely the most extreme case in these regards among the industrial democracies.... Fairness and balance in the American media system do not mean assessing all views and preferences on a given issue, but publicizing the dominant views that are readily accessible to the press.'[5] Corporations colonize the public sphere through media. Many judgments about the US, within and outside the country, are judgments about media representations rather than direct experience. Gore Vidal's 'United States of Amnesia' and James Bovard's 'Attention Deficit

Democracy' are judgments about the American media landscape and its memory holes. Conservative American backlash culture is also to a large extent a response to media representations. A strand of conservatism such as the emphasis on 'family values' is an attempt to make up for the imbalance of market media crowding out educational media.[6]

The control of the airwaves by the media Big Six is exhaustively researched.[7] FAIR, a media analysis organization devoted to fairness and accuracy in reporting, analyzed television news broadcasts during the week before and after Colin Powell's presentation at the UN in February 2003, a fateful period in the run-up to the Iraq war.

> Looking at two weeks of coverage (1/30/03–2/12/03), FAIR examined the 393 on-camera sources who appeared in nightly news stories about Iraq on ABC World News Tonight, CBS Evening News, NBC Nightly News and PBS's News Hour with Jim Lehrer. More than two-thirds (267 out of 393) of the guests featured were from the U.S. Of the U.S. guests, a striking 75 percent (199) were either current or former government or military officials. Only one of the official U.S. sources … expressed skepticism or opposition to the war.
>
> Similarly, when both U.S. and non-U.S. guests were included, 76 percent (297 of 393) were either current or retired officials. Such a predominance of official sources virtually assures that independent and grassroots perspectives will be underrepresented. Of all official sources, 75 percent (222 of 297) were associated with the U.S. or with governments that support the Bush administration's position on Iraq; only four out of those 222, or 2 percent, of these sources were skeptics or opponents of the war.[8]

Media perform a game of mirrors, with media as the main content of media. At times also media criticism becomes an exercise in hair-splitting. Part of the bubble is radio silence amid media noise – scandal after scandal but no follow-up; in Krugman's words, a culture of cover-ups. Investigations are left to politically embedded commissions. The media report (almost) everything but do so in muffled sound bites, short of public resonance. In societies with deep public spheres, significant events are gone over in print and talked through in radio and television roundtables and public meetings; in the US these are dominated by journalists or experts. The ratio of pundits to reporters and of opinion to information is in the order of ten to one. The Washington press corps is a bubble within a bubble. For the sake of access to government sources there is no rocking the boat. What is at stake is a black market in information. Trade books spill information from inside executive power houses and are operational rather than fundamental in nature, tweaking discourses and technologies of control and recycling paradigms. Operational questions are discussed ad infinitum; fundamentals (why, to what end?) rarely come up. In bookshops the politics shelf is three times the size of any non-fiction section, followed by business and management books. The American public sphere is long on politics and short on society.

With this comes a thoroughly bourgeois outlook and firm policing of the bounds of polite society. American media talk is for the college-educated. What once was the dog squad is now the 'canine unit,' under the skin is 'subcutaneous,' and thirst is now 'dehydration.' The *New York Times* may feature global warming by reporting on the problems it poses for restaurant chefs to fill their menus because some items are difficult to obtain. In the barbershop a haircut has become a 'precision trim.'

National Public Radio (NPR) reports in a style designed for a college-educated audience, presented with controlled diction, stripped of emotion, careful tiptoeing to avoid 'bias,' presenting the world news for dentists. Like most government agencies under the Bush administration, NPR was placed under neoconservative management and has been subject to similar neutering campaigns to the BBC.

Taking part in the public sphere is one of life's pleasures; it takes one out of one's individual zone into a roundtable sharing of concerns. In the US, however, it means participating in the ritual polarization of Republicans and Democrats, which are supposed to represent right and left. Reports and talk shows reproduce this divide and have to be 'evenhanded,' so on most issues both left-wing and right-wing views have to be presented, which is tedious itself and troubling because it disregards whether any view is based on valid information. Besides, 'Even most of the conservative parties in Europe are to the left of the Democrats in [the US]'[9] so by international standards the American right and left are *both* on the right. This divide is reproduced throughout American culture, where there is supposed to be a right-wing and a 'liberal' view on everything. In multiparty democracies the common framework is the roundtable in which many political parties and as many viewpoints take part and world-views don't neatly align or fall in predictable patterns. This makes for a wider, more varied, and to some extent less predictable conversation and spectrum of discourse, which matches the common sense of society.

In American discourse the social is instrumentalized as 'social capital,' trivialized as expressions of civic life, ritualized in sports, churches or parent–teacher meetings, choreographed in consumer behavior, and monitored through surveys and polls, as in the shopping season's and electoral reports. Robert Putnam's reflections on *Bowling Alone* parody social life as bingo and BBQ. If the social isn't depoliticized it is aggressively co-opted, as in Karl Rove's strategy of 'energizing the Republican base' by using wedge issues such as abortion and gay rights. The neutering and depoliticization of the social – the absence of labor and social movements and the stilted bent to public life – is so routine and ordinary that for many Americans it goes unnoticed.

Corporation nation

When a European court upheld the European Commission's antitrust charges against Microsoft in September 2007, the chief of the US Department of Justice antitrust division pontificated: 'In the US, the antitrust laws are enforced to protect consumers by protecting competition, not competitors,'[10] implying that the ruling would harm consumers and clearly adopting the corporate line, a reaction that the European Commission, in turn, deemed 'totally unacceptable.'

It is a cliché that the American political climate and legal conventions are far more pro-business than anywhere in the world with the exception of offshore tax havens. American society is a sweet deal for corporations, a labyrinth of arrangements crafted by corporations/special interests/lobbyist/lawyers/Congress. Under the heady motto of 'free enterprise competition' a byzantine grid of cartels prevails. Unlike anywhere else in the world one can hardly buy a mobile phone without a two-year service contract (and substandard services). Many Internet providers have local monopolies, services are expensive, and broadband speed is below international standards. Banks offer minimal services. Paying in shops even for the simplest services is lengthy; each state charges different sales tax, so beyond the marked price one has to pay taxes charged at the cash register, so no one knows in advance what to pay.

Where else in the world is government prohibited from negotiating drug prices with pharmaceuticals, as in the American Medicaid system? Health care and dental care are labyrinths of insurers and 'managed care.' The health-care system includes insurers, professional organizations, care providers, doctors and co-opts researchers and universities through elaborate arrangements of free samples, conference perks, free travel, and speaking fees. Marketing masquerading as education and research, using the patent system to sustain monopolies, and buying influence are part of the pharmaceuticals charade.[11]

Time and again American corporations opt for keeping established value streams going over developing new ones, to their own disadvantage. A case in point is the American auto industry and GM's electric car – a technology that was eventually developed by Toyota and other Japanese competitors after American companies had neglected it.[12] The bulky, clumsy design of many American-made products, for instance in consumer electronics and furniture, shows that the US is a sheltered market whose consumer products are not internationally competitive, apart from salient sectors such as software and movies. A third of small and medium-sized US manufacturers (which make up 99 percent of US manufacturing companies) don't sell or purchase internationally and two-thirds do less than 10 percent of their sales or purchases abroad, far less than their European counterparts. A report cautions that this insularity and lack of engagement with international markets puts these manufacturers at risk at a time when large US manufacturers derive most of their profits from overseas operations and sales.[13] US executives also 'lack a global perspective.' Even though 'most US corporate bosses are ardent supporters of globalization' few have experience abroad: 'only a third of US chief executives [in the Fortune 100] have lived or worked abroad for at least a year. In the UK, 67 percent of chief executives have had stints overseas.'[14] Thus, contrary to impressions of American corporate transnationalism, the American bubble envelops most American business too.

The superpower syndrome

In the bubble, muscular foreign policy talk is a performative standard. Policy analysts in talk shows discuss with unflinching seriousness what should be the terms for ultimatums to Iran, Syria or North Korea, or the terms of cooperation with assorted other countries.

The public is routinely primed for America's role as world arbiter. An annual theme of the syndicated *Parade* magazine, the country's largest-circulation magazine, is 'Who Are the World's Ten Worst Dictators?' in an inverse popularity contest. The list 'draws in part' on Human Rights Watch, Freedom House, Reporters without Borders and Amnesty International reports. The world's top ten worst dictators in 2004 are listed as the following: (1) Kim Jong Il, North Korea; (2) Than Shwe, Burma; (3) Hu Jintao, China; (4) Robert Mugabe, Zimbabwe; (5) Crown Prince Abdullah, Saudi Arabia; (6) Teodoro Nguema, Equatorial Guinea; (7) Omar Al-

Bashir, Sudan; (8) Saparmurat Niyazov, Turkmenistan; (9) Fidel Castro, Cuba; (10) King Mswati III, Swaziland. In subsequent years there are some newcomers, but most contestants remain the same.[15] Newcomers in 2005 include Muammar al-Qaddafi, Libya (6), and Pervez Musharraf, Pakistan (7); 2006 saw the entry of Islam Karimov, Uzbekistan (6), and Seyed Ali Khamanei, Iran (9); and in 2007, Bashar al-Assad, Syria (9) enters the list.

This exercise uses human rights as a stick, deploys liberal values for hegemonic ends, and naturalizes American moral superiority in a representation that recycles the trope of US/freedom/good versus totalitarianism/evil. It displays liberal imperialism as a cornerstone of American interventionism. The exercise is a monologue, for the American bubble is also American babble, a society engaged in nonstop conversation with itself. In mainstream media, foreign voices – other than the occasional government leader – are about as common as edelweiss in the prairie. During decades of American involvement in Iraq, how many Iraqis – other than US appointed officials – have been engaged in conversation on American media? Images of Saddam, usually brandishing a rifle, marked the lead-up to the war and after the war; images of combat and conflict have dominated. Allegedly this is about the liberation of Iraqis, but who are they?

This is not a minor point of opinion or taste; it concerns fundamentals of foreign policy and how it is conducted, and fundamentals of war and how it is waged. Underlying Uncle Sam's wars and how they are waged are abstract values such as democracy and freedom alongside profound lack of interest in or cultural affinity with other regions. This attitude has been described as a form of 'multicultural unilateralism.'

> Europe is rightly envious of America's multicultural society.… But the American multicultural model also generates an illusion.… It is always an American version of otherness that is encountered in the US. You will not necessarily learn anything about the culture and history of Vietnam by working alongside a Vietnamese doctor in the teaching

hospital at Stanford.... Foreign films account for less than 1 percent of
the American film market, and the figures are similarly low for books
and news from abroad. The impressive integrative power of American
society seems to generate a kind of obliviousness to the world, a multicultural unilateralism.[16]

This approach echoes in war-speak. 'An American soldier refers to
an Iraqi prisoner as "it". A general speaks not of "Iraqi fighters" but
of "the enemy". A weapons manufacturer doesn't talk about people
but about "targets".'[17] 'Geeks' and My Lai in Vietnam, 'towel heads'
and the massacre of Haditha, and abuses at Abu Ghraib, Guantánamo and Bagram airbase share a pattern: how does one control a
world that one isn't interested in, has zero affinity with, and sees
only through the prism of abstractions (democracy, freedom) or
through the narrow lens of geopolitics, pipelines, and the vizors
of F-16s?

The Israel lobby

In the American bubble it often seems that only two parts of the
world really matter, the United States and the Middle East. Other
regions are covered but the Middle East is on the front pages almost
daily. The habitual framework of reporting is the implicit identification of American and Israeli government viewpoints, which Anatol
Lieven calls 'the intertwining of American and Israeli nationalisms.'
This occurs at all levels and is cultural well before it is political.

The *Diary of Anne Frank* is discussed in primary school as early
as fourth grade. Schools in towns big and small organize collection
drives in malls to fund Holocaust exhibitions (I came across one
in a mall in Bloomington, Illinois). The Holocaust industry has a
vast, sprawling cultural presence that ripples through society and
makes the Holocaust the main portal through which to understand
history and relate to the world. My daughters grew up and went
to school in Amsterdam but in American culture Anne Frank is
a far greater cultural presence than in the Netherlands and plays
a different role. The Anne Frank Foundation in the Netherlands

is dedicated to anti-racism; it publishes books, organizes exhibits and takes part in debates on prejudices against minorities and immigrants and in recent years against Muslims, Moroccans, Turks, and Africans. It forms part of the politics of tolerance in the Netherlands which goes back to the seventeenth century, when people suffering religious persecution, such as Jews, Huguenots, and Pilgrims, were welcomed. In contrast, the Holocaust industry in the US is essentially concerned with anti-Semitism and Israel. Tolerance and genocide are part of its penumbra but have a second-ary cultural radius. Genocide is a label that is selectively used to target governments that the US and Israel are in conflict with, as in Darfur and Chechnya. The scrutiny of anti-Arab and anti-Muslim prejudices is parceled out to organizations such as the Anti-Arab Discrimination League.

The Holocaust industry syncs with another cultural habitus, the cult of the Second World War and America's role in it. Historians note that Americans keep fighting one war, World War II, and prefer to skip the Korean and Vietnam wars. The Second World War places the US firmly in the good camp as the liberator from evil. Thus the foundation myths of Israel (never again, redemption from evil) and of the United States as a global power are identical and increasingly (particularly since the 1967 war) reflect an elective affinity of cultural politics.

The cold-war category *totalitarianism* merged fascism and com-munism and became the anchor of American foreign policy, which Jeane Kirkpatrick fine-tuned by distinguishing between totalitarian and authoritarian governments (the difference is that with the latter there is light at the end of the tunnel). Upon the end of the cold war, Francis Fukuyama's *The End of History* concluded that since the US defeated fascism and communism there was no alternative but liberal democracy.

Efforts are made to fit every conflict within the World War II matrix. Hence the 'axis of evil,' references to Saddam Hussein as an evil dictator and as another Hitler or Stalin, and to Iran's president

Ahmadinejad as another Hitler. In the neoconservative paradigm, following Leo Strauss, threat assessment is based on the charac- ter of the regime, on its intentions rather than its capabilities. As Fareed Zakaria notes, 'Saddam was assumed to be working on a vast weapons program because he was an evil man.'[18] Hence the claim that 'American values are universal values.' To many Americans, reared in the penumbra of the Holocaust industry, this sounds quite reasonable. Thus the Afghanistan and Iraq wars are cast as 'wars for civilization,' the war on terror as 'the ideological war of our genera- tion' and as a war against 'Islamic fascism.' Paul Berman speaks of 'Muslim totalitarianism,' and Bernard Lewis, Fouad Ajami, Daniel Pipes and Christopher Hitchens hammer on 'Islamofascism,' which is gratefully echoed by neoconservative think-tanks. Given the cultural sprawl of the Holocaust industry it finds some resonance with the American public.

The American bubble is an applause culture rather than a debate culture. Debate on operational matters and details of fact and numbers is interminable; but in the scripted public sphere debate on fundamentals is a non-starter. Debate on the fundamentals of American policy in the Middle East and the relationship with Israel is off-limits. The pro-Israel consensus in Congress is 100 percent.[19] John Mearsheimer and Stephen Walt, respected mainstream politi- cal scientists, could not get an article on the influence of the Israel lobby published in an American journal, so it was published in the *London Review of Books*, where it created a major stir. When their book came out in 2007 their talks at several venues, such as the Chicago Council on Global Affairs, were cancelled. The Israel lobby exer- cises de facto veto power on American debate. Harvard law professor Alan Dershovitz successfully lobbied to have Norman Finkelstein, a well-known critical and serious scholar of the Holocaust industry, denied tenure at DePaul University and to deny the Muslim scholar Tariq Ramadan a professorship at Notre Dame University.

Consequently criticism of Israel's policies that is ordinary in Israel is taboo in the US. Books that are even mildly critical of Israel are consistently dismissed in the *New York Times Book Review*. The *New York Times*, the nation's paper of record and the newspaper of well-heeled, *bien pensant* New York society, is a consistent purveyor of pro-Israeli government perspectives and biased perspectives on the Middle East. The Anti-Defamation League publishes large ads in the *New York Times* such as:

> 38 REPORTERS ARRESTED last year in IRAN.
> And BRITISH JOURNALISTS are boycotting ISRAEL?
>
> 700 HUMAN RIGHTS ACTIVISTS DETAINED and TORTURED
> last year in ZIMBABWE.
> And BRITISH JOURNALISTS are boycotting ISRAEL?
>
> 400.000 MURDERED in DARFUR.
> And BRITISH ACADEMICS are boycotting ISRAEL?
>
> When BRITISH UNIONS single out ISRAEL for boycott...
> That's not activism. That's ANTI-SEMITISM.[20]

These ads equate criticism of Israel with anti-Semitism. They also illustrate the role of 'Darfur' and the politics of genocide. The Save Darfur organization published full-page ads in the *New York Times* targeting China for its role in the Darfur genocide.[21] Iran, Zimbabwe, and Darfur serve as lightning rods to divert criticism from Israel. The language is crass and in your face, and matches the style of the American right and the vitriol of conservative websites. The flipside of saving Israel's government from criticism is a lasting Middle East stalemate to the point of regional polarization.

Military culture

Hegemonic nations promote warrior cults. The Dutch cultivated admirals and seafarers, Britain admirals and generals, and American culture lionizes the military. In the US the military commands greater confidence than any public institution including the courts and universities. 'Americans' trust and confidence in the military has soared, even as it has declined in other institutions like corporations, churches and Congress.... In 2002, Americans who expressed a great deal or a lot of confidence in the military rose, to 79 percent from 58 percent in 1975.'[22]

Military budgets have grown steadily (aside from cuts during the early Clinton administration) while the state department's budget has shrunk. According to Joseph Nye, a former undersecretary of defense, the military is important, but not sixteen times more important than diplomacy.[23]

Among toys, GI Joe now appears in desert gear. From 2001 to 2002 there was a 46 percent spike in sales of GI Joe.[24] The company 21st Century Toys sells a toy called 'Mercenary.' Video games also transmit military culture. The Pentagon provides video wargames free to download for playing soldier online (a well-known one is America's Army, available at www.americasarmy.com). Since 2005 Dish Network broadcasts the Pentagon Channel, a government-run satellite TV service, to 11 million viewers 24/7 to keep them up to date with military news. James Der Derian refers to the military–industrial–media–entertainment network and Jackie Orr speaks of 'the militarization of inner space.'[25]

The popularity of the military is sustained by relations between the Pentagon and Hollywood and marketing firms. Movie-makers often use aircraft carriers, military helicopters and gear, and off-duty soldiers, at no or little charge. The Pentagon argues that 'promoting a positive image of the military is good for recruitment' and the CIA and FBI welcome such cooperation because it can 'help justify their partly secret budgets to a skeptical public.'[26]

> The Defense Department usually trades its cooperation at a nominal 'cost price' for influence over script and final cut. It has an elaborate PR liaison office for army, navy and air force in Los Angeles, which suggests dozens upon dozens of minor changes. Hiring ships, planes, tanks, personnel and consultants may otherwise cost millions, eating into Hollywood profits, so most producers silently submit to censorship and self-censorship.[27]

This cooperation turned *Black Hawk Down* from a film about American defeat in Somalia into a heroic rescue mission along the lines of a Rambo script. The Defense Department and Hollywood are the country's main purveyors of myths of nationhood. After September 11 their cooperation intensified. 'A group of Hollywood executives and producers, calling itself the Hollywood 9/11 International Messaging Group, started a public service commercial, promoting peace and tolerance, aimed at TV audiences in the Arab world.'[28] This cooperation produced trailers for the Navy and Marines such as 'Enduring Freedom.'

The Pentagon's public affairs efforts include spinning war with methodical organization and rigor 'much like a political campaign.'[29] The Pentagon hired PR firm the Rendon Group to explain Iraq war operations to the American public, and the Lincoln Group to disseminate information to Iraqis. Donald Rumsfeld ordered an Information Operations Roadmap to coordinate military psychological operations, information operations, and public affairs programs. Part of this is stage-managing stories such as the rescue of Private Jessica Lynch. Under the headline 'She Was Fighting to the Death' the *Washington Post* reported that Lynch 'fought fiercely and shot several enemy soldiers, firing her weapon until she ran out of ammunition,' and US Special Forces rescuing her from the hospital where she was kept endured 'a blaze of gunfire.' After the networks ran the story it turned out to be a complete fabrication.[30] The Rendon Group choreographed the scene of the fall of Saddam's statue in Baghdad, and, according to unconfirmed reports, the way Saddam was captured was staged as well. The Pentagon commemorated the death of football hero Pat Tillman in Afghanistan as a tragic death under enemy fire. Later it turned out he was killed at short range by one of his own soldiers, so it was a case of 'fragging' (a term used in Vietnam to describe soldiers attacking their officers) or, alternatively, a case of silencing a war critic.

One effect of chronic propaganda is chronic unreality – a $40 billion a year intelligence effort that doesn't produce intelligence, a preventive war in which there is nothing to prevent, an occupation cast as liberation, a coalition of the willing that isn't really willing and not much of a coalition, Iraq reconstruction efforts that don't produce reconstruction, a rollercoaster empire whose Kodak moments turn out fake, spending $3.5 trillion on wars in Afghanistan and Iraq (according to CBO estimates) for spurious reasons. Such is the twilight atmosphere of unreality that the best news and where most young Americans get their news are comedy shows such as the *Daily Show*, which makes the Comedy Central television channel the American bubble's main touchdown with Planet Earth. Blogs are another outlet – many document government chicanery on a daily basis with meticulous, obsessive detail, a sign of how pervasive exasperation and alienation have become.

Karl Rove's strategy for the Bush presidency was its total identification with the military as the country's most trusted institution, through speeches at military camps, flight suit photo-ops, and his self-description as 'war president.' This backfired when the war went wrong and when identifying with the armed forces came with neglect of the actual military, such as insufficient armor and equipment for the troops in Iraq, extended troop rotations, and inadequate health care for the wounded, even in the nation's top military hospital Walter Reed. This still leaves out – and leaves completely unreported – the damage done to GIs and to war theatres by the Pentagon's use of depleted uranium and other toxic munitions.[31]

Reflecting on Michael Moore's film *Fahrenheit 9/11* and the scene of Marine recruiters accosting black youngsters in a shopping mall in Flint, Michigan, Geoffrey O'Brien comments:

> I found myself recollecting an afternoon in late August 2001, in a laundromat at another shopping mall, in upstate New York. The wall-mounted TV tilting down over the dryers was tuned to a seemingly interminable documentary about the arduous training of American Special Forces, a kind of cinematic recruiting poster that evoked simultaneously the action aesthetic of the *Die Hard* movies and the ferocious camaraderie associated with the warrior cults of 1930s Germany and Japan. After the movie ended it was followed by another in identical style, devoted to the training of Navy SEALS. The afternoon began to take on a disorienting and disturbing quality. Between the

poverty of the people in the laundromat – a substantial portion of the town's population was on welfare and out of work – and the unrelieved stridency of the military infomercials, I'd had a sense of glimpsing a possible American future I hadn't quite dared to imagine, of increasingly limited economic prospects and a culture increasingly devoted to the worship of armed force.[32]

American apocalypse

Anatol Lieven describes America's response to September 11 as a 'wounded and vengeful nationalism.'[33] Robert Jay Lifton, a distinguished psychiatrist who treated Vietnam War veterans, goes a step further and views the Iraq war as 'an apocalyptic face-off between Islamist forces and American forces' which are both inspired by visionary projects of cleansing war. He reflects on 'an aggrieved superpower, a giant violated' and on the war on terror as an 'infinite war' driven by a mission to 'rid the world of evil' with 'a clarion call to total victory.' Lifton views the American apocalypse as part of the superpower syndrome.

> More than mere domination, the American superpower now seeks to control history. Such cosmic ambition is accompanied by an equally vast sense of entitlement – of special dispensation to pursue its aims. That entitlement stems partly from historic claims to special democratic virtue, but has much to do with an embrace of technological power translated into military terms. That is, a superpower – the world's only superpower – is entitled to dominate and control precisely because it is a superpower.[34]

The American apocalypse is part of the id of the American bubble. Marvel comics, superheroes like Superman and Terminator, science-fiction fantasies of novel combinations of domination and innovation feed the apocalyptic imagination.[35] Future weapons systems such as the Star Wars missile defense system, the Future Imagery Architecture, Total Information Awareness and the aspiration to achieve 'full spectrum dominance' carry its footprint. It runs through the testosterone pathos of Rambo movies. It is inscribed in the Daisy Cutter as the 'Mother of all Bombs,' the 15-ton Massive

Ordinance Penetrator that can smash bunkers 200 foot beneath the surface, or the 30,000 lb Big Blu bomb, the Powell doctrine of Overwhelming Force, and Shock and Awe, as it was in the Nazi Blitzkrieg that inspired these strategies. Apocalyptic imagination runs through black ops and 'strategies of tension' that promote instability and chaos. The fantasies of redeeming, cleansing violence turn on a script in which by unleashing unrestrained violence, the superpower, the supreme specialist in violence and master of technologies of destruction, eventually wins.

The deep strata of the bubble remind us of the Indian Wars, of Wounded Knee and the bloodletting that is part of 'how the West was won.' Robert Kaplan finds that the American grunts on the frontiers of empire invariably welcome him, whether they are on the ground in Colombia or Afghanistan, to 'Injun country.'[36] They remind us of Joseph Conrad's *Heart of Darkness* set in the Congo ('the horror, the horror') and its echoes in Francis Ford Coppola's *Apocalypse Now*.

To the violence that runs in the undercurrents of the American bubble there are many strands. At higher echelons it involves managerial result-oriented instrumental violence that inspires torture, water-boarding and Abu Ghraib allegedly in the name of efficiency, as it inspired 'stove piping' intelligence through the Pentagon Office of Special Plans. It involves driving forces at the top such as the secretary of defense calling for a 'nimbler and more lethal force.' It involves anxiety and reckless abandon in lower strata such as the youngsters from small towns in the American South who implemented Abu Ghraib abuses while their age mates back home turn to methamphetamine because industry jobs are gone. It involves the drill of violence specialists, such as American air marshals who train under the guiding principle 'Dominate, Intimidate, Control.'[37] In middle strata it involves control fantasies such as senior CIA analysts who call not just for more killing but for razing infrastructure as well, and defense intellectuals at the American Enterprise Institute who call for more robust military hardware and better

battle plans. It involves authors such as Robert Kaplan, who calls
for a pagan warrior ethos. Translation: pagan means non-Christian;
take no prisoners, this is a struggle to the death. For good measure
Kaplan explains that 'globalization is Darwinian.'[38]

The message of Blackwater's success in Iraq is Rambo-without-
apologies: 'The dirty open secret in Washington is that Blackwater
has done its job in Iraq, even if it has done so by valuing the lives
of Iraqis much lower than those of US VIPs. That badass image will
serve it well as it expands globally.'[39]

Mediating between the comfort zone of the American bubble
and the mission impossible of American expansion, violence helps
to keep the balance by destroying unwilling targets. Yet violence
also means violence against the self – which sprawls and manifests
in rising rates of domestic violence in soldiers' families, in soldiers'
chronicles of war, and rising suicide rates.[40]

The apocalyptic imaginary is not a mere sidetrack or adolescent
indulgence; it provides a rationale to violence and the background to
the tremendous outpouring of violence in the new wars – in arming
Iraq during the Iraq–Iran war; through twelve years of sanctions
when, according to state secretary Madeleine Albright, the lives of
50,000 Iraqi children lost were 'worth it'; the Gulf war; during Shock
and Awe and the chaos that followed; during war operations such
as the obliteration of Fallujah; and in Abu Ghraib and Guantánamo
Bay. The British medical journal *The Lancet* estimated the death toll
of Iraqi civilians from the Iraq war at 650,000. Adding the deaths
from sanctions brings the death toll to over a million. Add 2 million
Iraqi refugees, 2 million internally displaced, a middle class gone,
infrastructure razed, a society obliterated with bloody Balkanization
as the best-case outcome, and the American apocalypse has gained
another trophy. Indeed, the Fallujah operation, the largest and most
lethal battle in Iraq, 'earned Marines more Navy Cross medals for
heroism than any other action in Iraq.'[41]

A major source of American apocalypse is the Holocaust complex.
The Holocaust is critical to understanding the mindset of neo-

conservatives. Although neoconservative politics are much the same as those of realists and liberal hawks, as I argue later in this book, what is different is their *pathos* of civilizational alarm, their focus on the Middle East and 'global Islam' and doctrine of World War IV. The objective of radical Islamism, according to Norman Podhoretz, is 'not merely to murder as many of us as possible and to conquer our land. Like the Nazis and the Communists before him, [this new enemy] is dedicated to the destruction of everything good for which America stands.'[42] Hence the war cry of 'Islamofascism,' Richard Perle and David Frum's 'victory or holocaust,' and John Bolton's policy motto *No Surrender.* This mindset also links to Christian Zionism and evangelical themes of Armageddon and rapture.[43]

Presumably, from US and Israeli governments' point of view this is the point: dismantle the Iraqi state, Balkanize the nation; and by some reckonings, Iran and Syria are next. Alongside this deep strategy script, in the American bubble the violence of the Iraq war also serves apocalyptic cleansing, matching the World War II matrix of battling an evil dictator and an evil force. At this point, however, pretzel logic takes over (the evil wasn't there before we came, let's change the subject).

Numbers

Market societies live by numbers, prices, ratings, rankings and by the adage if you can't count it, it doesn't count. In tribal, peasant, feudal and court societies values are established through relationships, meanings, codes of honor and obligation, but market societies convert values into prices and numbers. Every day in America brings fresh numbers – commodity prices, market data, sales figures, scores, grades, survey data, demographic data, poll numbers, census data, health metrics, government statistics, numbers from conferences and scientific papers, and so on. Numbers and whether they are up or down mark the days. History appears as a parade of numbers. Sports such as baseball are experienced through numbers. Seminars and lectures don't count without numbers. When one gives a talk one is invariably specifically asked to 'repeat the numbers.' The numbers should be fresh; old numbers don't count. Print media meticulously document population data and mobility, and quantitative studies in social science yield intricate permutations.

In American society numbers fulfill more pivotal functions than they do in many other societies. American empiricism, positivism, and pragmatism hinge on numbers, as does market society. Although metrics seek to bypass subjective judgments and arbitrary evaluations, in the process numbers acquire totemic status even though their reliability cannot exceed the paradigm that guides them and the process that generates them. As befits an Enlightenment angle on the universe, statistics take on mystical value as glyphs with which to decipher the universe, high-modern equivalents of runes and Kabala. Meanwhile, important as metrics are, the US is a lone feet-and-Fahrenheit power in a metric world.

Leadership

American society assiduously cultivates leadership, not only by lionizing charismatic CEOs but throughout society. Leadership is cultivated from early school age on. Top-scoring high-school students are invited to 'leadership conferences,' 'student leaders' are singled out, managers and academics are evaluated on their leadership skills, bookshop fliers feature a selection of books on leadership. Social problems generate bureaucracies and the bureaucracies are typically headed by 'czars' – a drug czar, public diplomacy czar, Homeland Security czar, intelligence czar, war czar, and so on. Policy differences are often marginal and candidates running for office tend to be evaluated on their character rather than their policies. The 'Coalition for American Leadership Abroad' seeks to stem the tide of anti-Americanism through cultural diplomacy. The title of Zbigniew Brzezinski's book *The Choice: Global Domination or Global Leadership* contrasts leadership and domination. In the American bubble, leadership is moral and uplifting; in international affairs it translates as hegemony (from Greek *hegemon*, leader). Yet by international standards, leadership sounds authoritarian and carries a prewar ring. It recalls a conservative, old-fashioned world-view in which 'history is driven by the club of those in power.' This is how David Brooks describes G.W. Bush's view of the world as a stage for leaders and heroes: 'he loves leadership. He's convinced leaders have the power to change societies.... When Bush talks about world affairs, he talks about national leaders. When he is asked to analyze Iraq, he talks about Maliki. With Russia, it's Putin [or 'Vladimir']. With Europe, it's Merkel, Sarkozy, Brown and the rest.'[44]

The central institutions in 'the home of the brave and the land of the free' are profoundly authoritarian – the military, corporations, and the political system share a top-down pyramidal structure. The military serves as a role model for other institutions, from corporations to sports teams. Corporations are hierarchical institutions – manifestly so in times of downsizing. The presidential system (in constrast to the parliamentary system), executive privilege and the inclination towards mammoth bureaucracies share top-down features, which have been reinforced by the ramifications of post-9/11 securitization. The cult of winning and winners, prizes, honors and awards; the American idol and star system and the X of the year selection dramatize the leadership cult. The leadership culture doesn't explain what the others who are *not* leaders are supposed to do. Presumably they are implicitly tutored to be followers, unless all of society would consist of leaders, which seems impractical. Hence the implicit reality of leadership culture is a culture of followers.

Leadership, unlike coercion, carries a halo of moral example. Yet in the American case leadership in combination with Puritanism and backlash culture easily turns punitive and revanchist. For example, the 'war on drugs' emphasizes law enforcement, not treatment or care, and resources flow to the law and order system rather than to drug users as patients. So although the rhetoric is leadership, the reality is punishment. Indeed, 'the US leads the world in many categories that suggest violence and coercion as everyday facts of life: numbers of citizens in prison, numbers of troops in uniform, the numbers and types of law enforcement personnel, and the millions of guns on the streets and in night tables next to beds.[45] Likewise, American leadership abroad is marked by a peculiar combination of idealism and brutality, or 'punitive idealism.'[46]

The American bubble functions as a milkshake in which the contradictions that Americans face are blended. Due to the cost of campaigns only a wealthy elite can run for major office. The US is the land of the free, yet Americans, especially young Americans and minorities, face an overweening law-and-order regime with tight rules (no drinking in public, no drinking under 21, no drugs) and a police and judicial system that is exceedingly well organized and short of humor. 'Three strikes and out' results in major convictions for minor offenses.

The American bubble often works because it is self-reinforcing, assimilates foreign elements into the cultural continuum, and is sustained by the national entertainment state. Because of America's geographical insularity and historical rupture, low social density, and the sway of entertainment media, alternative views don't easily come in. Yet the American bubble isn't static or all-encompassing. Not everything works, or works all the time.

For at least a year following September 11, patriotism filled the air and flag fever, media deference, obedience culture, and rallying behind the leader prevailed. For about a year if I took a walk of two blocks in my suburban neighborhood I would count a hundred or so American flags in front of houses, in windows, or as car decals. Joan Didion spoke of the 'new normal' of the Bush years and several books sketch this eerie atmosphere.[47] Gradually normalcy returned, media became more matter-of-fact, though short of critical (old normal), and public attitudes sobered. The demand for 'Support Our Troops' yellow ribbons as car decals peaked in 2004 but had collapsed by late 2006.[48] The American culture of conformity transcends the trauma of September 11. As Susan Sontag observed: 'Our "United We Stand" or "Winner Takes All" ethos: the United States is a country that has made patriotism equivalent to consensus.'[49]

Two products that have been well past their sell-by date for some time have been the Bush presidency and the Iraq war. No matter how deft the packaging and sales pitch, they can't fix a lousy product. The Bush presidency has come with unprecedented stage management – a White House communications office that creates 'message of the day' backdrops, advance teams that seek out locations for photo ops, designs entire sets for backdrops and times speeches to catch 'magic hour light' that casts a golden glow on Mr Bush, a White House that stays 'on message' and doesn't divert from its 'talking points.'[50] Yet if the contrast between the package and the product is too large, deft propaganda becomes counterproductive and everything unravels, as summed up by Maureen Dowd: 'The president is on a continuous loop of sophistry: We have to push on in Iraq because Al Qaeda is there even though Al Qaeda is there because we pushed into Iraq. Our troops have to keep dying there because our troops have been dying there. We have to stay so the enemy doesn't know we're leaving. Osama hasn't been found because he's hiding.'[51]

Outside the Bubble

American tourists vacationing in Rome in June 2007 found 'some of the Eternal City's most famous streets and piazzas packed with tens of thousands of anti-war demonstrators protesting against a visit by President George W. Bush on his way home from a G8 summit.' The Americans were shocked and aghast at seeing the rage and anger against US government policies.[52] This is one encounter of the American bubble and the outside.

In an article written for the 2000 campaign, Condoleezza Rice wrote that American foreign policy should be guided by national interest and American values, and added in passing that 'American values are universal values.' This claim goes back to Roosevelt and Wilson.[53] In 2002 American intellectuals such as Samuel Huntington and Francis Fukuyama signed a statement according to which 'What We're Fighting For' is 'American values.' By collapsing 'American values' into universal values, Americans in effect claim to capture globalization. By this logic America's fight is the world's fight, and the US through the war on terror leads the world to freedom and democracy, 'with us or against us.' This dangerous illusion inflates the American bubble to a global balloon. Americans are socialized in the bubble, which comes with a sense of American superiority and leadership, as in World War II and a mission to free the world, which makes this the beacon in foreign relations and public diplomacy. Since most Americans are unable to exit the American bubble, they seek to *extend* it over other regions. Thus American discourse and propaganda seek to envelop other countries like a vast tent on the premiss that democracy and freedom are irresistible and the US leads the way. The Washington Consensus promoted the free market and democracy ('good governance') in tandem. This is often upheld with great sincerity and the deep conviction that the 'freedom agenda' is the destiny of the Middle East and other countries, as it has been of the US. The American bubble is oblivious to or routinely papers over the clash between means and ends. Even if many Americans are aware of the cynicism according to which the end justifies the means, many are inured to American foibles because, after all, the rest of the world consists of evil powers (as in the 'axis of evil') along with a spineless lot who fail to stand up to them.

Charlotte Beers, the 'queen of branding' from a major Madison Avenue firm, and then Margaret Tutwiler, a former US ambassador to Morocco, and Karen Hughes, a Bush confidante and former White House communications director, were appointed under-secretary of state for public diplomacy and charged with selling the image of the US abroad and especially in the Middle East. 'The problem of "Why they hate us" was rephrased, in ad-speak, as "How we reposition the brand." ... These endeavors will be guided by the best practice in advertising: to convey the emotional as well as the rational, frame all messages in the context of the audience, enlist third parties for authenticity and magnify a good result.'[54]

Invariably this runs up against one major obstacle: 'It's the policies, stupid.'[55] And it's precisely the policies that are not under discussion. An editor of the Egyptian newspaper *Al Ahram* left his meeting with Charlotte Beers 'frustrated that she seemed more interested in talking about vague American values than about specific US policies.' As Naomi Klein comments, 'the misunderstanding probably stemmed from the fact that Beers views America's tattered international image as little more than a communications problem. Somehow America still hasn't managed, in Beers' words, to "get out there and tell our story".'[56] The State Department's Middle East PR magazine *Hi* has failed to make any impact. American policies such as the Greater Middle East initiative have been stillborn because they were conceived in such self-seeking terms that even close allies such as Egypt declared them 'ludicrous.' By one assessment, the 'US failed to consult nations before making plans to change them.'[57] Time and again US officials at every level are unable to leave their comfort zone and continue to operate inside the bubble even if their mission is to reach beyond.

> Al Hurra television, the U.S. government's $63 million-a-year effort at public diplomacy broadcasting in the Middle East, is run by executives and officials who cannot speak Arabic, according to a senior official who runs the program. That might explain why ... the service has recently been caught broadcasting terrorist messages, including an hour long tirade on the importance of anti-Jewish violence ... the top officials in the network's chain of command could not understand what was being said on Al Hurra broadcasts.[58]

Rebranding the US runs into fundamental problems. First, long neglect of diplomacy can't be made up by a quick fix. Second, diversity and complexity are intrinsic to brand USA and authoritarian attempts at branding that may work for corporations are inappropriate and unworkable for a country. Third, such is the mismanagement and cruelty that is part of the way the US has been conducting war in the Middle East that no packaging can hide the product. No charm offensives or jazz concerts can possibly make up for Abu Ghraib and Guantánamo. No public diplomat can make up for the American secretary of state declaring, as Israel's devastation of Lebanon is in progress, that these are 'the birth pangs of a new Middle East.' Fourth, if American media don't show the devastation and casualties in Palestine, Lebanon and Iraq, channels such as Al Jazeera and Al-Manar TV do. Besides US policies, a fundamental obstacle on this course is the American bubble and its applause culture. Fifth, it is not possible to manage an empire from within a bubble, with an island mentality. Thus the US has long lost the battle for hearts and minds.

Teaching American undergraduate students I find them open-minded yet ignorant about the world outside America. They are keen to voice their opinions and values but since knowledge about the history and geography of foreign countries is short of elementary, the values and opinions remain abstract generalities with little bearing on reality. Teaching in Germany I find students well versed in high theory, from Hegel to Simmel, but often ignorant about empirical knowledge of the world beyond Europe. Teaching students from the global South, however, whether in Thailand, South Africa, Brazil, or in international programs, I find them often keenly political in their knowledge and aware of international political and economic trends. The South studies the North, but not vice versa. For the South this is survival knowledge, but not the other way round. The cultural climate in the prosperous northern hemisphere is essentially conservative and cultures can afford to follow their proclivities. In Germany and Japan this revolves around high theory. In France it involves philosophical reflection and speculation. In the UK it includes empirical, data-based knowledge. American common sense is ideological and centered on 'values,' often shaped by an implicit Sunday sermon morality.

What sustains the American bubble are, ultimately, America's geographic isolation, separated from the world by oceans, and its historical rupture, separated from the Old World by its departure from feudalism, monarchy, and the church. For the immigrants who continue to come to the US, the experience of rupture keeps being reproduced, so rupture, psychologically and existentially, remains a fundamental part of American experience. The US is large enough to keep most of its citizens busy and entertained. What further shapes the American bubble is American global power. This is also a paradox: the country that claims the greatest influence on world affairs is most ignorant of the world and culture outside its borders and unused to dialogue with it. No other advanced country translates so few books from other languages or views so few foreign films. The US echo chamber experience doesn't equip Americans to understand or deal with the world; hence the cliché of the ugly American, which dates from the nineteenth century.[59]

Polls report that the American image in the world is steadily declining – even among its allies, Britain, Australia, Italy, the US is not trusted and not ranked among the top ten nations. The UN is more trusted than the US. In the insularity of national cocooning, sound-bite analysis, polarized debate, extreme nationalism and right-wing drift become normal. But Americans cannot afford to think of American policies solely in the terms of the American bubble and through the lens of corporate media, for the international public views them in a light that is *not* deferential. The American bubble and the doublespeak ideology of freedom limit the capacity of Americans to understand the world and the resistance to their projects and limit their capacity for reflexivity and self-correction. This is the core problem of the American public sphere. All large countries inhabit a comfort zone cocooned from the world, but not all dabble in global hegemony, which requires a degree of mature debate, cultural openness and empathy.

TWO

Odd Numbers

In the early 1990s Edward Luttwak asked, 'When will the United States become a Third World country?' Noting American deindustrialization and 'a pervasive and increasingly accepted lack of skill in shops, banks, garages and workplaces,' he pinned the likely date as 2020.[1] However, for many Americans third-world conditions have begun already.

Around 1980 the US saw major shifts in economic and social policies, and since then income inequality has steadily increased. 'What is amazing,' notes Jack Newfield, 'is that this expansion of inequality took place without ever becoming a noticeable issue in American politics. This growing concentration of wealth has given the super-rich domination over politics through extravagant campaign contributions and media ownership, which has made large elements of the media sound like Republican echo chambers.'[2] Ben Bagdikian observes, 'The fact that such a gap exists gets into U.S. news occasionally, but as a routine statistic, like the corn crop in Kansas.'[3]

Whether one consults census data, congressional budget office reports, policy reports, or economic and sociological studies, they all echo the same findings of a sharp increase in social inequality since about 1980. Since 1975 almost all income gains in the United States have gone to the top 20 percent of income earners. Since 1979 the income of the top 1 percent of American income earners has tripled while the bottom 40 percent has seen its income rise by 13 percent. In 1979 the top 1 percent garnered 9 percent of the nation's income, which rose to 16 percent in 2004 and 17.4 percent in 2005. Between 1979 and 2000 the gap between rich and poor more than doubled.[4] 'Forty-seven percent of the total real income gain between 1983 and 1998 accrued to the top 1 percent of income recipients, 42 percent went to the next 19 percent, and 12 percent accrued to the bottom 80 percent.'[5] Paul Krugman notes, 'Between 1980 and 2004, real wages in manufacturing fell 1 percent, while the real income of the richest 1 percent ... rose 135 percent.'[6]

In the 1960s the pay of corporate chief executive officers was about 25 times that of hourly production workers. The ratio climbed from 93 times in 1988 to 419 times in 1999. At a time when the wages of ordinary workers barely kept pace with inflation or just rose in single digits, CEO compensation increased by 481 percent. In 2005 average CEO pay was about 500 times ordinary wages and 1,000 times for the top 100 CEOs.

Meanwhile the minimum wage was not raised for over a decade and was only marginally increased in 2006. 'Since 1968, worker productivity has risen 81 percent while the average hourly wage barely budged, adjusting for inflation, and the real value of the minimum wage dropped 38 percent.'[7] Again, between 2000 and 2006 labor productivity in the non-farm sector of the economy rose by 18 percent, but the inflation-adjusted weekly wages of workers increased by just 1 percent (or $3.20 a week).[8] Median household family income had been falling for six years in a row in 2004. Since the late 1970s the top 1 percent of the population has more than doubled its share of national income and the share of the top 0.01 percent increased by a factor of six. 'The top 5 percent of Americans now own almost 60 percent of the country's wealth.'[9]

Conservative commentators pooh-pooh such figures, for they only show that 'the rich are getting richer faster than the poor are getting richer, so what?'[10] But in fact it indicates a fundamental break in the pattern of American social stratification. Earlier, between 1949 and 1979, the incomes of the bottom 80 percent grew more rapidly than the incomes of the top 1 percent and those of the bottom 20 percent grew most rapidly of all. Between 1955 and 1980, the era of New Deal protections and high marginal tax rates (up to 90 percent in the 1950s and 70 percent in 1980), the middle class grew dramatically, income inequality decreased, and corporations enjoyed labor peace.[11] These are the golden years of capitalism, the era of the post-war boom, the American Dream, bipartisanship and political moderation.

In sharp contrast to the American Dream of upward mobility and a nation in which the majority belongs to the middle class, trends since 1980 produce a downwardly mobile society. Until 1980 the American trend was to move closer to the European welfare state; it would be a matter of time and there would be universal health insurance for Americans too. However, with the Reagan administration the US took a radically different turn and gradually reverted to the system of business power that existed during the gilded age – the time before the Wall Street crash of 1929 and the New Deal. While several of these trends took shape in the late 1970s they were institutionalized during the Reagan administration.[12]

Every indicator shows this period as a trend break. A report in the *San Francisco Bay Guardian* notes: 'The dead canary of structural American poverty was the sudden appearance of the homeless in the early 1980s.... In the early 1980s, in the new fervor for shifting everything possible to the free market, subsidized low-cost housing subsidies were cut by 92 percent.' The report continues: 'Other affluent countries lack a permanent underclass like the American poor. Why? The other rich countries have housing, employment, pension, and tax policies that prevent it.... The answers are not mysterious: official housing policies, deliberate shifting of wealth to the top through destruction of the national progressive income tax, mammoth special favors for corporations, and cynical treatment of the national minimum wage.'[13]

The outcomes are familiar. It has produced a society in which the level of inequality is higher than in any other industrialized nation. In the 1990s in Japan the income ratio for the top fifth of households to the bottom fifth was 4.3:1. The ratios in European social democracies were 6:1 or 7:1, in Germany 5.8:1, while the US ratio was 11:1 or higher.[14]

The US is the richest and most unequal country in the developed world, with the lowest life expectancy. Male life expectancy in the US is lower than in Costa Rica. Greece, with half the GDP per head, has a longer life expectancy than the US.[15] Nationwide in 2001, 16 percent of children were living in extreme poverty, the highest percentage among OECD countries – compare France's rate at 2.9 percent, Taiwan at 2 percent, and Sweden at 1.3 percent.[16] The poverty count in 2000 added another 5 million Americans to make a total of 37 million. According to the 2005 *Human Development Report*, infant mortality in the US is at the same rate as in Malaysia. Some 47 million Americans have no health insurance. In 2005 the US ranked 27th among 163 nations on the Index of Social Progress. According to a report on international quality of life studies, the pace of social development has been 'on hold' in the US since 1980, putting the US on the same level as Poland and Slovenia.[17]

Census Bureau data show that this nationwide pattern is reproduced in different states and cities. Since 1999 median household income in Illinois has fallen by 12 percent and in Michigan by 19 percent. Job growth in Illinois has been mostly in lower-paying occupations, even during the 1990s, and there is no sign this trend will reverse; this comes at a time when costs are rising for everything from transportation to housing.[18] In Manhattan, 'the top fifth of earners now make 52 times what the lowest fifth make… which is roughly comparable to the income disparity in Namibia…. Put another way, for every dollar made by households in the top fifth of Manhattan earners, households in the bottom fifth made about 2 cents.' Manhattan ranks fourth among American cities with the biggest income disparities, behind Atlanta, Berkeley, California, and Washington DC. Across New York State, 'the middle class is being depleted while the rich are getting richer and the poor are growing in number and barely getting by.'[19] This pattern of inequality is being reproduced within cities, with growing disparities between neighborhoods.

Rural America faces growing joblessness as farm size grows and industries leave. Wages have declined to such a level that it becomes competitive to set up call centers in rural counties. Economic decline in small-town and rural America manifests in growing use of methamphetamine, homegrown and imported, mainly from Mexico. Methamphetamine is a dead-end drug and its rising use is a major indicator of American decline and a factor in crime rates.[20]

The Fortune 400 list of the richest Americans 'no longer reflects a dynamic and elastic economy; instead, it reflects a growing concentration of wealth and economic power.' In the 1985 list, the wealth of the largest number of millionaires (103) came from manufacturing; in the 2005 list this dwindled to 22, with the largest number (95) owing their wealth to finance or investments. The combined wealth of the Fortune 400 is $1.13 trillion. Thus the combined net worth of billionaires worldwide is $3.5 trillion, of which almost 40 percent belongs to Americans.[21]

The multi-speed economy manifests itself everywhere. The effective federal tax rate for the top 1 percent of income earners fell from 69 percent in 1970 to about 40 percent in 1993, while the tax rate for the median family increased from 16 to 25 percent. Taking universities as a microcosm of American inequality, in 2002 the pay gradient ranged from $19,000 a year for janitors and housekeepers to between $300,000 and $500,000 for university presidents,[22] rising to $2 million in 2007.

Economist Robert Frank notes, 'As incomes continue to grow at the top and stagnate elsewhere, we will see even more of the national income devoted to luxury goods, the main effect of which will be to raise the bar that defines what counts as luxury.'[23] In a society where the wealthy set the norms for consumption and people at every rung seek to match the consumption of those just above them, this produces a society-wide arms race for goods.

The rich and super-rich, in contrast to the merely affluent, set new standards of extreme consumption. The luxury sector in the US has been growing at 12 percent for several years. The luxury market is booming with gargantuan real estate, Gulfstream jets, $20 million yachts, $3 million birthday parties, $600,000 watches, $24,000 sunglasses, and alligator-skin toilet seats. The rich (it takes about $10 million to be considered entry-level rich) are 'financial foreigners' in their own country. They have their own health care system with 'concierge doctors' and their own travel network of timeshare or private jets and destination clubs. Hotel magnate Leona Helmsley left the largest part of her estate of $12 million for the care of her Maltese dog. The merely affluent make do with $3,000 crocodile handbags and $1,200 designer jeans.

Please Don't Feed the Homeless

One of the ways in which the two-speed economy manifests is homelessness. It doesn't take much in America to fall from the middle class into homelessness – medical expenses, job loss, rising housing cost, and mounting debt drive many onto the streets. Punitive credit card rates penalize late payments and the bankruptcy law adopted in 2005 has made it more difficult to handle debt. According to a survey of twenty-five American cities, homelessness affects 3.5 million in any year, and among the fastest-growing segment of the homeless population are families with children (41 percent in 2003).[24] Yet the way the homeless are treated shows, instead of social solidarity in difficult times, a punitive attitude. Signs in Orlando parks read:

DO NOT LIE OR OTHERWISE BE IN A HORIZONTAL
POSITION ON A PARK BENCH... DO NOT SLEEP OR REMAIN
IN ANY BUSHES, SHRUBS OR FOLIAGE ...
per city code sec. 18A.09 (a) and (o).

According to the mayor of Orlando, homelessness 'adversely
affects public safety and economic development, and therefore must
be addressed.' More and more cities in the US are not only debating
or implementing laws on the homeless but are also putting restrictions on those who help them, even though not enough resources
are dedicated to helping the homeless and the hungry.

> Already, Dallas, Fort Myers, Fla., Gainesville, Fla., Wilmington, N.C.,
> Atlanta and Santa Monica, Calif., have laws restricting or outright pro-
> hibiting the feeding of the homeless. In Fairfax County, Va., homemade
> meals and meals made in church kitchens may not be distributed to the
> homeless unless first approved by the county. Other cities, including
> Miami, are considering similar anti-feeding measures.
>
> A 2006 report on 67 cities [by the National Law Center on Home-
> lessness and Poverty and the National Coalition for the Homeless]
> found an 18 percent increase since 2002 in laws prohibiting aggressive
> panhandling; a 12 percent jump in laws outlawing 'passive' begging; a 14
> percent rise in laws defining sitting or lying in public places as criminal
> acts.[25]

The Coalition's director comments, 'The idea is to drive the
visible homeless out of downtown America, so that cities can attract
developers, big money.' This matches a drive toward neoliberal
urban policies and transforming American cities into 'taut entrepreneurial spaces.'[26] An Orlando resident wrote on his website
'feeding the homeless only encourages more homelessness' and
then offered the equation 'Less Homelessness = Less Problems
= Better Place to Live.'[27] Similar restrictions and surveillance are
in effect in many other cities, notably in California and in tourist
towns such as Las Vegas. Sennett and Cobb referred to 'the hidden
injuries of class' to describe the subtle and emotional effects of
status distinctions.[28] This, however, is not a matter of 'the hidden

injuries of class' but rather a matter of ensuring that class and the injuries of class remain hidden.

Vagrancy laws have a long history and have been adopted particularly in times of social upheaval; yet the history of social solidarity and support for the vulnerable in society is longer and common to virtually all societies and religions. Vagrancy laws adopted in the early nineteenth century in the wake of the enclosures gave way to statutes of aid to the poor and eventually to the welfare state. But the present restrictions in the US are put in place at a time when welfare provisions have been cut back and the ranks of the homeless are swelling. The welfare reform of 1996 has taken many welfare recipients off the rolls and into work, but the jobs earn so little that all that has been achieved is the transformation of the welfare poor into the working poor.[29]

Ben Bagdikian notes, 'Most often the media refer to the homeless who are alcoholics, drug addicts, or mentally ill. But we have always had alcoholics, drug addicts, and the mentally ill before without large numbers of families living in the streets.' The trend of widening income inequality, the elimination of government-subsidized low-cost housing, and urban redevelopment wiping out affordable housing, together produce a growing divide between housing and income. The postindustrial economy and gentrification add to the number of the homeless.[30] War veterans make up only 11 percent of the adult population but a quarter of the homeless.[31]

With this growing divide comes a culture of blaming the victim and stereotyping the poor according to which poverty is a 'character flaw.'[32] Several myths about the poor 'explain why poverty is the fault of the poor.' One stereotype is that the poor are fat and 'Americans connect fat bodies with economic incontinence.' But 'if the poor are fat, it's because they're saving their money by buying cheaper food, which is often higher in fat.' Another stereotype is that the poor are not white – at times racism and classism are hard to distinguish. Or, the poor are that way by choice – which functions as a kind of internalized classism where poor people blame themselves for being 'bad with money.' Another claim is that the poor have it better now than they used to – but today, as in the past, 'the poor live near garbage dumps, suffer unequally from environmental cancers and diabetes, and are routinely kicked out of nice neighborhoods.'[33]

The genteel standards of the 'new urbanism' and the aesthetics of gentrification ban the homeless and the poor from the new urban designs. Segregation – spatial and social – is built into bifurcating economies and takes the form of surveillance of public spaces, gated communities, and the 'secession of the successful.'[34] Segregating the poor and the homeless serves several functions. Making the losers invisible enables the winners to claim their victory as *society's* victory, for besides some misfits doesn't everyone prosper? It enables the successful to monopolize urban space, set the terms of social cohabitation, and define the social contract. Furthermore, concealing the social cost of economic growth and tax cuts is aesthetic. Clearing urban and suburban spaces of misfits readies them for redevelopment and gentrification. The urban elites know that 'poverty rocks. Poverty is profitable. Poverty makes stocks go up and labor come down.'[35]

Explaining Inequality

Now that we've sketched the trends of social inequality in America let's consider how economists respond to growing inequality. A few economists deny the data and argue that inequality is a 'statistical illusion' or find minute blips in the data which they present as countertrends.[36] The common position, however, is to question not the data but their meaning.

One perspective acknowledges that income inequality has grown but questions its importance, for it is not reflected in inequality of consumption; nor, according to surveys of personal happiness, is it matched by inequality in happiness. Besides, less educated groups have more leisure time than do high earners, who work harder. Thus 'inequality as a major and chronic American problem has been overstated.'[37] That 'in terms of happiness – unlike income – Americans are really quite equal' keeps popping up in op-eds, for it demonstrates that income inequality is not nearly as important as Democrats make it out to be and that 'in terms of what really matters most to Americans, they may be more equal than they thought.'[38]

Conservative economists maintain that the rise at the top end of the scale is normal and appropriate – thus CEOs earn 500 times more than ordinary workers do because they multiply the company's value by a factor of 500. Not surprisingly, many CEOs share the view that income inequality reflects the returns on education and hard work.[39] In this reasoning the problem is not inequality (which is justified in view of the new economy) but poverty. Inequality reflects the new skills differentials that come with technological change. Poverty, according to Harvard economist Martin Feldstein, reflects poor education, family breakdown and 'low cognitive ability.' According to economists James Heckman and Alan Krueger in their study *Inequality in America*, it's all about 'raising the incomes of people at the bottom. Punishing those at the top doesn't help.'[40] However, blaming the educational system and particularly minorities for poverty is circular reasoning, for American early education – unlike in other industrial societies – is largely based on school district taxes. 'Rich schools often look like country clubs – with manicured sports fields and swimming pools. Poor schools often look more like jails – with concrete grounds and grated windows.'[41]

'There is no doubt that market forces have spoken in favor of more inequality,' according to Harvard economist Richard Freeman.[42] In effect, the leading accounts of inequality in economics are another form of segregating the poor and the homeless. Paul Krugman observes that the three main hypotheses to explain growing inequality are globalization, skill-biased technological change, and the superstar hypothesis;[43] yet each proves increasingly inadequate. Globalization can explain part of the relative decline in blue-collar wages, according to Krugman, 'but it can't explain the 2,500 percent rise in CEO incomes.' With the shift from 'managerial capitalism' to 'investor capitalism' during the 1980s and 1990s came the 'irrational quest for charismatic CEOs': 'Since the 1980s there has been ever more emphasis on the importance of leadership – meaning personal, charismatic leadership.'[44] The hypothesis that income inequality reflects a skills gap that follows technological change holds that inequality represents an increase in returns to 'investing in skills.' But, as Daniel Gross notes, 'It takes an optimist to find good news in the fact that the top 1 percent have steadily increased their haul while the other 99 percent haven't; after all, many more than one in every 100 Americans are investing in skills and education.'[45]

This focus on market forces conceals the role of non-market factors, in particular government wage and tax policies and the decline of unions. The market has a lot to answer for but is far from being the whole story. When the Reagan administration lowered marginal tax rates from 70 percent to 36 percent it opened the way to soaring remuneration for CEOs and changed the culture and expectations in boardrooms. With the decline in trade unions came a rise in performance-based pay, based on individual output rather than collectively negotiated wages based on job titles. Krugman notes that wages are determined by social norms and explains the rise of inequality through cultural and political changes: the unraveling of the norms of the New Deal 'replaced by an ethos of "anything goes"' and the rise of 'permissive capitalism' induced by the boom economy of the 1990s, reflected in changes in corporate culture and the growing polarization of politics.[46]

The income stratification at the turn of the millennium matches the concentration of wealth at the top during America's gilded age in 1915 and 1916 and the late 1920s, and for the super-rich even exceeds this by a giant factor. America's belle époque was an era of elite conspicuous consumption and elegant art deco architecture, and an era of capitalist tycoons, company towns, press barons, and the violent suppression of labor.[47]

In recent years the highest income increases don't go to CEOs but to hedge fund managers – 'like the 25 hedge-fund managers who each earned at least $240 million last year (the top dog took home $1.7 billion).' They are part of the super-rich 0.01 percent. 'The top five Wall Street firms (Bear Stearns, Goldman Sachs, Lehman Brothers, Merrill Lynch, and Morgan Stanley) were expected to award an estimated $36 billion to $44 billion worth of bonuses to their 173,000 employees,' an average of between $208,000 and $254,000, 'with the bulk of the gains accruing to the top 1,000 or so highest paid managers.' The *Financial Times* reports, 'CEOs of some of the biggest [S&P 500 companies] now earn up to $50m a year, while the going rate for the CEO of a top financial services company has reached $30m–$35m.'[48] Which points to an additional variable in rising inequality, the financialization of the American economy.

These steep inequalities have been a growing cause for concern and became an issue in the 2008 presidential elections. However, in public discourse and media far more attention goes to factors such as free trade, globalization, China's renminbi, and immigration than to Wall Street and the government policies that enable or allow Wall Street excesses. The Bush administration's tax cuts are discussed but this discussion is dwarfed by discussions of 'free trade' and ideas such as imposing high tariffs on imports from China.

The consensus on globalization is that technological change enables offshoring and outsourcing, which is beneficial to the overall economy. According to the Clinton administration mantra, workers must adjust to the new realities by retraining and re-education. This emphasis on education has been followed by steep increases in the cost of college tuition (by 30 to 70 percent during 2006 and 2007), making college education increasingly unaffordable.

A serious conversation on health care finally took shape in 2007; Democratic presidential candidates propose universal health-care

schemes and improved access to education. However, the tax base
that should fund these initiatives is not under serious discussion.
Legislation that would treat the earnings of hedge fund managers
not as capital gains taxed at 15 percent but as income taxed at
35 percent was blocked not just by Republicans and the White
House but also by Senate Democrats who receive funding from
Wall Street.

The conversation, rather, is about lowering corporate taxes.
Treasury secretary Hank Paulson argues for a lower corporate tax
rate and notes, 'Government should not pick economic winners or
losers; the marketplace has proven itself more than able for that
task.'[49] This was written at the time that the subprime mortgage
crisis ripped through Wall Street and the financial markets. Another
conversation is about releasing Wall Street from the strictures of
the Sarbanes–Oxley Act, which was to rectify the Enron-type
accounting excesses, on the argument that it hampers Wall Street
in its intensifying competition with London and other financial
centers.

According to Krugman, 'the division between the parties is
sharper now than it has been since the 1920s.' A central thesis of his
book *The Great Unraveling* is that the Republicans have moved to the
right and the G.W. Bush administration behaves like a conspirato-
rial and combative 'revolutionary movement.' Yet a few years later
he observes, 'For the last few decades, even Democrats have been
afraid to make an issue out of inequality, fearing that they would be
accused of practicing class warfare and lose the support of wealthy
campaign contributors.'[50] According to Kevin Phillips 'revolutionary
elections' have long vanished from the American political landscape
and have been overtaken by 'Permanent Washington':

> As Washington has entrenched, the old two-party system, revitalized
> by once-a-generation bloodless revolutions at the ballot box, no longer
> works. Governmental mechanisms, too, are losing their responsive-
> ness... Washington is now too big, too rich, too pride-set in its ways
> as arbiter of the postwar world, to accept another of the upheavals and

housecleanings that Thomas Jefferson predicted would be necessary every generation. Special-interest power just keeps consolidating.[51]

The last revolutionary election in the US took place in 1932. The 2005 Census identifies the seven suburban counties around the capital as among the twenty richest in the country. This wealth is bipartisan; more than half of the senior officials in the Clinton administration became corporate lobbyists.[52]

Inequality in America has reached gross proportions, as even a casual glance at the figures makes clear. As we've seen, the economy and market forces do not adequately explain the dramatic increase in social inequality. We'll look at what political transformations underlie this trend in the next chapter. The second part of this chapter also considers the rise of the financial sector as a factor in growing inequality.

THREE

Dixie Politics

IN THE 1980s the United States became a different country. Social inequality which had narrowed for decades began to widen. The American Dream became a memory. From a progressive country, or at least a country with major and growing progressive forces, the United States became a right-wing country – in an economic sense with policies that privilege corporations, and in a political and cultural sense with an authoritarian turn. What accounts for this profound shift in American politics and culture?

The usual explanation for this change includes various cultural and political factors but is essentially economic. The golden years of postwar capitalism were past and to recover from the recession of the 1970s (the OPEC oil boycott followed by stagnation and inflation) and restore the profitability of business required scaling back government regulation. The Reagan administration's deregulation, tax cuts, cutbacks in social services, and assault on trade unions changed the balance. Implementing similar policies in the UK, Margaret Thatcher proclaimed 'There Is No Alternative.' This inaugurated the neoliberal policies that have dominated from

1980 onwards. Accompanying this shift was the reorganization of capitalism from Fordist mass production and Keynesian regulation to post-Fordist flexible production and pro-market regulation. Also in international development policies the Keynesian consensus that had prevailed made way for the Washington Consensus and IMF and World Bank policies promoting the same policy package of deregulation, liberalization, and privatization that had become dominant in the Anglo-American economies, along with export-oriented growth.

Adam Tickell and Jamie Peck discuss the development of neoliberalism in three phases: an early phase of *proto-neoliberalism* from the 1940s to the 1970s in which the main ideas took shape; a phase of *roll-back neoliberalism* in the 1980s when it became government policy in the US and UK; and *roll-out neoliberalism* in the 1990s when it became hegemonic in multilateral institutions.[1] This account draws a straight line from Friedrich von Hayek and Chicago School economics to Reagan policy and neoliberalism. This is the standard interpretation of the rise of neoliberalism that is widely accepted in international political economy, development studies, geography and urban studies. David Harvey's work is a well-known example of this. This account poses fundamental problems. The line of interpretation is economistic. It assumes that profound shifts in American and British politics and culture are reducible to the needs of capitalist reorganization. In drawing a straight line from ideas to policies, it takes politics for granted and reads economic history schematically. It misreads the Reagan record and attributes influence to economic ideas (ideas inspire policies) that doesn't match the record. I agree with the diagnosis of neoliberalism as capitalism after cutting the social wage or 'liberalism without the poor'; but this is how neoliberalism functions, which is not the same as how it comes about.

Earlier, following Michael Lind and others, I argued that the turn away from Keynesian policies was driven by the appeal of *Dixie capitalism*: corporations in the north-east recovered profitability by relocating in the American South and south-west. In the South, the regime of low wages, low taxes, low services, and no unions went back to the nineteenth-century plantation economy and the policies of Reconstruction and Jim Crow. All along the South had been adamantly opposed to the New Deal and had kept conservative institutions and racially exclusive policies in place. These trends were in progress and the Reagan administration policies facilitated and institutionalized them.[2]

Let's take this argument further. In the wake of civil rights legislation in 1964 Southern Democrats flocked to the Republican Party; at the same time the Sunbelt grew demographically and economically. The Southern culture of fundamentalist and evangelical Christianity (with mammoth churches for the newcomers in the suburbs) and the Confederate traditions of militarism in the countryside infused the right-wing turn in the Republican Party. Keywords of the era are 'new federalism,' 'states' rights' and 'right-to-work states,' followed by social and cultural issues (right to life, family values, anti-gun control, pro-law and order). In the Republican Party this ensemble became known as the *southern strategy*. Government regulation was cut back for many reasons – undoing the New Deal was the aim of the conservative South all along; but the main reasons were cultural and political before they were economic. It was a *cultural* backlash against the 1960s (protest, sex, drugs, and rock and roll) and a *political* backlash against pro-government Democrats (undoing the New Deal).

In 1995 Norman Podhoretz, founder of *Commentary* magazine and godfather of the neoconservative movement, looked back:

> If anti-communism was the ruling passion of the neoconservatives in foreign affairs, opposition to the counterculture of the 1960s was their ruling passion at home. Indeed, I suspect that revulsion against the counterculture accounted for more converts to neoconservatism than any other single factor.[3]

According to Paul Krugman, 'right-wing economic ideology has never been a vote-winner. Instead, the [Republican] party's electoral strategy has depended largely on exploiting racial fear and animosity.'

> Ronald Reagan didn't become governor of California by preaching the wonders of free enterprise; he did it by attacking the state's fair housing law, denouncing welfare cheats and associating liberals with urban riots. Reagan didn't begin his 1980 campaign with a speech on supply-side economics, he began it – at the urging of a young Trent Lott – with a speech supporting states' rights delivered just outside Philadelphia, Miss., where three civil rights workers were murdered in 1964. And if you look at the political successes of the G.O.P. since it was taken over by movement conservatives, they had very little to do with public opposition to taxes, moral values, perceived strength on national security, or any of the other explanations usually offered. To an almost embarrassing extent, they all come down to just five words: southern whites starting voting Republican.[4]

Reagan became governor of California in 1966 in response to the violent riots in Watts and student protests in Berkeley. According to Norman Podhoretz, 'Reagan can also be considered one of the first neoconservatives, having been a liberal Democrat for most of his political life and then becoming a Republican only at the age of fifty-one.'[5] Reagan lost the New Hampshire primary in 1976 on a platform of transferring $90 billion from the federal government to the states, a program of states' rights. Reagan came to power in 1980 riding the wave of anti-government sentiment that blamed the excesses of the 1960s (Vietnam War and campus protest, feminism, environmentalism) and 1970s (Watergate, energy crisis, high interest rates, recession, inflation) on 'failures of government' and produced an anti-government revolt, overlooking the role of progressive government and the New Deal in attacking vested interests.[6]

In *Fear of Falling*, Barbara Ehrenreich provides a cultural profile of the rise of the New Right in the 1980s, again tracing its emergence to the culture shock of the 1960s. Political scientists like Samuel Huntington viewed the civil rights, students, and anti-war movements of the 1960s as 'excesses of democracy.' In cultural politics and pop psychology they were viewed as outgrowths of 'permissiveness,' the permissiveness of the parents of the Benjamin Spock generation and their hedonistic children who were incapable of self-control and deferring gratification. When 'permissiveness' entered discourse in the 1960s it represented moral laxity to explain rebelliousness and deviance; it was linked to the 'New Class' as the enablers of social permissiveness. Targeting the poor for 'welfare dependency' was a way of restoring discipline to society. The ideas of the New Right came to power with the Reagan administration. Cutting government programs was a way of depriving the 'liberal elite' of their power base and letting market forces provide the discipline that society and the poor needed. Targeting the liberal elite as the enablers of the culture of permissiveness became a political project: 'embrace the working class and the business leaders and cast out the "sickening" New Class.'[7] In Britain, Thatcher's reforms stemmed from a similar revulsion towards the 1960s; according to Thatcher the 1960s destroyed the Victorian values of self-discipline and restraint.[8]

Meanwhile the Democrats were also weakened when suburbanization contributed to the decline of urban political machines. The backlash against the 1960s coincided with the breakup of the liberal coalition as Jews seceded from their alliance with the civil rights movement. As American Jews achieved higher education and entered the professions they became less vulnerable to racial prejudice, even though they remained excluded from the boardrooms of blue chips and commercial banks. The political origins of neoconservatism are often talked about – former liberals and Marxists, Jews and Catholics, who moved to the right – but there were also cultural and racial subtexts to this secession. In the first major article Norman Podhoretz wrote, in 1963, 'My Negro Problem – and Ours,' he recalled his youth growing up in Brooklyn and how as a boy he felt intimidated by and feared blacks. He concluded, 'What kind of feelings do I have about Negroes today? What happened to me, from Brooklyn, who grew up fearing and envying and hating Negroes? Now that Brooklyn is behind me, do I fear them and envy them and hate them still? The answer is yes, but not in the same proportions and certainly not in the same way.'[9] This sheds light on the *emotional* tissue of neoconservatism.

Reflecting on neoconservatism in 1995, Podhoretz notes,

> By now most neoconservatives have pretty well given up on the welfare state – by which, as they see it, American society has been mugged just as surely as they themselves once were by reality.... There is hardly any disagreement over the harm the welfare state has done in fostering illegitimacy and all the terrible pathologies that flow from babies having babies.[10]

Again the same subtext emerges: prejudice and tandem revulsion of the counterculture and the welfare state.

The Reagan reforms, which are now called neoliberalism, thus originated not in economic designs but *primarily* in cultural sentiments and political schemes that sought to *use* market forces – unleashing market forces was a way of disciplining society. If the problem is excess of democracy and government is democratic, then trimming government is a way of bringing democracy back under control. Thus the general thrust was to instill social discipline by cutting social welfare and unleashing the 'free market' (aka corporate rule).

Reagan built on conservative trends going back to the 1950s with George Wallace, Richard Nixon, and Spiro Agnew.[11] The main six conservative families such as Scaife, Coors, and Mellon provided major funding for conservative campaigns and think-tanks, again motivated by cultural and psychological upset about the turmoil of the 1960s. The Heritage Foundation, American Enterprise Institute, Hoover Institution and Federalist Society, along with dozens of other conservative think-tanks, were founded during the 1970s.[12] The religious right with the Moral Majority, the Religious Roundtable, the Assembly of God churches and their direct-mail techniques bolstered the Republican Party.

The South's response to Emancipation was Jim Crow laws and the Dixie regime of low wages, low taxes, and low services. To secure the support of 'Dixiecrats' Democrat governments from Roosevelt to Truman implemented modernization projects in the South such as the Tennessee Valley Authority; yet the New Deal failed to alter institutions, labor laws, or taxes in the South.[13] In time, the Southern Democrats or Dixiecrats became the Southern flank of the Republican Party and the backbone of the Southern strategy. Thus the backlash against the 1960s merged with the backlash against the new wave of black emancipation and this combo set the stage for thirty-five years of American backlash culture and backlash politics. After civil rights legislation emancipated African Americans, the Dixie regime that had kept blacks in their place after Reconstruction in the South became the *national* policy, implemented by Republicans or Democrats who adopted a Republican platform.

Reagan economics gave a new twist to conservative economics. Supply-side economics provided a rationale for regressive tax cuts, which cut government to size, disciplined society by reducing social spending, and deprived Democrats of their power tools. Milton Friedman and the Chicago School inspired reduction in money-supply growth. Reagan's policies led to major recessions, the 'second slump' of 1982 and 1987, and deliberate budget deficits. Michael Lind views Reagan economics as a variant of 'Southernomics,' rooted 'in the older late-medieval plantation economies that Britain, Spain and other European empires established in the Americas in the 1500s and 1600s,' with the agribusiness of the American South and south-west continuing the traditions of rightless labor, whether in the form of slavery or the Bracero program (the labor program under which Mexican manual workers were temporarily allowed to work in the US in the 1940s). Lind notes another feature of the Reagan policies: 'Thanks to the predominance in national politics of the South and Southwest since the 1970s, what was once the foreign economic strategy of the Confederate States of America has become the trade policy of the United States as a whole.'[14]

Conservative campaigns and think-tanks amplified these trends by focusing on cultural issues rather than on economics or foreign policy. Paul Weyrich, godfather of the conservative movement, wrote, 'The most important political idea of the mid-eighties is cultural conservatism.'[15] In 1988 Reagan scrapped the Fairness Doctrine that had sheltered the airwaves from corporate takeover, and right-wing talk radio took off. In 2003 Weyrich boasted that there are 1,500 conservative radio talk-show hosts and on the Internet 'all the successful sites are conservative.' 'In all, according to a study by the National Committee for Responsive Philanthropy, Heritage and other conservative think-tanks – the best known being the libertarian Cato Institute and the neoconservative American Enterprise Institute – spent an estimated $1 billion promoting conservative ideas in the 1990s.'[16]

As Norman Podhoretz notes, 'We are all Gramscians now.'[17] Thus the awareness on the left that moral leadership matters and that political leadership has to be gained by gaining influence in civil society was adopted by the right, which also turned to cultural strategies. The conservative campaigns, mushrooming talk radio stations and polarizing media like Fox News cannot be simply interpreted as business and corporate strategies. They reflect cultural pathos and political designs, driven by attempts to re-establish elite authority through a combination of cultural propaganda, economic discipline, and political control. Policies to instill economic discipline included avoiding full employment (by adjusting interest rates), demobilizing trade unions, and cutting social spending, along with virulent attacks on 'welfare deadbeats,' which turned the Johnson administration's war on poverty into a war on the poor. Backlash politics did not merely introduce economic changes but cultural changes as well. A recent editorial in the major daily of Illinois state capital sums up these changes:

> Not happy with your lack of health insurance? Eat healthier and you won't need it. Not happy because your workplace closed and now you're forced to work two jobs to make as much as one used too? It's your own fault for not getting that master's degree in business. Not happy because the color of your skin seems to draw the attention of the police

as you drive? Quit whining – you should be more careful where you
drive. You're not happy because it's impossible for your power chair to
negotiate the curb cuts in your neighborhood? Blame your mother for
taking thalidomide. Not happy because it's getting more expensive to
gas up your car? Blame the environmentalists for blocking drilling off
the coast of Florida. Not happy because that low-paying job you had
laid you off to hire new immigrants? Don't blame the owners; blame
the new immigrant. And so it goes. They've got us so turned around
that for the first time in history the have-nots are blaming folks who
have less for our dissatisfaction. In fact, many of us are more likely
to identify with the rich and powerful than with our neighbors and
co-workers.[18]

The cultural and political backlash against the 1960s merged with
Dixie capitalism to produce *Dixie politics*. Thus a dark twist to America's right-wing turn is that it is the revenge of the Confederacy.

The sociologist Daniel Bell interpreted the cultural changes
of the 1960s as part of the *Contradictions of Capitalism*. As capitalism matures to a mass consumption stage, media and marketing
promote consumerist, hedonistic values that are fundamentally different from the work ethic that is the underpinning of capitalism's
production stage, the ethic of deferred gratification and savings
and investment rather than consumption. Thus the irony is that
the permissiveness that conservatives blamed on parents and liberal
elites was in part built into the dynamics of American capitalism.
The second irony is that the turn to authoritarianism was implemented in the name of 'freedom' and corporate rule was established
in the name of the 'free market,' recycling the anti-communist
rhetoric of the Free World. The third irony is that deregulation
set in motion a different kind of permissiveness. Commenting on
the widening income inequality, Paul Krugman faults 'permissive
capitalism': 'Since 1980 the U.S. political scene has been dominated
by a conservative movement firmly committed to the view that
what's good for the rich is good for America.'[19] In effect, the 'liberal
elite' and those who sought to use government to help the poor
were pushed aside for an elite that was business-friendly (lobbyists,

lawyers), upwardly mobile (yuppies), invested in Wall Street and the defense industries, and innovative (financial wizards, dotcom entrepreneurs). In Reagan style, ideological optimism went together with political authoritarianism. It is 'morning again in America' meant betting on the strong and celebrating winners; hence the accompanying cult of *leadership*. Thus the federal government sanctioned and institutionalized the apartheid economy that existed in the Southern model. Thus began the great corporate give-away and the return to the gilded age – the shift from social welfare to corporate welfare, the shift from the welfare society to the warfare society, the shift from entrepreneurial capitalism to crony capitalism. Eventually new elites walked off with the winnings. Indeed, the terminology 'permissive capitalism' is deeply ironic for it was against permissiveness – the permissiveness of the liberal elite, the Benjamin Spock generation, and welfare dependency – that the conservative reforms were implemented. With the right-wing turn came not just a growing concentration of wealth but also a steep concentration of power with ripple effects throughout society and with the corporatization of media and Wall Street and the Pentagon as major beneficiaries.

Easy Money

In the 1990s finance, insurance and real estate overtook manufacturing in US national income. Financial services became the largest sector of the economy at 20 percent of GNP, larger than manufacturing at 12.5 percent and larger than the next largest sector, health care at 14 percent.[20] Financialization, 'a process whereby financial services, broadly construed, take over the dominant economic, cultural and political role in a national economy,'[21] carries several meanings. First, it is a trend that is common to mature economies; economies build their strength in agriculture, then commerce, then manufacturing, and finally in financial instruments.

Second, in the era of accelerated globalization financialization is a global trend.

> According to the McKinsey Global Institute, the ratio of global financial assets to world output soared from 109 percent in 1980 to 316 percent in 2005. The value of the global stock of equities and bonds reached about $140,000 bn by the latter year. On top of this mountain is piled yet another, made of derivatives, whose face value reached $286,000 bn in 2006, up from a mere $3,450 bn in 1990.[22]

Third, financialization is the final phase in cycles of hegemony, the 'endgame of champions.' Hegemons build their strength in agriculture, industry and military capability, and when competitors begin to match their lead, the hegemon's financial lead remains and outlasts the others. This applied to the Spanish Hapsburg Empire, Dutch hegemony, the British Empire, and for some time to the United States.

Fourth, the US has been a trendsetter in the financialization of the world economy. Riding the wave of late-twentieth-century globalization, Wall Street, the Treasury, and the IMF worked in concert to further American financial interests. IMF conditions and World Bank structural adjustment programs promoted the liberalization of capital markets, dismantling barriers to foreign investors and banks in developing countries. This entailed the monetization of economies, making assets tradable, the rise of stock markets, and the entry of international banks, easing the flow of speculative capital ('hot money'). While the deregulation of capital markets benefited Wall Street enormously, it prompted financial crises from Russia to Latin America, culminating in the Asian crisis of 1997–98 and Argentina's collapse in 2001.[23] When financial crisis ensued, major financial interests were bailed out while local assets were sold off in fire sales.

Fifth, financialization has been furthered by innovations in financial engineering, made possible by the combination of information technology and deregulation. Information technology, 24/7 global banking, and the interconnectivity of markets gave a tremendous boost to the financial sector. Deregulation of the financial sector from the Carter and Reagan administrations onward removed the barriers between different financial institutions (such as banks and insurance companies), allowed financial institutions to operate across state borders, lifted limits on the fees that credit card companies can charge, and unleashed finance. This set the stage for mass marketing campaigns for consumer credit and innovations in options, futures, derivatives, and hedge funds built on derivatives with increasingly inscrutable mathematical models and quantitative investment. The deregulation of telecoms and energy contributed to the feast. 'During the boom, the energy and telecom sectors each issued roughly one trillion dollars' worth of new debt, manna for the financial services industry.'[24] This set the pace for the financial wizardry that produced Enron, WorldCom, and HealthSouth. Sixth, neoliberalism as the dominant form of capitalism since 1980 has been characterized by the return to hegemony of the financial sector.[25]

Thus finance matters in several ways – as an economic sector (just as industry, agriculture, and retail), as a sector that mediates between other sectors, as a leading field, as a field that is closely linked to the rise of the US, and as an arena of global competition.

In the US financialization has been closely linked to government policies; its path has been smoothed by the policies of the Federal Reserve and especially its chairman Alan Greenspan. Between 1854 and 1945 the US was in recession 42 percent of the time; since 1945 the US has been in recession only 14 percent of the time. If recessions have gone out of fashion, they have been replaced by a series of financial fixes (Box 3.1). A pattern these interventions share is that the credit instruments are privately owned whereas major credit risk is socialized. This is one of the intriguing features of the financial sector. First, several financial institutions win whether the market goes up or down because they earn a fee from *any* transaction. Second, the casino rule applies – the house usually wins. Third, because the payments sector is essential to the stability of the economy, finance is treated as a public good and large financial

---

Box 3.1   Financial fixes in the United States

- The decoupling of the dollar from gold (1971)
- The oil-dollar standard adopted when OPEC agreed to price oil in dollars (1974)
- The Plaza Accord that devalued the yen (1985)
- The 'reverse Plaza Accord' that increased the value of the dollar (1995)
- Bail-outs of domestic financial institutions (Continental Illinois Bank 1984, Savings & Loan 1989–92, Citibank 1990, Long Term Capital Management 1998, Amaranth 2006)
- Bail-outs of international financial crises (Mexico 1984–95, Brazil, Argentina 1989–92, Asia 1997, Russia 1998, Brazil 1999, Argentina 2001)
- Emergency interest rate cuts (1987, 1989–92, 1995, 1998, 2001–03, 2007, 2008).[26]

---

interests are politically sheltered. Thus central banks guarantee the deposits in commercial banks through arrangements such as the Federal Deposit Insurance Corporation in the US, a buffer against system crisis that also makes bank failure difficult. Fourth, major Wall Street institutions are usually represented in government and the Treasury. Fifth, the financial sector has the wherewithal to fund political campaigns and buys political influence regardless of the party in power.

The 1990s' boom was followed by the Greenspan era of easy credit. During the Clinton years with Robert Rubin as treasury secretary the new economy boom was accompanied by fiscal conservatism. When this ended with the Asian crisis, the collapse of Long Term Capital Management and the crash of the dotcom stocks in March 2000, Greenspan's easy money policies papered over the cracks. The Nasdaq bust was followed on its heels by two other shocks, the attacks of September 11 and the Enron spate of corporate scandals. Greenspan's easy credit smoothed over these bumps as well.

It was Mr Greenspan who, in the aftermath of the dotcom bust, practically drowned asset markets with a tidal wave of liquidity and easy money. It was Mr Greenspan who drove the Federal funds rate – the rate charged by United States banks for lending to their peers – down to 1 percent in 2003–04, a four-decade low. And it was Mr Greenspan who opened the floodgates of liquidity that might have saved the United States equity market, for a time, but that also triggered an unsustainable boom in government and corporate debt, residential property and a carnival of mortgage lending unimpaired by anything approaching prudence.[27]

Greenspan endorsed the Bush tax cuts for the wealthy and helped Bush economics along with low interest rates. The Federal Reserve's policies furthered the deindustrialization (Greenspan wondered why industry is necessary) and financialization of the economy and set the US firmly on its course of foreign borrowing. The massive deficits built during the G.W. Bush administration are the crowning achievement of this era. Under the motto 'deficits don't matter' state and local debt rose to $1.7 trillion and the savings rate, which had been around 10 percent in the 1970s, dwindled to −0.5 percent in 2005 and −1 percent in 2006, a negative rate that was only matched during the depth of the Depression in 1933. Mortgage debt stood at $4.4 trillion in 2000 and rose steeply to $7.5 trillion in 2004, while total household debt rose from $6.5 trillion in 2000 to $10.2 trillion in 2004 – both almost doubled in four years.

In 2005 the national debt stood at $13.5 trillion, 115 percent of GDP. In 2007 the current account deficit was $800 billion per year and the US borrowed $70 billion per month and $3 billion each trading day. In 2006 alone the US borrowed 60 percent of all global credit. The interest on the debt is $7 billion per week. This means that poorer countries are funding American overconsumption. It also means increasing foreign ownership of American assets.

Foreign credit enables the US to keep interest rates low. The Federal Reserve's low interest rates (at 1 percent during 2003–04, below the rate of inflation) turned the boom into a bubble – 'the credit bubble, the mortgage finance bubble, the hedge-fund bubble, and the systemic liquidity (money supply) bubble.'[28] Low interest rates flooded the market with liquidity and enabled companies to borrow to buy other companies (leveraged buyouts), which ushered in a wave of mergers and acquisitions that, in turn, pushed the Dow Jones index over 13,000, lifting Wall Street to unprecedented levels at a time when the 'real economy' of American workers was shrinking. The second effect of low interest rates was that it made mortgages cheap, which led to rising house prices; rising real estate enabled home owners to refinance their mortgages, which supported consumer spending and rising debt. Paul Krugman noted in 2005, 'the fact is that the U.S. economy's growth over the past few years has depended on two unsustainable trends: a huge surge in house prices and a vast inflow of funds from Asia. Sooner or later, both trends will end, possibly abruptly.'[29]

According to Kevin Phillips, 'the evidence is that once a great economic power goes so far down the deficit-and-debt route, Pandora's fiscal box cannot be closed. The Spanish, the Dutch, and the British, each in turn, proved unable to turn back their public debt once it gained momentum because the vested interests involved were too great.' Also in the US, 'For most firms, federal debt has meant gravy, not hardship.' Hence 'As massive debt becomes a major national problem, it also becomes a financial opportunity and vested interest.'[30]

Easy money is the foundation of what has been called the 'borrower–industrial complex' but should be termed the 'lender–borrower service complex' for it accompanied the transformation of the American economy into a service economy. Easy money conceals the actual value of this economy. Greenspan's legacy, according to *The Economist*, 'will be the biggest economic imbalances in American history.'[31] Greenspan's low interest rates ushered in a phase in which part of America's economic prosperity 'is based not on genuine gains in income, nor on high productivity growth, but on borrowing from the future.'[32] When Greenspan left the Federal Reserve, Princeton economists called him 'the greatest central banker who ever lived,' whereas Senate minority leader Harry Reid called him 'one of the biggest political hacks in Washington,' only to be shushed by fellow Democrats.

Extreme capitalism is built in many layers, but easy money connects most of them. While easy money made corporations awash with funds it didn't improve their productivity, efficiency, capacity utilization, or profitability. It did change corporate governance and reinforced the financialization of corporations and the rise of the chief financial officer alongside the chief executive officer. In 1950 profits from the financial sector accounted for 8 percent of total US corporate earnings, for 20 percent in 1990, and for 31 percent in 2006.[33] Another assessment notes, 'The money that's made from manufacturing stuff is a pittance in comparison to the amount of money made from shuffling money around. Forty-four percent of all corporate profits in the U.S. come from the financial sector compared with only 10% from the manufacturing sector.'[34] Leading American manufacturers such as the automakers made their profits no longer from selling cars but from selling finance. These changes eroded cohesion within firms. According to the CEO of Costco, 'obscene salaries send the wrong message through a company. The message is that all brilliance emanates from the top; that the worker on the floor of the store or the factory is insignificant.'[35] The super salaries at the top, the growing role of the CFO and the financial department, and the cost-cutting exercises of the new incoming MBAs all combine to concentrate corporate power at the top. The mergers and acquisitions that prop up stock values do not necessarily improve corporate efficiency but in some cases erode productivity.

Another manifestation of the easy money era is the rise of hedge funds, overtaking commercial and investment banks. A former chair of Deutsche Bank referred to financial markets as the fifth estate. Wall Street campaign funding cements links with Permanent Washington and Congress; lobbies and media are other components of this constellation. Hedge funds' lobbyists have been active gathering 'political intelligence' in Washington. Wall Street influence is being consolidated through political appointments. The G.W. Bush administration was nicknamed the 'Goldman Sachs administration' because of the many executives from this firm in political appointments, from Hank Paulson on down.[36]

Easy money and soaring Wall Street were the basis for the growth of a rentier class and a new phalanx of American billionaires. The entry level of the Forbes 400 stands at $900 million (2007); their total wealth adds up to $1.1 trillion. Most fortunes among the 374 American billionaires are in real estate and oil. Easy money underlies the conversion of debt into financial opportunity, the growth of super incomes, and the steep rise in income and social inequality. Finance as the largest economic sector has profound ripple effects on the structure of society:

> Its narrowing employment base, some 8 million in 2004 out of a national workforce of 131 million, stood in sharp contrast to the much broader uplift of manufacturing in, say, 1960, when good production employed 17 million Americans out of a workforce of 68 million.
> This too is in keeping with the later stages of previous leading world economic powers: finance distributes its concentrated profits to a much smaller slice of the population.[37]

Since the funny money bubble of the new millennium has been accompanied by growing economic apartheid, it has been described as 'class warfare by the rich.'[38] The implication is that increasingly social inequality is the foundation of the new American economy and not a mere sideshow.

Information Rules

Financial services hinge on information: 'Information is both the process and the product of financial services. Their raw materials are information: about markets, risks, exchange rates, returns on investment, creditworthiness. The products are also information: the result of adding value to these informational inputs.'[39]

A central assumption of neoclassical economics is that market forces provide superior circulation of information. Markets allocate resources more efficiently than government planning because information circulates more swiftly and widely through market mechanisms, hence free-market competition is superior. Revived by Hayek this view entered Chicago School economics. It applies on the assumption of 'perfect competition,' which assumes in turn that market actors have adequate and symmetric access to information. Meanwhile several Nobel prizes in economics have been awarded for research that demonstrates that this assumption doesn't hold and that asymmetric information is the rule.

It is no coincidence that the crime of the epoch is distorting and falsifying information: insider trading, backdating stock options, inflating earnings, and fudging the numbers. 'Pretexting,' backdating, 'market timing' are Wall Street weasel words for cheating, or keeping information as asymmetric as possible. The Enron, WorldCom, HealthSouth, and Global Crossing scandals share key features.

> Though extraordinarily diverse, these crimes all have a common trait: they were sins of information. Most of them involved an expert, or a gang of experts, promoting false information or hiding true information; in each case the experts were trying to keep the information asymmetry as asymmetric as possible.[40]

Manipulating information takes myriad forms, such as insider trading, inflated earnings reports, backdating stock options (to enhance CEO remuneration), mixing consulting and auditing so accounting firms join the party, Wall Street investment firms rewarding good customers with lucrative trading favors, and generally fudging the numbers. In 2005 sixty major corporations with a stock market value of $3 trillion restated their earnings.[41] Thus fraud is an intrinsic part of contemporary financial hegemony. Creative accounting enabled Enron, WorldCom, HealthSouth, Global Crossing, and Parmalat to soar. Fraud was an ingredient in the savings-and-loan collapse, and again in the subprime mortgage crisis of 2007.

> Fraud has been detected up and down the financing chain: just as borrowers have lied to get better rates and larger loans, mortgage

brokers and loan officers have lied to borrowers about the terms of their loans and may also have lied to the banks about the qualifications of the borrowers. Appraisers, likewise, have lied about the value of the properties involved.[42]

Bernanke, the Federal Reserve chairman, conceded that 'the recent rapid expansion of the subprime market was clearly accompanied by deterioration in underwriting standards and, in some cases, by abusive lending practices and outright fraud.'[43] Part of the problem is the 'expert service problem' in which the expert who diagnoses the problem is the same who will be paid to fix it and may have an incentive to misrepresent the flaw.

If the central bank sets the standard by providing easy money the economy gradually turns into a giant pyramid scheme, which hinges on continued expansion for its functioning and hinges on fraud for its continued expansion. Eventually this spills over into every sector. Student loans have been another link in the chain. Universities enter into lucrative arrangements with student loan providers. Students take on inflated loans to fund their studies and then inflate their credentials to obtain jobs that enable them to pay back the loans. Thus gradually fraud trickles down through society. In winner-takes-all markets the gains of winning are so huge that winning (or making the numbers) becomes an end in itself and the end justifies the means. Athletes take drugs and teams take sponsors. This involves an American tradition: 'Forget the cowboy. The true all-American hero is the confidence man: breezy, self-invented, ambitious, protean,'[44] as in Herman Melville's novel *The Confidence Man*. But at some point the music stops.

The main components of the 2007 credit crunch are similar as in the Asian crisis of 1997–98: easy money, a real estate bubble, and a weak banking system. The latter isn't usually associated with the United States, but 'having gorged on overly easy money for years, Anglo-Saxon financial markets are suffering from indigestion.'[45] The payback comes in two forms: a liquidity crisis – which is actually a crisis of confidence and solvency – and a weakening dollar. Central banks intervene by injecting liquidity or lowering interest rates – stretching the easy money cycle and fixing the problem with the same method that caused the previous one, so each further extension of easy money weakens the foundations of the American economy.

According to Kevin Phillips, the Clinton administration came in on a platform of challenging Wall Street but changed course while in office. According to Stiglitz, the New Democrats were obsessed with financial markets from the outset, and to demonstrate their New Democrat credentials policymakers leaned pro-business. The deregulation of telecoms and financial markets led to the boom that fed into the dotcom and Enron crises. The political system is not merely unable to challenge Wall Street; it enables Wall Street, just as Wall Street enables Washington. Washington has relaxed financial regulation under both Democratic and Republican administrations.[46] Public forums to spell this out are scarce. As major Wall Street forces, the media big six are not wont to turn the tables on themselves. Directing blame elsewhere is politically more convenient. Blame China and the value of the renminbi, blame free trade and immigrants. This matches other Washington conventions, such as blame attacks from Iran for the debacle in Iraq; blame Pakistan for the debacle in Afghanistan; blame Hamas for the impasse in the Middle East. Meanwhile, it is in this setting of extreme capitalism that policymakers and advocates from the right and center moved to the left, such as Kevin Phillips, Paul Craig Roberts, and Clyde Prestowitz. For all the attention bestowed on left-wing intellectuals who turned neoconservative, this is another side of the American equation.

Subprime and the World Economy

Foreign credit has been entering the US via Treasury bills, bonds and other credit instruments at $3 billion per trading day (2007). This inflow enabled the Federal Reserve to keep interest rates low, at 1 percent in 2003–04. Low interest rates fuel the American economy in two major ways. Cheap credit enables firms' leveraged buyouts and mergers and acquisitions, which in turn prop up the stocks of the firms buying and bought and the middling banks. Second, low interest rates made mortgages cheap, and larger mortgages fuelled a housing bubble. Rising real estate values, mortgage refinancing, and easy credit boosted consumer spending. American consumer spending, in turn, kept the world economy spinning and Asian exports and Asian vendor financing going. This charmed circle has kept the world economy in thrall.

The subprime mortgage sector was the latest extension of the easy credit bubble, the latest extension of funneling credit through the consumer grid, on terms that might be viable if the housing market continued its rise, but since it is the last and lowest segment of the money pyramid this was unlikely from the start.

Subprime mortgages grew massively during this period. Adjustable rate mortgages represented 40 percent of mortgages during 2004–05 (at $390 billion). Most of these were due to reset beginning in 2007 (involving $1 trillion). The subprime default rate was 10 percent already in 2006. The subprime market in the US is 20 percent of mortgages (in the UK it is 8 percent). The loans were sold to banks who securitized them as bonds ($800 billion in 2007) and derivatives and resold them in structured loans and collateralized debt obligations, and so forth (incurring a loss of 40 percent in 2007). In late 2006 the housing market began to slow and 2007 brought payback time. The collapse of subprime mortgage lending prompted a wider credit crunch.

> At the root of the subprime problem was easy credit: lenders and their brokers were often rewarded for generating new mortgages on the basis of volume, without being directly exposed to the consequences of borrowers defaulting. During several years of strong capital markets and strong investor appetite for high-yielding securities, lenders became accustomed to easily selling the risky home loans to Wall Street banks. The banks in turn packaged them into securities and sold them to investors around the globe.[47]

Earning higher commissions on subprime mortgages, brokers offered them also to borrowers who qualify for normal fixed-rate
mortgages. Automated underwriting software, a technique that was
first developed in the 1970s to process car loans and credit card ap-
plications, was used to generate as much as 40 percent of subprime
loans. A leader in the subprime mortgage market, New Century
Financial, on the brink of bankruptcy in 2007, 'promised mortgage
brokers on its website that with its FastQual automated underwriting
system, "We'll give you loan answers in just 12 seconds!"[48]

Speculative home buying by 'flippers', who borrow money or
leverage their own homes with double mortgages to buy properties,
make some improvements and then expect to sell them quickly,
joined the pyramid scheme, again on the premiss of continuing
expansion. False advertising and nonfunctioning credit-rating agencies compounded the situation.

The collapse of the subprime sector is a symptom of a wider
problem: 'The real issue has been the excess liquidity created by
the central banks through a decade of ever-more ambitious crisis
management. The risks created by those "solutions" were not identified, let alone measured, by their econometric models.'[49] Robert
Wade points to the institutional dimension of the situation: 'The
basic problem is that finance has moved from servant to master,
from tail to dog. It has acquired so much structural power as to
shape the conditions of existence of everyone else.'[50]

Securitization, or mortgages bundled in credit packages and derivatives sold to other banks, facilitated the real estate bubble. The
vanishing boundary between commercial and investment banks
and between banking and non-bank forms of finance facilitated
sprawling derivatives, hedge funds, and Quantitative Investment,
supported by insurance companies and pension funds. Hedge funds
became larger players than banks even though their risks were
underwritten by banks through arcane methods of splicing debt.

The current crisis resembles the savings and loan crisis of the
early 1990s, Japan's real estate bubble bursting, and the Asian crisis

of 1997–98. Long-term finance provided on short-term conditions is vulnerable to short-term market fluctuations, as in Thailand's hot money crisis. In this financial crush, however, 'Emerging market debt is the new safe haven.'[51] For a change, emerging markets have been unaffected because, having learnt from the Asian crisis, they built cash buffers. Sovereign wealth funds in China, Singapore, Qatar, Abu Dhabi and other places now emerge as new sources of stable liquidity.

American consumption accounts for at least 20 percent of world consumption.[52] The chilling American housing market since the end of 2006 has withdrawn $800 billion from consumer spending. American retail sales were down in 2007. A cycle is ending. The world economy is slowly decoupling from American consumer spending and shifting gear to growing demand in China, India, and Asia. High petrol prices create surplus liquidity in oil-exporting countries and the United Arab Emirates has emerged as a financial hub. In September 2007 the Borse Dubai and Qatar together bought a 48 percent share of the London Stock Exchange. Financial centers from London to the Netherlands vie to attract Islamic banking. With the rerouting of financial flows Shanghai and Hong Kong come to the fore as financial centers. The headlines have been changing for some time: 'Overseas investors lose taste for U.S. securities.' 'Gulf liquidity offers glimmer of hope for subprime relief.' 'China and India will shield GE from US downturn.'[53] One risk is that American easy credit spills over into the world economy in a massive global oversupply of dollars. The ramifications of the gradual decoupling of the world economy from American consumers are taken up in Chapter 8.

FOUR

The Trouble with Hegemony

ACCORDING TO DEEPAK LAL, professor of development economics at UCLA, 'the major argument in favor of empires is that, through their pax, they provide the most basic of public goods – order – in an anarchical international society of states.' However, observes Lal, 'empires have unfairly gotten a bad name, not least in U.S. domestic politics. This is particularly unfortunate, as the world needs an American pax to provide both global peace and prosperity.' On this note he concludes his lecture *In Defense of Empires* at the American Enterprise Institute in 2002.[1]

British historian Niall Ferguson also argues that the world needs 'liberal empire' and the US should fulfill this role. Both refer to the British Empire, view empire in a benevolent light, and seek to 'sell' empire to reluctant and skeptical Americans with some advice on how to do empire better. Thus American neoconservatives find overseas support for their argument for benevolent hegemony. Empire for the sake of stability and prosperity is a classic thesis. The reverse is at least as valid: empires are destabilizing because they come about through conquest, and the prosperity they generate is lopsided. Besides, this thesis has already been examined by American political scientists, notably under the heading of hegemonic stability theory. This chapter resumes the debate on hegemonic stability and asks what its implications are for the United States now.

In the next chapter we discuss the distinction between empire and hegemony; here the focus is on hegemony. Hegemony is usually defined as a state exercising unrivalled leadership in economic, political, and military spheres. Thus, according to Wallerstein, hegemony is a situation where 'one power can largely impose its rules and its wishes (at the very least by effective veto power) in the economic, political, military, and even cultural arenas.'[2] The three instances of hegemony in recent history are the United Provinces (1620–70), the British Empire (1820–70), and the United States (1948–71). Hegemony is also increasingly understood as based at least in part on consent and not just coercion. This extends Antonio Gramsci's idea of hegemony as moral leadership to the international domain. Thus hegemony in this sense of consensual leadership exists 'when the hegemonic state creates an order based ideologically on a broad measure of consent.'[3]

Charles Kindleberger combined international leadership and stability. Robert Keohane rephrased this as a theory of hegemonic stability, which holds that 'a relatively open and stable international economic system is most likely to exist when there is a hegemonic state with two characteristics: it has a sufficiently large share of resources that it is able to provide leadership, and it is willing to pursue policies necessary to create and maintain a liberal economic order.'[4]

The keynote of hegemonic stability theory (HST) is the liberal market system. The theory has been in dispute from the outset. Arguably this theory is how American political science recovers from the Vietnam War by finding a new rationale for American power, now with an emphasis on economic stabilization rather than security. The main proponents of HST, such as Robert Keohane and Robert Gilpin, were also critics. In Gilpin's view, hegemonic stability applied to the US early on but this changed in the late 1960s.

> For two decades following the Second World War, the United States, largely for political and security reasons, subordinated many of its parochial economic interests to the economic well-being of its alliance partners.... In the late 1960s, however, the United States began to pursue economic policies that were more self-centered and were increasingly denounced by foreign critics.... By the 1980s, the United States was pursuing protectionist, macroeconomic, and other policies that could be identified as appropriate to ... 'a predatory hegemon.'[5]

This chapter reviews the hegemonic stability thesis to examine whether it now applies to the US. This is worth examining because it scrutinizes hegemony in terms of its major justification, its stabilizing effect. The idea that hegemony is stabilizing and specifically that American hegemony is stabilizing is shared by advocates of power – historians with a penchant for empire, realists who worry about problems of order, liberals who endorse the liberalism of power, neoliberals with a weak spot for strong states such as Deepak Lal and Thomas Friedman, and neoconservatives in pursuit of another American century. Hegemonic stability theory is their kind of theory. The irony is that HST does justify hegemony, but, according to its proponents, not American hegemony. When HST was formulated in the 1980s it didn't apply, according to its proponents, to the United States.

HST involves several components: hegemonic capacity (resources, competence), intention (willing), policies (implementation), and outcome (a liberal economic order). Since the US is not a unitary formation there is no single or homogeneous intent. Intention is a necessary but not a sufficient condition for stability to materialize, which also involves resources, implementation, and parties other than the US. The theory is prescriptive rather than descriptive and the hegemon's actual behavior may range from benevolent to coercive and exploitative.[6] There are more fundamental problems as well. What does it mean to say that the global economy has been 'relatively open and stable' if hegemony comes with a growing North–South inequality gap, clearly so since the 1980s? Relative openness may hold true from the viewpoint of the economies of the North, but for the global South 'hegemonic stability' has meant structural adjustment under the auspices of the Washington Consensus. Agricultural subsidies in the North ($1 billion per day in 2006) don't add up to openness and have been the stumbling block in the WTO Doha round.

In viewing economic effects as beneficial (a liberal order) and the effects of power as stabilizing, HST *assumes* that which is to be demonstrated. HST is by definition a top-down perspective. The world's underprivileged have little store in stability and their proposals for reform, such as the New International Economic Order in the 1970s, have come to naught. Hegemonic stability is a view from the North. *Hegemonic compromise* among the leading powers would be more straightforward and less candy-colored terminology. Along the lines of hegemonic compromise the European Union and Japan *grosso modo* accept American policies in the context of the IMF, G8, and WTO because they share overall benefits such as concessions on trade and agricultural policies (in the case of the EU), find shelter under the US military umbrella and benefit from American economic growth (in the case of Japan). This doesn't rule out disputes but they are not large enough to upset the applecart.[7]

Hegemonic stability theory describes a postwar constellation in which developing countries were kept from exit through the financial discipline of the IMF and that held sufficient promise, or insufficient frustration, as long as promises of reform provided a silver lining, such as in recent years the WTO Doha round (and the promise to cut agricultural subsidies in the North) and the Millennium Development Goals. Yet somehow the promises of reform never materialize as if they primarily serve as decorative elements to cheer up the status quo, just as the 'Roadmap to peace in the Middle East' has become a ceremonial gesture. Over time the cracks in hegemonic stability have widened – what of hegemonic stability in view of recurrent financial crises in emerging markets, American withdrawal from international treaties and chronic stalemate in the Middle East? What of hegemonic stability in view of the US doctrine of preventive war?

Proponents of the theory already found that hegemony stability ceased to apply to the US since the Vietnam War. Since the Reagan years of military rollback, the US military build-up after the end of the cold war, the G.W. Bush administration's aggressive unilateralism and mounting deficits, the role of the US has increasingly changed from hegemonic stabilization to destabilization. Pollack refers to the paradox of the 'revisionist hegemon': the hegemon is supposed to uphold the status quo, but the US government's preventive war and attempts to expand US dominance show the behavior of a revisionist state and thus suggest that the US is *not* hegemonic.[8] This holds implications for how we understand hegemony; should we replace hegemonic stability theory with a theory of hegemonic destabilization and replace the notion of the benign hegemon with that of the predatory hegemon? And if hegemonic stability was supposed to produce a 'relatively open and stable' international economy, what kind of world is hegemonic destabilization creating? This leads to the question of the unraveling of hegemony and the afterlife of hegemony, which is taken up in Chapter 8.

Predatory Hegemony?

Hegemonic stability theory holds that 'in the absence of a world government the global economy can be stabilized when a powerful nation plays the role of flywheel.' I quote from a precis by Robert Kuttner:

> The hegemon, in this conception, performs several stabilizing functions: it serves as quasi-central banker, providing the system with financial liquidity in times of stress, as well as credit to temper

exchange-rate instability; it serves as market of last resort and encourages other nations to keep their markets relatively open; being a rich
and technologically advanced nation, the hegemon is a net source of
development capital as well; and it also has a special responsibility for
keeping the peace. A hegemon, in Kindleberger's sense, is relatively
benign. Affiliation with its system is not coerced, but invited on the
basis of benefits that the hegemon offers other member nations. Indeed,
what differentiates hegemonic leadership from Caesarism is precisely
that the hegemon uses carrots rather than sticks and makes sacrifices to
preserve the system. Chief among these is that the hegemon endeavors
to be the system's best behaved free trader.[9]

Let's take each of these components and see whether they apply
now. This is a brief treatment in vignettes (a full treatment would
have to be book-length).

The hegemon provides the system with financial liquidity in times of stress.
Arguably this was the practice during the Bretton Woods system,
which ended when the US abandoned the parity of the dollar and
gold in 1971. During the 1980s and into the 1990s the US did provide
liquidity, although it came at a price of market conformity according to the stipulations of the Wall Street–Treasury–IMF complex.
The IMF bailout of Mexico's Tequila Crisis is a case in point. The
IMF interventions in crises in Asia in 1997–98 followed by Russia
and Latin America, were of a different character: with reluctant
and meager support in Congress they provided more sticks than
carrots, more financial discipline than largesse. Opening up developing country capital markets as part of IMF lending conditions
enabled American banks and hedge funds to play an increasingly
destabilizing role.[10]

Over time the US financial position has deteriorated sharply.
During the Clinton administration reducing the budget deficit was
a priority, but the Bush administration followed the Reagan administration in practicing extreme deficit financing. The US has become
the world's largest borrower, draining the world of liquid capital on
an unprecedented scale of $600 billion per year and $3 billion per

trading day. Year after year the IMF warns Washington that its budget deficits 'pose "significant risks" not just for the United States but for the rest of the world.' A 2003 IMF report notes: 'Higher borrowing costs abroad would mean that the adverse effects of U.S. fiscal deficits would spill over into global investment and output.'[11] In a brief period the financial situation has deteriorated to a level that destabilizes the world economy. Looking back, the hegemon's provision of liquidity has come with destabilizing effects all along: the liberalization of capital markets exposed developing countries to risk and speculative capital, along with the consequences of American credit bubbles.

The hegemon is a net source of development capital. The US has been one of the stingiest foreign aid donors among OECD countries and this function has long changed from minimal to negative: 'since 1972 the American economy has been a net importer of capital (to the tune of 17 percent of gross national product last year).'[12] On balance the US has been *draining* capital from developing countries. More significant is that, as I argue elsewhere, the American model has become a bottleneck for international development.[13]

The hegemon serves as market of last resort. While this has been true for quite some time, it has taken on a darker hue. By importing far more than it exports the US has built up a massive trade deficit. The US share of world output declined from 25.9 percent in 1960 to 21.5 percent in 1980 and continues to shrink.[14] The rapid rise of Asian Pacific Rim economies has been based on exports to the US. American and Asian dynamics dovetail: the rise of Wal-Mart to the status of the world's largest retailer has been paralleled by the rise of Chinese and East Asian imports in the US. But, coupled with American deindustrialization, loss of manufacturing jobs and increasingly also white-collar jobs, and growing American indebtedness at every level from households to the federal government, this is not a sustainable pattern.

The American economy has been deindustrializing on a massive scale and suffers structural job loss. 'The United States has lost 3 million manufacturing jobs in recent years.'[15] 'From 1995 to 2002, the number of factory jobs rose 22 percent in Canada and 24.6 percent in Spain, versus a loss of 11.3 percent in the United States.'[16] The differential is too large to be accounted for in terms of industrial maturity. Manufacturing jobs are cheaper in Mexico since NAFTA and cheaper still in China since China joined the WTO. Offshoring and outsourcing now extend to back office and software jobs that are cheaper in India. At Microsoft the motto is 'Think India' ('two heads for the price of one'). Blue-chip companies such as IBM have been moving jobs offshore; even state labor bureaus whose mandate is job creation outsource their information-processing jobs. A US senator outsourced a speech (on 'The impact of globalization on the Oregon economy') to a firm in Bangalore; the UK government outsourced election-related work to a Bangalore firm.[17] American Catholic churches, with clergy in short supply, outsource prayers: 'American, as well as Canadian and European churches, are sending Mass intentions, or requests for services like those to remember deceased relatives and thanksgiving prayers, to clergy in India.'[18]

One expectation is that '3.3 million services jobs in America will move offshore by 2015,' led by the information sector, as part of 'a trend that is real, irreversible and another step in the globalization of the American economy.'[19] In the 1990s vanishing manufacturing jobs seemed to be made up by new economy jobs, but this prospect faded with the dotcom bust. The standard Clinton-era response to job loss in manufacturing was what you earn is a result of what you learn. This is invalidated by recent trends or refers to yet a higher learning curve; the jobs that are now moving offshore include straightforward software programming and code reading, whereas software design remains onshore. But the American educational system is not prepared to take up the slack. The flexibility that enabled the US economy to generate many jobs during the 1990s now moves jobs offshore with the same agility. Flexibility, a post-Fordist codeword, applied to corporate agility all along. The present wave of job losses affects a middle class that is already burdened by debt, so this undermines consumer purchasing power, as became apparent in 2007–08.

The hegemon uses carrots rather than sticks. Like beauty, carrots or sticks are in the eye of the beholder. What have been the carrots for Central America, Nicaragua, Panama, El Salvador, or Haiti? Particularly since American victory in the cold war, Treasury and IMF policy increasingly became a political instrument to reward allies and discipline foes.[20] The US budget for foreign aid and diplomacy has been shrinking as steadily as military spending has been growing. American military expansion since the late 1980s results in a million soldiers in 350 bases and 800 military facilities in 130 countries. Does this suggest carrots or sticks?

The hegemon endeavors to be the system's best behaved free trader. The Clinton administration heralded the WTO as the spearpoint of American-led globalization alongside NAFTA and APEC. The G.W. Bush administration, in contrast, replaced reliance on the WTO with 'competitive liberalization' and bilateral free trade agreements.[21] Its recourse to steel tariffs and farm subsidies clashed with the WTO and steel tariffs have been repudiated by the WTO. The unilateralism of the Bush administration has a general negative impact on international trade; trade policy has increasingly become an instrument of power politics.[22]

The hegemon has a special responsibility for keeping the peace. If we think of the Vietnam War this claim borders on absurdity. After the end of the cold war the US defense strategy posture for unrivalled military dominance (proposed by Paul Wolfowitz as undersecretary of defense) was repudiated by Congress, only to be resurrected in subsequent doctrines of Overwhelming Force, Achieving Rapid Dominance, full spectrum dominance and preventive war. The keynote of the 1990s, humanitarian intervention (in Bosnia, Kosovo, Haiti, Somalia, and Kurdistan) has been selective in application and marred by ulterior motives.[23] A related problem is that the American military are trained for war and not for peacekeeping.

American military commitments are limited. Paul Kennedy refers to 'imperial overstretch': 'the sum total of the United States' global interests and obligations is nowadays far larger than the country's power to defend them simultaneously.'[24] The American investment in unrivaled military superiority since the end of the cold war has destabilizing ramifications of its own: it comes with neglect of diplomacy, a pattern of investments that distorts the US economy, and mammoth projects to sustain the military–industrial complex such as Plan Colombia and billion-dollar non-functioning weapons systems such as Raytheon's Patriot missile system and the Missile Defense Shield. The adoption of the preventive war doctrine in the 2002 National Security Strategy and the Pentagon strategy of 'permanent war' imply a growing militarization of foreign policy that is destabilizing. First, within the US, 'Mix the open-ended costs of war and reconstruction with huge tax cuts, shrinking tax revenues and a stalled economy, and you get a budget deficit bound to explode.'[25] Second, it has regional and international effects. According to the IMF, 'a prolonged war in Iraq could depress financial markets and put global economic recovery into jeopardy.'[26] This is recognized in the business press. In its *Risk Map 2004* report, Control Risks, an international security consultancy based in Britain, describes US foreign policy as 'the most important single factor driving the development of global risk.' In the private sector many 'believe that US unilateralism is creating a security paradox: by using US power unilaterally and aggressively in pursuit of global stability, the Bush administration is in fact precisely creating the opposite effect.'[27]

The hegemon makes sacrifices to preserve the system. Hegemony in the Gramscian sense of consensual leadership means that potentially all stand to benefit and that the rules of the game are perceived to be fair. But in the present American dispensation 'sacrifice is for suckers,'[28] and this applies also internationally. Political and electoral opportunism prevails in the US; applied in international affairs this approach flaunts the very rules and institutions that the US has helped to build over many years. American failure to comply with international law, a zigzagging and instrumental attitude to international institutions such as the United Nations, and withdrawal from or nonparticipation in international treaties and covenants, produce an opportunistic hegemony.

In its original formulation, hegemonic stability theory focuses on the global economy, which it views and represents from the standpoint of the North, and underplays the political and military components of hegemony,[29] which it views and represents in terms of their benign impact. If we consider that the original setting of hegemonic stability theory is the Vietnam War and its aftermath (1967–77), this is a remarkable bias. Consider hegemonic stability from a regional viewpoint and the picture doesn't get better. US hegemony in the Middle East has come at the expense of Palestinians and democratization in the region and is unstable. We can view hegemonic stability theory as a matrix in which the overall premises remain constant, the strategic emphases shift over time, and foreground and background change places. In hegemony thinking, economic and security considerations ('keeping the peace') have mingled all along. During the Clinton administration the geopolitics of the 'indispensable nation' functioned alongside neoliberal globalization; during the G.W. Bush administration the emphasis shifted to geopolitical concerns.[30] Thus hegemonic stability claims keep being reproduced in different guises: on political and security grounds, as conservatives and liberals alike applaud the expansion of American power 'in a chaotic world,' or alternatively on economic grounds.

Hegemonic stability thinking keeps reproducing the same bias: fascinated by the displays and machinations of power it is oblivious to the cost in human suffering and insecurity that domination and global hierarchy entails. In viewing the world from the top down, from establishment comfort zones looking outward, hegemonic stability thinking does not see and does not count the sacrifices that the underprivileged have been making to sustain stability, as part of the 'collateral damage' of stability.

Maintenance and Repair

Thus taking each component of hegemonic stability theory it is clear that the US has long ceased to perform this role. This erosion of hegemony is widely perceived and there are many diagnoses of and explanations for this sea change. Surveying the literature we can identify several clusters.

- *Hegemonic reform* A major preoccupation in American political science is repair and maintenance of hegemony, or 'getting hegemony right' – by using more 'soft power,' exercising restraint so hegemony is less offensive to other powers, strengthening cooperation with Europe via NATO, or using hegemony more benevolently.[31] These perspectives tend to focus on power politics, are usually short on political economy, and rarely question whether hegemony is in fact reparable.
- *Hegemony critique* According to Danner, the US is stuck in the cold war and imposes on the world a mindless hegemony, predominance for its own sake, or an 'empty hegemony.'[32] A large literature is political or political–military in emphasis and concerned with recent US administrations, sometimes in combination with an overall critique of American imperialism.
- *Hegemonic incapacity* While upbeat assessments of American primacy remain in ample supply,[33] a growing number of critics argue that the US has insufficient capacity to continue to perform a hegemonic role and several observe that the aims set

forth in the 2002 National Security Strategy outstrip American capacities.[34]

- *Hegemonic transition* Occasionally this is combined with a perspective on hegemonic transition towards trilateralism or multilateralism.[35] Kupchan offers guidelines the US should follow to ensure that American unipolarity can peacefully give way to a benign tripolarity, which goes beyond hegemonic reform towards international power sharing. However, reviving 1980s' trilateralism is not a valid option in twenty-first century globalization.

- *Hegemonic decline* This perspective has been prevalent in neo-Marxism and world-system theory and is long-term, systemic, and grounded in international political economy. In this view 1971, when the Bretton Woods system ended and the Tet offensive signaled defeat in Vietnam, was the 'signal crisis' of American hegemony. Wallerstein re-theorizes 'crisis of capitalism' as hegemonic transition.[36] Hegemonic decline may follow from a crisis of overproduction or from broader economic and political frailties.[37] The decline of American hegemony has been foretold since the 1970s and then faded as a theme, to re-emerge in the 1980s when Paul Kennedy raised the question of imperial overstretch. When this was overtaken by the boom of the 1990s, pundits proclaimed the 'decline of declinism' and the 'end of endism.'[38] Then the boom turned out to be a bubble.

Neoliberal globalization involved international institution-building that claimed legitimacy, even if it rested on the ideological grounds of market fundamentalism. It could boast appeal in view of the alleged dynamism of Anglo-American capitalism (never mind that inequality was rising steeply) and its pull in international financial markets, thus giving countries a stake in the project while leaving them little choice. The project of endless war is short on all these counts – legitimacy, appeal, and closure. With the US placing itself outside international law and international institutions and surrendering the pretense of legitimacy, what remains is rule by force.

This is global authoritarianism that dismantles the international institutional framework that the US has helped build over decades. American capitalism now commands as much appeal as Enron does. There is no charm to Uncle Sam's hard line and unwillingness to revise policies, particularly in the Middle East. By disregarding allies and international institutions the US gives countries an exit option. They may not be able to opt out of international financial markets and credit ratings, but they can opt out of exercises of power that don't include them.

The unraveling of hegemonic stability is built into the working of hegemony over time; hegemonic stability cannot last indefinitely. Hegemony tends to produce a concentration of power that becomes increasingly unaccountable. Several trends accumulate over time: the entanglements of the cold war, the military–industrial complex, domestic power plays, the 'Washington connection,' and transnational corporations overseas, all carry consequences for American political economy. The status of the dollar as world money allowed the US greater financial license than any other country. Such benefits accrued to American elites that checks and balances and safeguards gradually fell by the wayside; the political *portée* of the 'Reagan revolution' and subsequent deregulation is the gradual erosion of accountability, enabling elites to pursue increasingly narrower interests. In the ensuing economic decline the US becomes opportunistic and at times protectionist, regaining domestic stability at the expense of transnational stability. As a fair-weather ideology, neoliberalism has no provision for setbacks, so political and institutional resilience are in short supply. Thus the declining hegemon may purchase domestic stability by means of transnational destabilization.

This suggests the following main lines of hegemonic destabilization theory. As a process hegemony involves the accumulation of commitments over time, which produce imperial overstretch. In the domestic balance of forces hegemony privileges the security apparatus and fosters the development of a state-within-the-state;

illustrative episodes are the Pentagon papers, the Iran–Contra episode, and the intelligence foul-ups leading up to the Iraq war. The decision to attack Iraq marks a peak in the rise within the US of a massive concentration of unaccountable power that represents the biggest threat to the constitutional system since Watergate.[39] This raises the old question of '*quies custodiet*, or how to control authority'[40] and how to regulate the regulators. The domestic concentration of power offers economic and financial opportunities (for Wall Street, big oil, Halliburton, Bechtel), which furthers growing social inequality. At a late stage of hegemony it may be necessary to rebalance these disparities for electoral reasons, but short of fundamental changes in the power structure the tendency is to do so at the expense of external parties – by blaming globalization, free trade, immigrants, or the Chinese renminbi. This results in further hegemonic destabilization.

FIVE

Does Empire Matter?

THE PERPLEXITY THAT THE ACCOMPANYING CARTOON DEPICTS has become habitual. The task is finishing the job, but what again was the job? Accomplishing the mission, but what is the mission? Weapons of mass destruction, regime change, democracy in the Middle East, the freedom agenda, stay the course, combat terrorism, fight terrorism there or else it will be fought here, no appeasement – the rationales for the Iraq war change so often, they are hard to keep up with. It's over to plan C or D also because few remember what plan A was. A technical hitch is that the covert agenda of war is classified and not part of polite conversation.

There has been much talk about empire – is the US a reluctant empire, an inadvertent empire, empire in denial, arrogant empire, inarticulate empire, empire lite, benevolent empire, bipartisan empire, informal empire, empire of capital, empire without colonies, empire of bases, Wilsonian empire? Yet in many accounts 'empire' is a broad-brush description. An empire, according to the *American Heritage Dictionary*, is 'a political unit, often comprising a number of territories or nations, ruled by a single supreme authority.' American

TIME 3:17

TEMP 37°

TODAY'S WAR RATIONALE INVADED IRAQ TO PREVENT GAY MARRIAGE

By permission of Mike Luckovich and Creators Syndicate, Inc

power has gone through several, overlapping, stages – an early phase of imperial settler colonialism (manifest destiny) and regional expansion (including the Monroe Doctrine, the Spanish–American war and colonizing the Philippines); the cold war system of national security states wired through the 'Washington connection'; the network of neoliberal globalization under the canopy of the Washington Consensus, structural adjustment policies and the reach of multinationals; and the empire of bases, the grid of regional commands, airbases and 'lily pads' through which the US seeks to shape global security. Thus there are various strands to US hegemony – shaping countries' security policies and domestic and regional politics (cold war), economic policies (structural adjustment, aid, trade policies and trade pacts); but empire in the sense of controlling territory and sovereignty has been rare. This distinction is not unimportant; the fact that the US 'does not conquer' is one of the reasons why counterbalancing coalitions have been rare. This is why the new wars and the US exercising sovereignty over Afghanistan and Iraq, for brief periods, have been exceptional. This explains the surge of empire in the literature, but also indicates its limited purchase.

Arguably, then, the issue is not empire but hegemony and primacy. Empire is but one form that primacy takes and we shouldn't focus on the form. Aside from variations on the theme of empire the question that is more important is, does empire matter? The background of this question is the large place the new wars (war on terror, Afghanistan, Iraq) occupy in the US and the sprawling literature on empire. In relation to American problems and economic prospects, does empire matter? In relation to global concerns, does empire matter? Is empire the main street of history, a side street, or a cul-de-sac? Does empire make sense, is it important, and in what way is it important?

If the reference is to settler colonialism in North America, then the US has been imperialist from the outset. Some argue that the US has been imperialist all along (Appleman Williams, Chomsky, Zinn, Parenti, Petras, etc.) so the new wars are like a latent truth becoming manifest. This implies a soft-focus, wide-angle understanding of empire in which empire is a metaphor for domination and coercion.[1] Yet, though the US has experienced multiple imperial episodes and exercises global hegemony, the continuous-imperialism argument uses empire loosely, overstates the continuity of US policies, and understates the marked turn that recent policies and the Iraq war represent. I will use 'empire' generally interchangeably with hegemony and in a loose sense the way most literature does.

At the World Economic Forum in Davos in 2005 a major theme was the sinking dollar; in 2006 and 2007 it was the rise of China and India; and in 2008 it was the crisis of the Western financial system and the rise of sovereign wealth funds. In the World Social Forum during these years, mostly held in Porto Alegre, Brazil, most attention went to criticisms of neoliberal globalization. In either meeting American geopolitics hardly figured. If muscular foreign policy plays big in the US it doesn't necessarily matter in the rest of the world, or matter in the sense that many Americans think it would.

This chapter reflects on the implications, domestic and foreign, of the American pursuit of primacy. The Iraq war is widely perceived as having made the world more dangerous, war weariness is commonplace, and the literature on empire is staggering, so this treatment is pointed. The first section discusses the relationship between the new wars and corporate globalization. I question whether there is a rational relationship between the new wars and American capitalism. The second section addresses another major hypothesis for interpreting the new wars, the superpower syndrome and path dependence on the national security apparatus. The third section resumes the theme of the American bubble and argues that the extraordinarily high civilian casualty rates in Iraq and Afghanistan occur at the confluence of the US seeking land power on a distant continent, the tendency to view countries as strategic real estate, and American lack of cultural savvy.

Neoliberal Globalization

Does empire matter in light of the dynamics of contemporary globalization? Imperialism is a particularly clunky form of globalization, so nineteenth-century. In the twenty-first century is empire a viable project? Does neoliberal globalization – effected via international financial institutions and the WTO – need empire? If the main project is freeing up markets, especially capital markets, does empire matter or is control over territory and sovereignty rather a risky and costly burden and an unnecessary distraction? In 2003 the *Wall Street Journal* reported, 'Iraq's occupation government unveiled a plan to transform the country into a low-tax economy wide open to foreign investment' (21 September). If the aim is to create a free enterprise economy with an open capital market, does imperialism make sense in terms of cost–benefit analysis? In fact, if

Table 5.1   Policy profiles of recent US administrations

	Economics	Projects	Interventions, wars
Carter	IMF, WB	Carter Doctrine	Afghanistan, Lebanon, Iran
Reagan	IMF, WB	Rollback	Afghanistan, Nicaragua, Iran–Contra, Central America, Grenada, Angola, Libya
Bush	IMF, WB	New World Order	Gulf war, Panama
Clinton	IMF, WB, WTO, NAFTA, APEC	Enlargement, crisis response	Bosnia, Kosovo, Haiti, Somalia, Kurdistan, Iraq sanctions, Sudan, Libya
Bush 2	FTAs (WTO)	Preventive war, war on terror	Afghanistan, Iraq (Haiti, Yemen)

the objective is obtaining Iraq's oil, isn't it much cheaper to buy it? A rejoinder is that what matters to US policymakers is not oil per se but the *control* over oil supplies. Still, this is a reasonable question in view of cost estimates of the Iraq war that range from $1.6 trillion to $2.4 trillion and rising.[2]

American policies have been multitrack all along, corporate and military, as a comparison of recent US administrations in terms of economic and security policies shows (Table 5.1). These administrations all have in common a strong military–industrial complex, expansive foreign policies and interventions, and aggressive international trade and economic policies. Yet recent decades have not been imperial in the sense of lasting territorial occupation. Neoliberal globalization since the 1980s has taken the form of market domination exercised through the IMF, World Bank, WTO and transnational corporations without assuming control over sovereignty. The G.W. Bush administration continued the usual preoccupations but deviated from past policy in *how* it handles economic and military policies; in both spheres it has been more unilateral and aggressive, relied less on multilateral institutions, valued bilateral free trade agreements over the WTO, and has taken hegemony to the point of empire.

The idea that imperialism is intrinsic to capitalism is much too generalizing. David Harvey interprets imperialism and the Iraq war as 'accumulation by dispossession' and as part of capitalism survival and crisis management strategies. The assumption that empire is profitable has been a thesis since Hobson, Lenin ('imperialism is the highest stage of capitalism'), Rosa Luxemburg, and assorted propagandists of empire. War and empire represent huge transfers of resources and a redistribution among capitals, so a fundamental problem is the *aggregation* of capitalism – *which* capitalism, which faction of capital? Harvey's *New Imperialism* doesn't identify the agent, besides a brief reference to oil interests, while assuming the character of the overall process and outcome. That there is a 'rational' relationship between American military expansion and American capitalism (rational in the sense of proportional in cost–benefit terms) has been a general assumption of neo-Marxist takes on American hegemony. This is a difficult assumption. Economic actors are many and diverse (banks, institutional investors, corporations, government agencies) and rallying them behind a single project is easier said than done. The circuits of political power overlap with those of capital but not in a linear fashion. Material gain needs to be demonstrated, or, more precisely, what needs to be demonstrated is that the faction of capital that gains most from war is the one that holds the trumps in power. General-level explanations of the capitalism-equals-imperialism variety don't measure up; explanations can refer only to particular segments of capital.[3]

The close links between the Bush administration and Wall Street have been apparent in campaign funding, appointments, economic policies, and tax cuts.[4] But in relation to war there have been steep differences among factions of capital. Business media and circles have been divided on the Iraq war with the *Wall Street Journal* in favor and *Business Week, Economist, Financial Times* and the libertarian Cato Institute opposed or skeptical. From the viewpoint of corporations the winners are substantial (military industries, big energy, Halliburton, Bechtel, subcontractors), yet many are indifferent unless the cost of military expansion becomes excessive (Wall Street), or are damaged by American militarism (exporters).[5]

In business-speak the steep loss of American legitimacy over recent years represents a failure of managing 'brand USA.' That American brands worldwide are no longer 'cool' is a matter of growing concern for American business groups. An advertising executive notes, 'We know that in Group of 8 countries, 18 percent of the population claim they are avoiding American brands, with the top brand being Marlboro in terms of avoidance. Barbie is another one. McDonald's is another. There is a cooling towards American culture generally across the globe.'[6] Knock-off products in Europe and the Middle East imitate American products while appealing to anti-American sentiments.

Why, then, the Iraq war? According to Noam Chomsky and Tariq Ali, the Iraq war was not about oil but about hegemony and was to serve as an exemplary action to demonstrate imperial might. That the target is a military midget follows the logic of what Todd calls American theatrical micromilitarism with targets such as Grenada and Panama.[7] The GNP of Iraq equals that of Kentucky. This argument cuts two ways: because the target is a midget the demonstration of might is not particularly effective, yet if the demonstration fails it has the opposite effect of displaying US weakness.

In the case of Iraq this alone is not a convincing enough thesis. It is more appropriate to situate this show of force in the context of American geopolitics. Zbigniew Brzezinski reiterates the British political geographer Mackinder's heartland theory: 'He who controls Eurasia controls the world.'[8] The Great Game of the Russian and British empires lives on in current conflicts. The Carter Doctrine declared the Persian Gulf to be in the vital national security interest of the United States.[9] The wars in Iraq and Afghanistan follow long-term American involvement in Iraq, Afghanistan (by one account the US lured the Soviets into the 'Afghan trap'), Iran and Pakistan, strategic interest in the energy-rich Caspian basin, expansion into Central Asia, and pressure on Iran, Syria, and Lebanon. With Central Asia and the Caspian Basin, Iraq and the Gulf form a strategic triangle. Yet let's note that these objectives are not part of polite conversation.

Another consideration is segmented elites – different elites, institutions, and databases prevail in security, economics, and finance; which produces knowledge segmentation and policy compartmentalization. Grand strategy, but no correlating economics; expansionism, but no area studies or analysis of domestic dynamics, and so on. So this remains a fundamental question. All along, geopolitics, the war economy, and war-as-business interact with corporate globalization. But how sustainable is this? In the case where military interventions are brief and successful it doesn't necessarily matter, but lengthy unsuccessful military quagmires, as in Iraq and Afghanistan, multiply the economic and political cost.

American views on the new wars have been diverse. Table 5.2 gives a schematic overview of perspectives during the early stages of the Iraq war, with some provisos. Most perspectives (realism, security, conservatives, neoliberals, nationalists) typically yield mixed views; the ideological consistency that marks the neoconservatives is rare. Over time, war supporters became critics (such as William Buckley, Francis Fukuyama; several liberal hawks have become internationalists, such as Zakaria); some listings are indicative (some publications have published diverse views; neoliberals hold diverse views); and it isn't easy to plot all positions (where for instance to place the Concord Coalition that opposed the war for budgetary reasons?).

Each paradigm can be questioned on its premises and on what it leaves out. Realists typically leave out questions of legitimacy, international law, and political economy. Perspectives centered on security may suffer from threat inflation and are weak on

Table 5.2 American perspectives on the new wars

Paradigms	Keywords	Sources
Realism	Grand strategy, geopolitics	*Foreign Affairs, National Interest*, East coast Republicans (Scowcroft, Eagleburger, Kissinger); Brzezinski, Cordesman, Nye, Ikenberrry, Newhouse, Mearsheimer, Walt
Military and intelligence	Security	*Survival*, Bacevich, Brown, Peters, Hersh, Scheuer, Kupchan
Neocons	Prolong unipolar moment, regime change	*Weekly Standard, Commentary, National Interest*, PNAC, American Enterprise Institute, Heritage, Kagan, Kaplan, Krauthammer, Kristol, Perle, Podhoretz, Boot, Adelman, Ledeen, Fukuyama, D. Brooks, Frum, Christopher Hitchens, H. Mansfield
Conservatives	American values, Christianity	*National Review, Chicago Tribune, Washington Times*, Buckley, Limbaugh, southern Republicans
Neoliberals	Free markets	*Wall Street Journal, Economist*, Cato Institute, Deepak Lal, J. Bhagwati, F. Bergsten
Nationalists	National interest	Buchanan, Dobbs
Liberal hawks	War on terror, democracy	*New York Times, New Yorker, New Republic, Foreign Policy*, P. Berman, T. Friedman, M. Ignatieff, B. Keller, M. O'Hanlon, Pollack, Safire, Zakaria
Liberal internationalists	International institutions	*NYRB, Harper's, Dissent, Nation*, CFR, Barber, M. Mann, Krugman, C Johnson, Lieven
Neo-Marxism	Capitalist resource war	*Nation, Monthly Review, Z Magazine, Socialist Register*, Harvey, Klare, Parenti, Panitch, Zinn
Hegemony	Demonstrate power	Chomsky, Tariq Ali, Todd
Israel factor	Israel first	Christian Zionism, evangelicals
	Dog wags tail	Mearsheimer & Walt, Chomsky, Falk, Soros
	Tail wags dog	Petras, Michael Lind
Clash of civilizations	Islam as threat	Huntington, B. Lewis, Ajami, D. Pipes
Contingency	Rightwing coup	Michael Lind, Greg Palast
Hegemonic decline	Global political economy	*Le Monde Diplomatique*, P. Kennedy, Khanna, Amin, Arrighi, Soros, Todd, Wallerstein

peacekeeping. Neoconservatives gloss over the cost of interventions. Liberal hawks face the problem of wanting to replace the bullet by the ballot via the bullet. Neoliberals face the contradiction of establishing free markets by coercion; hence *The Economist* and the Cato Institute opposed the Iraq war. Liberal internationalists face the question, internationalism on whose terms? A question for neo-Marxists is, which faction of capital matters and is war cost effective? As regards the Israel factor, many concur that Israel probably influenced the US in going to war in Iraq, but some go further in attributing a general 'tail wags dog' influence to Israel. A question for the clash-of-civilizations view is whether conflict is *necessary* in view of American cooperation with Islamic governments, a wider configuration that Timothy Mitchell refers to as 'McJihad,'[10] or the long-term collusion between the US government, American oil companies and conservative Islamic governments and forces. The contingency perspective poses the deeper question, what are the structural parameters and trends that made this happenstance possible? The hegemonic-decline view prompts the question, what is the time frame and what comes after hegemony?

A reasonable question is, 'Why is the juggernaut of the West so preoccupied by the flea of al-Qaida?'[11] The war on terror instills fear and creates an enemy narrative that serves as a successor to the cold war and does everything the cold war did: uphold executive power, sustain the national security state, shield secrecy, instill patriotism, dim criticism, cement alliances, and create an ideological framework. Zygmunt Bauman suggests that 'politicians have abdicated any responsibility for moderating the impact of the inherent insecurity and instability of market capitalism, so they offer to assuage other types of insecurity.'[12] As corporate globalization marches on, the regime of fear diverts attention from growing corporate and financial concentration of power. As social insecurity grows, social government shrinks – through tax cuts, jacking up deficits, and removing barriers against corporate malpractice – and military government expands. Not social or human security, but military and private security is the biggest growth industry. If the war on terror is a perpetual war, security budgets can only grow and the security state directs funds and talents away from social services and education. In this broad sense, neoliberal globalization (finance capital and growing corporate power, both unaccountable) and the fear regime of the war on terror are tandem operations. Corporate logics dovetail with the logic of war directly (military industries, big oil, construction) and indirectly in that military and homeland security controls the airwaves and trumps social concerns. One option for interpreting the situation is that a new merger, *neoliberal empire*, has been taking shape.

> Neoliberal empire twins practices of empire with those of neoliberalism. The core of empire is the national security state and the military–industrial complex; neoliberalism is about business, financial operations, and marketing (including the marketing of neoliberalism itself). The IMF and World Bank continue business as usual, though with less salience and legitimacy than during the Clinton years; so imperial policies come in addition to and not instead of the framework of neoliberal globalization. Neoliberal empire is a marriage of convenience with neoliberalism, indicated by inconsistent use of neoliberal policies, and an attempt to merge America whose business is business with the America whose business is war, at a time when business is not doing great.[13]

Part of Reagan's legacy is the lean state. Reagan's rollback of communism coincided with government rollback, decimating state capabilities except security capabilities. The question is whether a lean state can be an imperial state, is it up to the task, is it possible to have hegemony on the cheap? What indicators there are of neoliberal empire – particularly along the lines of war-as-business[14] – suggest that it is an improvisation rather than a sustainable strategy. War is the 'continuation of business by other means'[15] but business is about the bottom line. A case in point is the 180,000 private military contractors in Iraq (2007), which exceed the US military presence (130,000); a third of the private military contractors are fighting forces. Yet this privatization of war is not sustainable, if only in view of its cost.

Superpower Syndrome

A different interpretation is that the American rendezvous of power operates autonomously from the rendezvous of capital and has a momentum of its own. This is a conventional state power thesis and has been the general drift in American political science.[16] Part of this is a *historical depth* that goes back to postwar American globalism and the cold war. It involves a *regional depth* in American security commitments, particularly in the Middle East and Israel, anchored in the regional commands that orchestrate its empire of bases.[17] The *strategic depth* has been summed up as 'OIL (oil, Israel, logistics).' It involves *political depth* in that support for the military–industrial complex and forward policies is bipartisan and long-term and involves many Washington beltway careers. This, in turn, is founded on *cultural depth* and the ingrained self-perception of the US as world arbiter, embedded in the American bubble. Finally, it involves secret agendas and the discreet charms of grand strategy.

The G.W. Bush administration has been characterized like no other by secrecy and the multiplication of command and intelligence units such as the Special Operations unit in the Pentagon and the Special Forces Command in Iraq.[18] The pattern is that of a state within a state within a state, or concentric command-and-control circles, in which the outer circles perform legitimate tasks and inner circles pursue covert agendas.[19] This sheds some light on the twilight surrounding this administration: vague policies clustered around grandiose ideals (freedom, democracy, stability) that are rarely elaborated; policies that are blatantly at odds with ideals; and recurrent clashes between overt and covert agendas.

Superpower path dependence implies that American foreign policies must be interpreted primarily, though not exclusively, in terms of institutional drives in the national security establishment. The Soviet Union losing the cold war arms race leaves the question, what happened to the victors? For the US the prize of cold war victory was *not* a peace dividend, not 'the end of history,' but hardened reliance on the path that allegedly brought victory. In the inaugural volume of *The National Interest* in 1985, Irving Kristol contrasted liberal internationalism and nationalist isolationism and advocated a third position, expansionist nationalism. Charles Krauthammer wrote about the unipolar moment in 1990 and resumed his article twelve years later in an essay on 'prolonging the unipolar moment.'[20] The US, according to Krauthammer, should adopt a policy of *democratic realism* and intervene 'where it counts.' Looking back, Fukuyama recast this episode as the 'neoconservative moment.'[21]

As part of the script of unipolarity, American governing elites invest in grand strategy and mega-power symbolism. This involves grandstanding as international style and noncooperation with international treaties such as the Kyoto Protocol. It reflects, in Robert Cooper's terms, a paradigm of defensive state modernism, in contrast to postmodern state trends (pooling sovereignty, international cooperation, treaties and covenants such as the International Criminal Court, etc.) that prevail in Europe and other parts of the world.[22] American governing elites tend to view the world in terms of *strategic* challenges (nuclear Iran, nuclear North Korea, energy supplies, etc.) rather than economic, ecological or cultural challenges. Economic challenges are left to corporations and to international trade policy, which is also cast in strategic terms. Cultural change, too, is viewed in terms of its strategic implications, as in the post-9/11 preoccupation with 'cultural extremism,' which inspires 'tough liberalism.'[23] Strategic challenges are typically talked about in military terms of worst-case scenarios, necessity, and fatality, rather than in terms of trade-offs and the cost–benefit of alternative ways of handling world order such as strengthening international organizations and international law. Unipolarity as premiss means that American governing elites tend either to ignore alternative ways of handling world order or to treat them as rivals to American power.

This is the case regardless of winning or losing the new wars; what is 'winning' has itself become problematic and unclear. It follows from the script of unipolarity that strategic aims become functionally autonomous and detached from their actual attainment. Is the war on terror and 'democratic realism' actually intended to succeed and what defines success? With the shifting reasons for war (weapons of mass destruction, regime change, democracy in the Middle East, war on terror, stability), how is one to keep track of the objective? On what terms is it supposed to succeed, in terms of its overt objectives or covert aims (geopolitics, geo-economics)? It is likely that the administration is divided on the objectives. The Iraqi state falling apart, unable to control its oil industry and ethnic factions jostling for position ('soft partition'), may be an outcome Situation Room strategists have been aiming at all along. Thus American objectives in Iraq are inherently contradictory: geopolitics and democracy, a mishmash of covert and overt aims. This mishmash, too, is calibrated into the script; yet the unintended effects have proved to be more erratic than bargained for.

In 1999 Richard Haass, then director of policy planning at the State Department, observed that globalization diffuses power to diverse actors and asked 'what to do with American primacy?' He argued that empire would not be a feasible policy.

> As power diffuses around the world, America's position relative to others will inevitably erode.... Other nations are rising, and nonstate actors – ranging from Usama bin Ladin to Amnesty International to the International Criminal Court to George Soros – are increasing in number and acquiring power. For all these reasons, an effort to assert or expand U.S. hegemony will fail. Such an action would lack domestic support and stimulate international resistance, which in turn would make the costs of hegemony all the greater and its benefits all the smaller.[24]

Nonstate actors in Iraq and Afghanistan proved to be more formidable foes than planned for. The Iraq war has turned into an asymmetrical people's war, involving different peoples and forces in the region. A lesson of Vietnam is that in protracted people's war popular support, logistical supply lines, culture and time are all against the invader; one can bleed but one cannot win. In Afghanistan, the American game of musical chairs, first supporting the south (the Pashtun and mujahideen) against the Soviet Union and their northern allies, and since 2001 the Northern Alliance against the south, produces localism and enduring structural stalemate. As protracted people's wars, both wars will likely yield decades of instability without clear outcomes.

'Democratic realism' means pursuing American national interests while respecting democracy, which easily translates into an instrumental take on democracy – democracy if it matches American interests or as an abstract value in which the end justifies the means and the label redeems the package. In the Middle East it means controlled democracy, vetoing inconvenient outcomes such as Hamas in Palestine.[25] Arguably this is not unlike democracy as practiced in the US. The Congress has a 32 percent approval rating (11 percent in 2007) but a 98 percent re-election rate thanks to intricate gerrymandering and shrinking voter turnouts.

Is the US actually at war or is war a symbolic exercise – a war of choice, a vanity war with vanity trappings? Elaborate airport security checks by screeners who haven't been screened themselves. Halliburton trucks peddling up and down Iraq empty to jack up costs. The war on poverty, war on crime, war on drugs, war on terror, No Child Left Behind, display similar traits: 'war' as the only available software, symbolic overdetermination, a mismatch between purpose and resources, more fluff than action, yet involving mammoth profits, real consequences, and a punitive streak.

The wars in Afghanistan and Iraq show bungling at every level: in pre-war intelligence, diplomacy, post-war planning and operations, in every respect except major combat. The US spends more on the military than the next twenty-one biggest military spenders combined and accounts for half the world's total military spending (48 percent in 2005). How is this spent? With a national security budget of over $500 billion for 2004–05, 'the military says it has run $1 billion a month short over the last year paying for the basics of war fighting in Iraq: troops, equipment, spare parts and training.' The Pentagon runs 77 major weapons programs at a cost of $1.3

trillion, '11 times the yearly bill for operating and maintaining the American military.'[26] This includes boondoggle projects such as the multibillion Missile Defense Shield. The preparations for future wars leave no money for actual war. Some 80 percent of Pentagon spending is with six major corporations and over 40 percent is in no-bid (and cost-plus) contracts.[27] The revolution in military affairs or the technological modernization of the armed forces means large private-sector technology contracts, which increase the cost to the Pentagon, and troop cutbacks, which means that with two major engagements the military is overstretched.

As naval strategy analyst Thomas Barnett notes, American strategic precepts focus on another great power opponent whereas real-world adversaries are small-scale guerrillas, so there is a fundamental mismatch between capabilities and threats.[28] In military circles, group-think prevails.[29] Generals who say more troops are needed are retired prematurely and troops serving in Iraq are threatened or demoted if they present the situation as a guerrilla war or civil war. Another factor is institutional culture. A CIA truism is that 'operations that include diarrhea as a way of life don't happen.'[30] As the public whipping boy of presidential failures, the CIA has 'battered child syndrome,' so morale is low and risk aversion high. Thus the steady upward curve of American military spending doesn't match a parallel increase in military capabilities. The point should not be exaggerated but a reasonable question is to what extent the military–industrial complex exists in a parallel universe as a military preoccupied with science-fiction warfare and with the Pentagon as another Enron, shuffling numbers.[31]

Reports from mainstream sources point to anomalies. By September 2004 the central CIA unit of the war on terror had no more staff than it had before September 11; by September 2004, of the $87 billion allocated for Iraq reconstruction only about $1 billion had been disbursed; by September 2004 the Pentagon office responsible for training and gearing up the Iraqi forces had only a third of its staff, and so forth. The usual explanation for these anomalies is

plodding bureaucracy, but another option is that US government ineptitude is systemic. After all the campaigns against big government
and continuous downsizing of its functions, personnel, and prestige,
is it still a capable government? Downsizing government means
eroding state capabilities and institutions. By this logic neoliberal
capitalism is institutionally incapable of empire or nation-building;
and if it does, it is a make-believe operation in which more effort
is dedicated to marketing and propaganda than to delivering the
product. Is an advanced nation that is incapable of keeping one of
its major seaports from collapse in the face of anticipated disaster
capable of rebuilding other nations in distant and alien cultural and
geographical settings?

Wall Street and the Pentagon are America's luxury liners, two
circuits that have benefitted from reorganizations since the 1980s;
other beneficiaries have been corporations and the law-and-order
system. By assuming an identity or harmony of interests between
the two, the capitalism-as-imperialism argument takes for granted
precisely that which is problematic. *Neoliberal empire* refers to a
strategic intersection of the two but as a field of contention rather
than a harmonious relationship. The Pentagon follows a paradigm
of defensive state modernism whereas Wall Street – transnational
in its operational circuits and postnational in its commitments
– operates according to a postmodern paradigm. Both pursue state
beneficence, but the Pentagon follows a state script whereas Wall
Street follows a post-state script. This fundamental tension in the
American project is further explored in the next chapter.

Stuff Happens

We all now have postmodern savvy enough to know that what
matters is not just what is said but *how* it is said, what matters is not
just what is said but what is done, and not just what is done but how
it is done. This sheds light also on the new American wars.

An obvious interpretation of the failure of the Iraq war is that the objective of bringing democracy was unreal and its implementation inept. From the start the failure to provide post-war security, peacekeeping and policing, dismantling the Iraqi armed forces, and compulsive de-Baathification had disastrous consequences for establishing order and democracy. These shortcomings are so glaring that the alternative scenario makes sense: geopolitics and oil as the primary agenda of the invasion. In this script Iraq is a large airbase with oil underneath. Sending forces to protect the oil ministry where the plans of the oil fields are kept, but not to protect other ministries, hospitals or the national museum matches these priorities, and so do the Abu Ghraib, Nama airbase and Guantánamo prison regimes, Special Forces and private security firms as mainstays of the occupation force, and a 'free press' disseminating American propaganda.

Americans have become increasingly capable of protecting their own soldiers (force protection) but not Iraqi forces and civilians. The American rules of engagement show little regard for Iraqi lives. In Haditha in November 2005, after losing one of their men to a roadside bomb, Marines burst into houses in the neighborhood and indiscriminately killed twenty-five civilians including women and children. The deaths were first attributed to insurgents, and the truth came out much later when a *Time* correspondent interviewed local witnesses. Raids in Iraq and Afghanistan have involved numerous episodes where American forces claimed to hit terrorists, while locals mourn the death of relatives gathered in family celebrations. The obliteration of Fallujah was prompted by retaliation for the death of Blackwater paramilitaries. The My Lai episode in Vietnam has been multiplied by many others in Iraq. The almost consistent American silence on Iraqi casualties, not counted, not reported, rarely mentioned, in contrast to daily mourned Fallen Heroes on the American side, dramatizes the American bubble island effect. While the Abu Ghraib episode and the Guantánamo Bay regime had a deep emotional impact worldwide, the attorney who authorized these war crimes was appointed US Attorney General.

A tragic feature of the Iraq and Afghanistan wars are the extraordinarily high number of civilian casualties. In Iraq the casualties of twelve years of sanctions and the war may add up to a million civilians. Add to this the ruthless detention regimes of Abu Ghraib, Guantánamo Bay, and Bagram airbase in Afghanistan. Should we view this as 'just so' circumstances (stuff happens) or do they betray fundamental characteristics of the American project? They show features of guerrilla war and urban war in which combatants shelter among civilians. The French war in Algeria displayed similar cruelties (American forces use *The Battle of Algiers* as a training film). Collective punishment of civilians in retaliation for hostile actions was a feature of the Nazi occupation in Europe and has been part of Israeli operations in Lebanon and Palestine, as in the obliteration of Jenin. British forces in southern Iraq have probably engaged in similar conduct as the Americans, so we shouldn't exaggerate the degree to which this is an American problem. In the American case this occurs at the convergence of several elements: the US attempt to gain power on a distant continent, the tendency to view countries as strategic real estate, and the narcissism of the American bubble.

For the US, the quest for world power in the Eurasian heartland, seeking land power on a distant continent, is a chancy project. By definition the supply lines are long. Because of lack of geographical contiguity and shared history, cultural affinities are non-existent. The US's main ally in this project, Israel, is itself isolated in the region. Not just the countries under attack but neighboring states feel threatened and their regional networks and supply lines come under pressure, creating an incentive to seek alternative security and energy networks. Thus if gaining control of Eurasia is central to American designs to prolong the unipolar moment, this is a high-risk project of the caliber of Napoleon's Russia campaign. As mentioned before, American forces have traditionally failed in ground combat. The US military has been successful in airborne operations and interventions using 'overwhelming force' followed by quick withdrawal, but not in sustained ground operations.[32]

The US tries to compensate for these weaknesses through an ideological offensive of 'bringing democracy to the Middle East' which seeks to convert lack of cultural affinity into an asset. American Orientalism is an attempt to extend the American bubble over the Middle East like a vast tent. Courtesy of Bernard Lewis, Fouad Ajami and many others it places Islam on the margins of modernity, denigrates Mideast culture and stars the US in the role of bringing the region freedom, democracy, modernity, and security.[33] This glosses over the interdependence of American influence and authoritarianism in the Middle East (as in Saudi Arabia, Egypt, and Jordan), ignores the area experts who counsel that democracy at this stage brings Islamists to power, and papers over the clash between ends and means in US policy.

Does Hegemony Matter?

Let's draw up a balance sheet, does hegemony matter? It does not in that imbalances in the US are large and belligerence aggravates them. Consequences of the American rendezvous of power include the opportunity costs of empire, or what the US government could do instead of unilateral aggression. Economic consequences include the neglect of economic policy, loss of manufacturing, and neglect of education, which results in loss of American competitiveness. That the largest American company is a retail company that sells Chinese goods with a logistics system that runs on Indian software is telling. Not all of this can be attributed to investment in hegemony; the absence of industrial policy is an expression of American laissez-faire. At any rate it leads to import dependence, growing trade and current-account deficits, and the weakening status of the dollar. The armed forces as avenue of social mobility (the nation's main affirmative-action program) and centerpiece of public culture gradually transforms American culture into a garrison culture that is out of sync with world trends. Valuing brawn over brain runs counter to global trends and to the rise of the knowledge economy.

Yet, empire does matter if security ranks above other concerns and if military power is viewed as a productive change agent. It does matter in that American hegemonic expansion stimulates re-grouping on the part of social forces and countries that increasingly work *around* the US, so empire accelerates global realignments. Gregory Clark writes, 'The US adventure in Iraq should have been welcomed since its probable failure, like the failure of the US intervention in Vietnam 30 years ago, will probably discourage further US military adventures for another generation or so.'[34]

Peter Gowan cautions that we should not underestimate Ameri-can grand strategy in pursuit of global primacy; September 11 pro-vided an opportunity to implement that goal.[35] Tony Benn, however, at an anti-war demonstration in London on September 27, 2003 suggests, 'Don't overestimate the intelligence of the powers that be.' One of his examples is that President Bush introduced the war on terror by calling for a crusade against terrorism, at which point some 30,000 people on Trafalgar Square roared with laughter. So do we under- or overestimate the makers of strategy? Both may be true. We may underestimate US long-term goals but overestimate the coherence between means and goals. For instance, a $500 billion military may be of limited usefulness. One level concerns strategy and another the way it is implemented; Tony Benn's comment deals with the implementation of strategy. An Irish newspaper notes, 'It's hard to imagine a greater management failure than that of the Anglo-Americans in Iraq. Seldom have so many resources been squandered so quickly and for so little effect.'[36]

Since the late 1940s the US has spent $12 trillion on the military. A large military apparatus was understandable during the cold war and the superpower arms race; but since then the crucial decision was taken to maintain a military force that would be capable of de-feating any rival or combination of rivals. When this was set forth in a 1992 Defense Policy Guidance (drafted by Paul Wolfowitz, under

Secretary of Defense Cheney) and leaked out, it led to an outcry in Congress. In 2002 it was incorporated in the National Security Strategy. Discussion of this document has focused on the doctrine of preventive war; the principle of American unrivaled military superiority is not discussed as if it is already taken for granted. The 2003 budget allocated $396 billion to military spending. Out of the discretionary budget 49 percent was dedicated to the military and 7 percent to education. The military budget increase by $48 billion (larger than Japan's entire defense budget and the largest increase in American military spending in twenty years) received a warm welcome in Congress.[37] The National Missile Defense System may cost more than $238 billion over the next fifteen to twenty-five years, although the system is known to be unworkable. In 2006 41 percent of US taxes went to military expenditures, compared to 5 percent on social programs and 2 percent on science, energy, and environment.[38] The 2008 defense budget is $766.5 billion if we include the supplemental budget to pay for war in Afghanistan and Iraq. When military-related allocations in departments other than defense are added, the total exceeds $1 trillion.

> The Department of Defense's planned expenditures for the fiscal year 2008 are larger than all other nations' military budgets combined. The supplementary budget to pay for the current wars in Iraq and Afghanistan, not part of the official defence budget, is itself larger than the combined military budgets of Russia and China. Defence-related spending for fiscal 2008 will exceed $1 trillion for the first time in history.[39]

Out of the $2.5 trillion budget for 2008, $1 trillion is dedicated to military or military-related expenditures. With so much national treasure spent on the military, why is there no sustained national debate about its purpose and the consequences for the American economy and society?

Privileging military contracts means that the US economy becomes uncompetitive. The military–industrial complex has been a major source of distortion; it has been a factor in the economic shift from the Frostbelt to the Sunbelt and the rise of the conservative South.[40] The price of pursuing Number One status is that the US has become an authoritarian society. Overinvesting in the military has incapacitated the country in many other spheres. It is under-educated, culturally backward, inward-looking, economically on its knees, and dependent on foreign lending. An implication of the threat–profit, war–business connection is that distinctions between public and private domains have eroded; the public domain is privatized. The growing role of private military contractors, operating outside national and international law, implies that private actors could unleash global instability or crisis. Ultimately the world's hyperpower can become a global warlord. The twenty-first century faces problems of poverty and ecological challenges in relation to which hegemony is irrelevant or counterproductive. War is not the answer to the world's problems, but 4.5 percent of the world population that spends 50 percent of world military spending may have no other answers to give.

Advocates for American power, such as Michael Mandelbaum who makes a 'case for Goliath,' argue that the US acts in effect as the world government and requires maximum resources to maintain order and security. In reality the US just as much sustains or creates the problems that it purports to need to control. The Pentagon spends the entire annual budget of the United Nations in approximately 38 hours, which sums up both the government the world gets and that which it doesn't. The issue is not world government or not, but what kind of world government; the kind the US provides is an arsonist–fireman world government, a problem that is taken up in the next chapter.[41]

SIX

Political and Economic Brinkmanship

THE NEOCONSERVATIVE CASE for American power, as set forth in
the Project for a New American Century, is a straightforward geopolitical argument alongside a Wilsonian argument for 'benevolent
global hegemony' to spread democracy. The former is relatively
easy to deal with; since it doesn't claim legitimacy it is plain
geopolitics. The latter dominates in policy speeches and is a harder
nut to crack because it resonates with a wider constituency that
shares the liberal case for hegemony. Many liberals (and not only
Americans) also endorse strong American power. According to
Michael Ignatieff, it is the 'lesser evil.' According to Paul Berman,
in response to terrorism war is just. This also resonates with
a long-standing idea that spreading democracy is an 'American
mission.'[1]

At the 2006 meeting of the American Political Science Association Joseph Nye said, 'The United States cannot win by hard
power alone, but must pay more heed to soft power and global
communications.' As discussant I asked him why should the United
States win, and he replied, 'The United States must win because it

is the world's largest democracy and this is a dangerous world.' This is a tenet that runs the gamut of political positions.

While much criticism targets the neoconservatives, criticism should rather focus on the liberal position because it claims a legitimacy that the neoconservative view lacks, is shared by many more than neoconservative views, is used by neoconservatives to garner support for forward policies, and underpins bipartisan and public support for the defense industries. The focus on the neoconservatives is understandable because they propagated the new wars and inspired conservative overreach; yet the furor is misplaced for it suggests that the neoconservative positions are unusual or extreme, though in fact they aren't. Mounting criticisms of the Iraq war have brought Republican realists and progressive internationalists together in platforms such as the Coalition for a Realistic Foreign Policy.[2] However, their joint criticism of the neoconservatives overshadows deeper problems of power. The neoconservatives may have been the loudest voices in millennial Washington but what they have been saying isn't all that different from the views of realists and liberal hawks. Realists focus on national interest, liberals on democracy and human rights; combine the two, national interest and democracy, and it captures 98 percent of Washington's policy spectrum. Neoconservatives advocate democratic realism while progressive internationalists propose progressive realism or ethical realism. To sell intervention, neoconservatives take democracy and human rights on board; to sell promoting democracy, progressives take national interests on board, so *all* positions that get any mileage in Washington combine different dosages of Woodrow Wilson and Henry Kissinger.

This poses the larger problem of *liberalism and power* or liberalism and empire. As Bhikhu Parekh shows in relation to Locke and John Stuart Mill, 'liberalism contains contradictory impulses … not just between liberal thought and practice, but within liberal thought itself.'[3] Uday Mehta has examined liberal thought and practice in British India and Bernard Semmel has scrutinized the encounter of liberal ideals and imperialism generally.[4] Liberalism is not only an ideology that defies power but also an ideology held by hegemons, an ideology that defends power and the power to act by vested interests. A case in point is Hugo Grotius' doctrine of freedom of the seas (*mare liberum*). Nineteenth-century Britain, in upholding *free trade*, played on its advantages as workshop of the world, just as the twentieth-century US and its open-door principle.[5] With the turn-of-the-century ethical policy it became appropriate to clothe colonialism in benevolent garments, as *trusteeship* and a mandate to bring dependent peoples to development and self-government, beyond classic justifications of imperialism such as the civilizing mission, the White Man's Burden and manifest destiny. At this juncture Wilson's liberal internationalism intersected with Old World colonialism. From Truman (announcing the era of economic development) to Kennedy (Alliance for Progress) and beyond, liberalism became a keynote of American interventions. Liberal hegemony represents a broad arc of American expansion from Jefferson's empire of liberty to Wilson's internationalism. It produces an anti-imperialist imperialism, interventions to promote democracy that hold wider public appeal than sheer power and gain. Yet in the process liberalism itself evolved. Over time American liberalism has become a liberalism of fear[6] and a liberalism of power. Notes David Ludden, 'The confidence with which American feminists promoted the criminalization of the Taliban and the conquest of Afghanistan is a good indication of how liberal Americans support imperial expansion. Liberal democrats led the fight against communism at home and abroad. Liberals and conservatives equally support the US empire.'[7]

Against the shared backdrop of liberal imperialism, the difference between liberal hawks and neoconservatives is mostly party affiliation. Krauthammer's democratic realism is barely distinguishable from Richard Holbrook's 'muscular liberalism' and the Clinton administration's human rights interventionism. In foreign policy a Democratic administration in 2009 will dent operational matters but not likely fundamentals. Attempts to redefine a 'liberal grand strategy' (Farer) or to recast ethical realism (Anatol Lieven) turn, after all, on tweaking the terms of what Michael Ignatieff calls the 'righteous use of force.'[8]

'Promoting democracy' is controversial because exporting democracy and 'democracy from the barrel of a gun' are difficult propositions. This may be a dangerous and chaotic world, but do American hegemony and preventive war make it less or more dangerous? The problem with this conversation is not just that it is disingenuous but the fiction that it is somehow sufficient to establish *intentions* (or policies). First, this poses a language problem, for words not only reveal but also conceal (as in the 'Roadmap to peace in the Middle East'). Second, it doesn't match the record of US interventions – which shows a trail of dictatorships, not democracies; and it is inconsistent with US cooperation with authoritarian regimes. Third, it poses an implementation problem – if this is the intention, can it be delivered? – which is what this chapter focuses on. If we take liberal reasons seriously it follows that interventions must show a meaningful and proportionate relationship between means and ends which should find expression in respect for the international liberal order including international law, legality in process, and international conventions with regard to combat, rules of engagement, and the treatment of POWs.

The liberal view should be examined not in terms of its declared intentions but in terms of its implementation. The first section of this chapter discusses the views and methods of American security professionals and argues that these stand in contrast to the declared liberal aims of American policy. This is not merely a matter of unintentional messiness of action on the ground but is often intentional and, I argue, part of a posture of political brinkmanship, which goes back at least to the Kennedy administration. The Vietnam War, too, was part of Kennedy's 'global liberalism.' Entering hegemony through the service entrance reveals the friction between ends and means and exposes fundamental flaws in the liberal position.

The term 'brinkmanship' entered American policy during the Cuban missile crisis. Brinkmanship, according to the Merriam–Webster Dictionary, refers to the art or practice of pushing a dangerous situation or confrontation to the limit of safety, especially to force a desired outcome. Brinkmanship was part of the American stance during the cold war and has since become part of the habitus of superpower. During the Reagan years American foreign policy shifted from containment to rollback, pushing back Soviet influence. Support for the mujahideen in Afghanistan, the Contras in Nicaragua and the Iran–Contra affair, interventions in Grenada and Angola were part of this.[9] Rollback means going on the offensive, war of maneuver, risk-taking and brinkmanship. The unilateral policy which the US increasingly adopted after the end of the cold war may be considered a form of brinkmanship, too. Prolonging the unipolar moment, advocated by Charles Krauthammer, and the grandiose defense policy guidance formulated by Paul Wolfowitz in 1992 to build American military preparedness beyond rival challenges represent brinkmanship elevated to strategic posture. The Project for a New American Century is part of this series. It is a project for turning American cold war victory into lasting supremacy and the willingness to take bold risks to achieve this.

There is ample discussion of the outcomes of American policies but this treatment focuses on the intentions driving policies. Brinkmanship is a strong interpretation because it assumes calculated risk-taking on the part of policy elites. It can be described as political 'maximalism.'[10] It may be difficult to demonstrate because the intentions of policymakers are often classified. At times they are implied in policy statements and conceded retroactively, in memoirs and biographies, though usually only in relation to policies that have proven successful. As a source I use the views of security professionals, which are less guarded than those of policymakers.

The cumulative effect of American economic policies has been that exports become imports, the trade deficit deepens, the economic base shrinks, income inequality widens, and external deficits rise to unsustainable levels. Can we view recent American economic policies, too, as brinkmanship? Political brinkmanship, though difficult to verify, is reasonable in outline and familiar as a theme. Economic brinkmanship is a more difficult and unusual hypothesis. In the second section I argue that laissez-faire and neoliberal policies represent willed risk-taking by policy elites. As a source I use the arguments of economists who say that current trends and American debts are actually positive signs.[11]

These hypotheses raise new questions in particular about the relationship between intentional and unanticipated risk. The risks accepted by policymakers and their adherents are often different from the public record, and the unanticipated consequences that follow are different again. This means that three scenarios are in play: the public one, which is usually couched in terms of liberal hegemony and promoting democracy; the classified script or the hidden transcript held by policy and security insiders; and the script of actual processes as they unfold and the political and operational responses they elicit. Another question concerns policy coherence. I don't assume coherence; rather I think policy is multi-level and set and implemented by inner and outer circles. Public discourse and insider representations diverge more the greater the risks that are at stake. The closing section considers whether brinkmanship is a matter of rational choice or policy extremism.

Political Brinkmanship: Producing Instability

On matters of defense the agendas of the two political parties are virtually indistinguishable. A Democratic Party policy study in anticipation of the 2000 elections opens with a chapter on defense policy which asks, 'Why is it necessary to spend so much? The answer is that the US is the world's only global military power and it is in the nation's – and the world's – interest that the US remain a global power.'[12] The national interest and its conflation with global interest are asserted rather than argued.

But a major test of the liberal approach to American power is the reality test: how do lofty political aims such as bringing stability and democracy translate into practice, how are they implemented by security professionals? Much attention devoted to the neoconservatives focuses on their role as ideologues and policymakers rather than on the implementation of their projects. But whether it is hard power or liberal hegemony, it must be implemented by a professional security apparatus.

The exercise of American power involves both deliberate ('Shock and Awe') and unintentional heavy-handedness, such as the abuse of Iraqi detainees in Abu Ghraib prison. More precisely, much heavy-handedness that is portrayed as accidental and unintended is intentional because it is part of the culture of inner circles of the military and is sanctioned through the chain of command.[13] From security professionals one typically hears quite different rationales for military action and different action programs than from public platforms. Thus, according to Michael Scheuer, a senior CIA analyst who headed the Afghanistan desk until 2004, 'the way ahead' is

> To secure as much of our way of life as possible, we will have to use military force... Killing in large numbers is not enough to defeat our Muslim foes. With killing must come a Sherman-like razing of infrastructure. Roads and irrigation systems; bridges, power plants and crops in the field; fertilizer plants and grain mills – all these and more will need to be destroyed to deny the enemy its support base. Landmines will be massively reintroduced to seal borders and mountain passes... such actions will yield large civilian casualties, displaced populations, and refugee flows.[14]

Ralph Peters, a former army intelligence major assigned to future war who is widely admired in security circles for his outspokenness, outdoes George Kennan by formulating a philosophy of *constant conflict* in these terms: 'We are entering a new American century, in which we will become still wealthier, culturally more lethal, and increasingly powerful. We will excite hatreds without precedent.... The de facto role of the US armed forces will be to keep the world safe for our economy and open to our cultural assault. To those ends, we will do a fair amount of killing.'[15]

In an article titled 'Stability, America's Enemy' Peters notes, 'Our insistence on stability above all stands against the tides of history, and that is always a losing proposition.... Historically, instability abroad has been to America's advantage, bringing us enhanced prestige and influence, safe-haven seeking investment, a peerless national currency, and flows of refugees that have proven to be rivers of diamonds.'[16] He criticizes diplomatic tradition and realism as morally corrupt and not in the national interest, and discusses several regions in which 'the quest for stability may prove antithetical to American interests', such as the Balkans, Russia ('demand an accountable Russia'), China ('a fractured, squabbling China would be less threatening to US strategic interests in the region and might well emerge as a far more advantageous business partner (or partners)'), Africa ('separatism is a natural and healthy force, until it is perverted by delay'), the Middle East ('would a peaceful resolution of the Middle East confrontation benefit the US, after all? ... Wouldn't we lose critical leverage?'), Indonesia ('the ultimate illogical state ... [the US should] manage and facilitate Indonesia's breakup').

This perspective offers a casual mix of moral-sounding arguments ('what on earth is wrong with people wanting their freedom') and American self-interest. Geopolitical opportunism masquerades as democracy, with large helpings of opinion unhindered by area knowledge, unlimited self-confidence ('we are a phenomenally strong and resilient nation,' 'our country is a force for good without precedent') and plain aggression ('We wish to wage war with tweezers, but combat remains the province of the ax'). In November 2004, Peters told Fox News that in Fallujah 'the best outcome, frankly, is if they're all killed.'[17]

Robert Kaplan offers a grim horizon:

two dynamic classes will emerge under globalization – the entrepreneurial nouveaux riches and, more ominously, the new sub-
proletariat: the billions of working poor, recently arrived from the
countryside, inhabiting the expanding squatters' settlements that
surround big cities in Africa, Eurasia and South America.... Disparities
will be enormous, while the terrorism that arises from such disparities
will enjoy unprecedented technological resources.

He concludes, 'there is nothing more volatile and more in need
of disciplined, enlightened direction than vast populations of
underpaid, underemployed and badly educated workers divided
by ethnicity and beliefs.' This, then, is what the war on terror is
to provide, 'disciplined, enlightened direction.' Thus Kaplan calls
for *Warrior Politics*, advocates ruling empire by stealth, and offers
romanticized accounts of robust Special Forces on the outposts of
empire.[18] Naval strategy analyst Thomas Barnett offers a similar
angle with a slightly different inflection. In the new American
economy 'exporting security' will be a major industry. 'As jobs move
out of the U.S. the primary export product of the nation will be
"security". Global energy demand will necessitate U.S. control of
the oil producing regions.'[19]

Thus security professionals echo the neoconservatives *without*
the Wilsonian trappings. Their rationales for military action are
to preserve the American way of life, to build a new American
century, or simply that the United States specializes in security
operations. Their tactics on the ground match these rationales and
bear little or no relation to the liberal aims enunciated in media
and diplomatic forums. 'Saving' or 'improving' countries is not part
of the vocabulary of Special Forces in combat theatres.[20]

Scheuer, Peters, Barnett, and Kaplan are not extreme fringe
voices; they write best-sellers and are frequent and respected media
commentators and security consultants. Conservative think-tanks
and administration policies amplify and reinforce these views.
Withdrawal from the International Criminal Court, declaring
the Geneva Conventions inapplicable in the war on terror, legal

justifications of torture, secret overseas interrogation of terrorism suspects, using depleted uranium munitions, cluster bombs
and white phosphorous ammunition, private military contractors
operating in legal limbo, limited prosecution of soldiers accused
of homicide of Iraqi civilians, expanded surveillance and future
combat planning that relies on robot technologies, all point in the
direction of unencumbered military force.

The culture of violence is sustained and nourished by the
normalization of hate speech since September 11 and depictions
of Islam as a religion of war and violence. Developments in the
Pentagon approach reinforce this culture. A 1996 strategy document,
'Shock and Awe: Achieving Rapid Dominance,' dealt with 'how to
destroy the will to resist before, during and after battle.' The force
modernization of the military combines advanced technology with
deploying more Special Forces.[21] Neoconservative defense intellectuals advocate a downsized military that is leaner, nimbler, and
more lethal as the successor to the Weinberg–Powell doctrine of
Overwhelming Force.[22] Ruthless methods have been part of American counterinsurgency and low-intensity conflict all along. Now
Special Forces and smart weapons should make up for fewer boots
on the ground. This was the reasoning behind the reluctance to
deploy large numbers of troops in Iraq *and* the White House and
Pentagon instructions to sidestep the Geneva Conventions. This
institutionalizes Special Forces and covert ops techniques so covert
standards become overt and what was background becomes foreground.[23] A second trend is to apply corporate standards of lean,
efficient, and flexible production to the organization and delivery of
force, a Wal-Mart approach to military force economy and an armed
forces productivity squeeze. Thus technowar, troop cutbacks, using
toxic munitions, economizing on veterans' benefits and medical care,
secret detentions and torture are part of a new 'economy of force.'[24]

The third variable that drives the American military is the
invocation of political will. Ever since Vietnam, hawks have argued
that the real cause of the defeat was a 'failure of will.' The Project

for a New American Century is a call to rearmament, but more importantly it is an invocation of political will. Repeatedly invoking September 11 serves this purpose and media products such as the television series *24* establish ruthlessness as a performative standard in American culture. Rumsfeld calls for a military that is speedier and deadlier and Scheuer pleads for 'manliness.' The culture of force intimidation is the backdrop to the abuses in Abu Ghraib, Guantánamo, and Afghan prisons. Abusing prisoners is a military tactic. While such exhortations and policies produce real abuses, they are also symbolic performances and postures.

This high-risk approach faces growing opposition within the military, particularly in the Army where many adhere to the Powell doctrine.[25] It is brinkmanship also because it exposes military personnel and policymakers to prosecution under international law. The force economy approach is at odds with patriotism and the media rhetoric of 'Fallen Heroes.' Besides, this approach is not particularly effective on the ground. The American military has traditionally been a naval and air power and ineffective in fighting ground wars on foreign soil.[26] Institutionalizing abuse and malpractice as doctrine don't make a stronger case. On the contrary, wars fought without legitimacy are more costly and invoke more resistance, and trumped up patriotism provides a feeble foundation.

Eight hundred American bases and 370,000 troops deployed in 120 countries, putting pressure on Iran, Pakistan, Syria, and North Korea, military operations in the Niger delta, Somalia, counter-terrorism operations in North Africa, establishing a new Africa Command, offensives for democracy in the Middle East and other flashpoint regions, establishing a missile defense shield on the Polish border, push positions to the brink of regional instability and military overstretch. Brinkmanship is not a fanciful interpretation. The brink is virtually daily news. Why this high-risk strategy is chosen is a different question.

Brinkmanship and producing instability carry several meanings. The US military accounts for 48 percent of world military spending

(2005 and ongoing) and represents a vast, virtually continuously growing establishment that is a world in itself with its own lingo, its own reasons, internecine battles, and projects. That this large security establishment is a bipartisan project makes it politically relatively immune. That for security reasons it is an insular world shelters it from scrutiny. For reasons of deniability the president is insulated from certain operations.[27] That it is a completely hierarchical world unto itself makes it relatively unaccountable. Hence, to quote Rumsfeld, stuff happens. In part this is the classic theme of the Praetorian Guard and the shadow state.[28] It includes a military on the go, a military that seeks career advancement through role expansion, seeks expansion through threat inflation, finds rationales for ruthless action in inflated threats, and is thus subject to feedback from its own echo chambers. Misinformation broadcast by sections of the security apparatus boomerangs to other intelligence and policy circles, where it may be taken for real.[29] Inhabiting a hall of mirrors this apparatus operates in a perpetual state of self-hypnosis with, since it concerns classified information and covert ops, limited checks on its functioning.

The American rules of engagement are self-serving. The military inhabits a parallel universe, embedded reporters are prohibited from reporting on rules of engagement, and defense experts clog the media, so discussion of these tactics and the capacity for self-correction is limited. The military stage manages swift victories to feed the news cycle. The pyrrhic victories come at a price of lasting instability, broadly according to the same logic that leads corporations to fudge numbers to look good for quarterly earnings reports. In Afghanistan the US staged a swift settlement by paying the Northern Alliance millions of dollars, which brought warlords and drug lords to power, embedded the new administration in a corrupt power structure, created another failed state and drug state, and precipitated the comeback of the Taliban.[30]

The third dynamic is scripting destabilization into operations on the assumption that politics of tension play into the hegemon's hand, which is obviously a wishful assumption. In Iraq the US backing the Kurds and permitting Shiite militias to operate (until the Samarra bombing in April 2006) created conditions for lasting instability. The autonomous Kurdish region in northern Iraq strengthens Kurds in the region and increases pressure on Turkey and, in time, other countries, which is built into the equation. The assumption is that the dealer controls the game because he has other leverage (economic, financial, diplomatic). Yet this underestimates US dependence on Turkish support for regional stability and operations in Iraq. Similar equations apply to Iran. Persuading Russia that placing a Missile Defense Shield on its borders in Poland ('against a missile threat from Iran') is in Russia's security interests is fanciful.

Part of the backdrop is the gradual erosion of state capacities because of twenty-five years, since the Reagan era, of cutting government services except the military and security. The American laissez-faire state has created an imbalance in which the military remains the major growing state capability, which leaves military power increasingly unchecked because monitoring institutions have also been downsized or dismantled. When recently the Pentagon wanted to review all the subcontracts it has outsourced, this task was outsourced too. This redistribution of power within the US government played a key part leading up to the war and in the massive failure in Iraq. Diplomacy was underresourced, intelligence was manipulated, and the Pentagon and the Office of Strategic Planning ignored experts' advice and State Department warnings on the need for post-war planning.[31]

American military posture and action on the ground, then, do not merely fail to implement a well-intentioned project because the real world is messy and chaotic but may be *designed* to achieve the reverse of the liberal mission. Real-time hegemonic operations are bipolar double acts: establishing order while pursuing politics of tension. The security institutions are layered in formal and informal cultures, overt and covert operations. Liberal hegemony is about bringing stability whereas security insiders may produce instability as part of a strategy of tension. Emmanuel Todd characterizes this script as 'America the arsonist–fireman.'

> The limited military, economic and ideological resources of the United States leave it no other way of affirming its global importance than by mistreating minor powers. There is a hidden logic behind the drunken sailor appearance of American diplomacy. The real America is too weak to take on anyone but military midgets.... Conflicts that represent little or no military risk allow the United States to be 'present' throughout the world. The United States works to maintain the illusory fiction of the world as a dangerous place in need of America's protection.[32]

Note the relative magnitudes in the distribution of military spending. In 1998 the US spent 33.7 percent of the global total while 'rogue states' (defined as Cuba, North Korea, Iran, Iraq, and Libya) spent 1.7 percent.[33] The three scripts and three rings of hegemony – public, operational, and classified – intersect in various, at times unanticipated ways. The State Department in Iraq relies for its security on the private military contractor Blackwater – that is, an alliance between diplomats and Rambos. Hamid Karzai's government in Afghanistan relies on protection by DynCorp.

The United States uses trade, aid, debt, and international financial institutions as strategic instruments to enforce its hegemony and there is usually a sizeable gap between American rhetoric and American policies. A cliché in the global South is that American and Western interventions usually result in the weakening and Balkanization of states, as in former Yugoslavia, Afghanistan, Iraq, and Somalia. IMF and World Bank policies, while ostensibly geared to promoting economic stability and development, impose Washington orthodoxy and often trigger economic chaos, financial crisis, and political upheaval. Campaigns for democracy and human rights through agencies such as the National Endowment for Democracy tend to focus on geopolitical flashpoints (the Middle East, Sudan, the republics bordering Russia, Central Asia, Venezuela, and Colombia) and foment political instability. In the global South,

American strategies of tension are familiar experiences; here I focus on the boomerang of brinkmanship for the US.

The declared intent of the Reagan project of 'getting government off our backs' was to release market forces, but since it coincided with cold war victory it also produced a military turn in government. Over time this brought about two paradoxical effects. With the military turn in government came a relative disconnect from Wall Street and corporations other than defense and energy, which leaves a narrow economic foundation and gradually institutionalizes a war economy. The second paradox of the neoliberal state is the retreat of the state as a strategic economic actor. Laissez-faire and preoccupation with geopolitics in effect leave national economic strategy and terrains such as innovation and research and development to other states, so in effect the state becomes less and not more market-oriented, which may be interpreted as another form of brinkmanship.

Economic Brinkmanship: Laissez-faire

The United States faces a current account deficit of unprecedented proportions, and if this is costly (with interest payments of $300 billion per year) and precarious (in view of an unstable dollar), the trade deficit ($818 billion in 2006) is more problematic because it is embedded in the structure of the economy. To finance its current account deficit the US borrows $3 billion each trading day, which absorbs 75 to 80 percent of the world's net savings. Manufacturing in the American economy at 10 percent of GDP is smaller than the health-care sector.[34] In cars and electronics American producers have lost out to Asian producers. The new economy has not made up for the decline of manufacturing. In service jobs there are wide skills and pay gaps.

These outcomes are the result of policies of risk-taking. We can distinguish different levels and stages of economic brinkmanship:

laissez-faire economics as a general trend, Dixie capitalism since the 1970s, shock capitalism, and G.W. Bush administration policies. Each represents deliberate risk-taking or economic brinkmanship; I argue that in combination with political brinkmanship they bring the US into the uncharted waters of unanticipated risks.

- *Laissez-faire economics*   Laissez-faire economics is anchored in American exceptionalism and reflects a society in which other power centers (feudalism, monarchy, court) were absent or weak (church), so business forces and their ethos occupy a much larger social, cultural, and political space than in other societies. Laissez-faire is brinkmanship because it assumes that the market is self-regulating and provides minimal safeguards to mitigate economic crisis and no provision for the losers in the process. This policy generated the 1929 Wall Street collapse, which led in turn to the New Deal and Keynesian policies.
- *Dixie capitalism*   In response to the 1970s' profit squeeze American corporations turned to the part of the country where the New Deal reforms were never implemented, the American South and south-west and its anti-union, low-wages, low-taxes, low-services approach. The Reagan administration turned these corporate strategies into government policy. Government rollback to 'unleash market forces' eventually became an international policy known as the Washington Consensus. The southern strategy satisfied corporate profits as well as the Southerners' long-term campaign of dismantling the New Deal. It generated economic and population growth and accumulated conservative political capital in the South, was institutionalized by subsequent administrations and in Clinton's welfare reforms, while its shortcomings were papered over by the new economy boom.
- *Shock capitalism*   Emmanuel Todd's characterization of political brinkmanship as the arsonist-fireman syndrome has a parallel in economic policies, too. IMF shock treatment *creates* crises as much as it seeks to remedy them; in Naomi Klein's words,

'Disaster capitalists share [and use] this inability to distinguish between destruction and creation, between hurting and healing.'[35] The general account going back to Marx and Schumpeter is 'creative destruction.'

- *Bush economics* The G.W. Bush administration resumed the Reagan policies of tax cuts and jacking up deficits so high that it becomes a matter of fiscal necessity to cut social spending. Hence 'deficits don't matter.' They don't matter because the objective is to 'starve the beast.' Cutting social government deprives the Democrats of their policy tools and would bring about a lasting political realignment that would make the GOP the party of government.

Because laissez-faire and the Southern strategy distribute risks to vulnerable groups with little electoral clout, they entail limited risk for elites. Elites underestimate the need for capable government intervention or national economic strategy. As long as corporations have a free hand, dire consequences for the economy and jobs will be temporary and things will be for the better eventually. This is ideological economic brinkmanship. Republicans believed that by manipulating 'cultural issues' they could offset the political damage of economic risk,[36] a gambit disproved by the 2006 elections. It is a risk-prone strategy because federal tax cuts defer taxes to states and local governments where deficit spending is ruled out by law. States remain solvent by postponing maintenance of infrastructure and cutting social programs and education. The results are neglect of infrastructure, growing inequality and hardship, and mounting debt. The country finds itself ill-prepared for natural disasters such as the Katrina hurricane because safety margins have been crossed.

Plant relocations to the Sunbelt have been followed by offshoring and outsourcing overseas. Tax incentives and declining corporate tax rates deepen the fiscal crisis of the state. A fundamental dilemma of laissez-faire capitalism is that corporations have no intrinsic commitment to the nation and this becomes manifest in accelerated globalization. The 'pro-growth' business-friendly policies that the Democratic Party adopted in the 1980s no longer necessarily benefit the American economy. In the throes of turbo-globalization – now recast as competition from China – they bring the American economy to the brink.

This is the passing of an accumulation era. Mass production went with post-Fordism. This is working itself out through the cumulative impact of offshoring and outsourcing, a layered process in which the Norman Rockwell capitalism of the New Deal is making place for the turbo-capitalism of Enron and Wal-Mart. Wal-Mart, a signal success of this era, the country's largest company and the world's largest retailer, represents a Southern strategy of low wages, no unions, extracting government subsidies for infrastructure and worker benefits, and cut-throat prices from suppliers, shippers, and employees. Its logistics system runs on Indian software. As a retail company that functions as an intermediary between American consumers and low-cost producers in Asia it makes superior profits by underpaying its workforce. It offers consumers low prices according to methods that, pushed to their logical extreme, eventually erode their capacity to be consumers. 'The sad truth is that people earning Wal-Mart-level wages tend to favor the fashions available at the Salvation Army. Nor do they have much use for Wal-Mart's other departments, such as Electronics, Lawn and Garden, and Pharmacy.'[37]

In the American case, the neoliberal state is a national security state, which carries economic implications in itself. The political economy of political brinkmanship raises several questions. Are the defense industries a wise future investment and do they have a sound multiplier effect? By comparison to the post-war decades the military economy multiplier is shrinking and the 'military Keynesianism' of the past is no more. The mammoth military–industrial complex makes leading industries uncompetitive by drawing them into military contracts and the military is also a major technology importer.[38] Does geopolitics make money and for whom? Some 80 percent of Pentagon spending is with six major corporations, and over 40 percent is in no-bid contracts. Does it halt the decline in American manufacturing? Can it turn the trade deficit?

Deficits Don't Matter

Business reports describe the world economy as a Ponzi scheme, 'a giant pyramid selling scheme,' 'a strange cycle in which trade deficits help fund the US budget deficit and make up for its low savings rate.'[39] The massive American debt is sustained by dollar surpluses and vendor financing in China, Japan (about $1 trillion each), and East Asia. Not only are American levels of debt high – including states' debt, corporate debt, and household debt (at $650 billion) – but manufacturing capacity is eroded, there are no reserves, and the savings rate turned negative in 2005 for the first time since the depression. Ten percent of Americans, those in the lowest income bracket, spend 40 percent of their income on debt.

One reasoning is that the problem is not American deficits but a 'savings glut' in Asia and Europe. Developing countries hold surplus dollars as a safeguard against financial turbulence, and Asian countries do so to sustain their exports to the US. According to the 'dark matter' hypothesis, the numbers are wrong and underestimate American earnings from foreign investment.[40] Even so, the US is deeply in the red to Asian central banks and the general understanding is that these deficits are unsustainable. The debate is whether it will be a soft or a hard landing. What optimistic readings there are of the situation don't generate consensus, nor do forward policies such as increasing the savings rate and reducing the value of the dollar. The main policy responses under discussion are: boosting exports, assuming dollar loyalty, new investments in technology, and imposing tariffs on imports.

Boosting exports   A common argument is that free trade will boost exports. 'Each new trade agreement has been heralded as a market-opening breakthrough that would boost US exports and thus move toward balanced trade. That is not what happened – not after NAFTA (1993) and the WTO (1994), not after China normalization (2000). In each case, the trade deficits grew dramatically.'[41] Another view holds that a lower dollar will reduce imports and boost exports. But for this to take effect the dollar should fall to the level of €0.55. Yet even then the *capacity* to significantly expand exports doesn't exist.[42] Besides, offshoring and outsourcing limit this option because they turn the production of American corporations into US imports. Outsourcing is export substitution.[43]

Assuming dollar loyalty   Alan Greenspan's mantra was that the fundamentals of the American economy are sound. As a safe haven and market of last resort the US remains so attractive that it can sustain large deficits. Indeed, indebtedness may be a virtue: 'the world's appetite for US assets bolsters US predominance rather than undermines it.'[44] Assuming dollar loyalty is vintage economic brinkmanship. It is the belief that *external* deficits don't matter. Take this a step further and the record American debt becomes an economic strategy. In plain language, incur mounting deficits and let foreign governments and investors hold the bag because creditors are hooked to the dollar as world currency and to the US as the largest market and the 'consumer of last resort' propelling the world economy.

Financial trends don't confirm dollar loyalty. A 2005 survey of the leading sixty-five central banks indicates that they are diversifying currency reserves, with a decline from 70 percent of world reserves held in dollars in 2002 to 63 percent in 2004 and further expected declines. Central banks in Russia, Switzerland, Italy, and the Arab Emirates have announced plans to diversify out of the dollar, and similar signals come from China, Iran, South Korea, and even Japan.[45] Venezuela prices its oil in euros. The 2007–08 credit crunch has weakened the dollar further.

Dollar loyalty is vulnerable to the emergence of alternative currencies and alternative markets. European investors reduced their dollar holdings and several countries have adopted the euro as trading currency. The Chiang Mai Initiative established an Asian Bond Fund. At the initiative of Venezuela, Latin American countries have set up a Bank of the South. Japan, China, and South Korea may develop a yen–yuan–won based Asian reserve fund. Alternative markets are taking shape in the economic powerhouse of ASEAN+3 (Southeast Asia plus China, Japan and South Korea) and the growing trade between Asia and the European Union, Latin America, the Middle East and Africa. Recovery in Germany and Japan (and meeting the rising cost of aging populations) and growing demand and inward investment in China and Asia are turning their savings inward. The pessimistic expectations of Stephen Roach, Morgan Stanley's chief economist who long anticipated a hard landing for the US economy, have come true by 2008.[46]

New investments inflow Some economists expect that private investment into the US will resume: 'a renewal of private inflows responding to the next stage of the information technology revolution.'[47] Foreign direct investment in the US has recovered from the new economy crash and corporate scandals and resumed at $110 billion in 2005 and $190 billion in 2006. Although the US continues to attract almost a quarter of all FDI flows, China has overtaken it as the preferred destination of FDI. Besides, over the past ten years the flow of funds into the US has shifted: central banks, and more recently sovereign wealth funds, have taken the place of private investors. 'These banks are not buying dollar-denominated bonds because they are attracted to U.S. economic strengths … they are buying them because they fear U.S. weakness.'[48] Unlike in the 1990s, these are not productivity-enhancing inflows but simply fund the budget deficit through Treasury bonds.

Imposing tariffs Fred Bergsten lobbies for a 50 percent tariff on imports from China as a negotiating tool to press for revaluation of the renminbi. The commerce department and Congress plan to impose tariffs on several products from China. This goes against the grain of WTO rules and against the interests of corporations that depend on imports (Wal-Mart imports alone make up 15 percent of the US trade deficit with China). Since a significant share of the trade deficit with China concerns intra-firm trade by American multinationals, an appreciation of the renminbi would have limited impact. Since it would reduce the incentive for exporters to hold dollars it would expose the US current account position.

None of these options is likely to turn the tide. Raising the American savings rate is unlikely and depreciating the dollar (which is overvalued by 20 percent) would increase interest rates. The Federal Reserve raised the benchmark rate twelve times since June 2004 (from 1 to 4 percent), yet the medium interest rate has barely risen. Central banks' dollar holdings have decreased and foreign investors reduced their US investments. Where, then, is the $600–700 billion per annum that the US borrows externally coming from? A major factor is the high oil price and the recycling of oil revenues into dollar assets. 'The current account surplus of the oil producers will be about three times that of developing Asia in 2006 and close to that in 2007.'[49] This suggests that the American economy is borrowing time from a precarious conjuncture. According to the United States comptroller general, 'debt on debt is not good.'

> The American currency must be slowly, carefully managed lower to boost U.S. exports, but without triggering a sudden plunge in the greenback that could spark a devastating jump in inflation. Interest rates must gradually rise to ward off inflation and encourage consumers to save more of their earnings. Spending must be reined in, but not so severely that it compromises U.S. security and other public priorities. And taxes must be raised, but not so drastically that they stunt economic growth.[50]

None of these matches current policies. Seeking a solution implies admitting there is a problem. Implementing a solution implies a bipartisan grand bargain which clashes with the Republican agenda of shrinking government. The majority in Congress still favor maintaining tax cuts. In 2007 the comptroller general referred to the US's financial position as a 'burning platform' of unsustainable policies and with striking similarities to the factors that brought down Rome.[51] The remaining scenario is to close the trade gap by reducing imports and that only happens through a recession.

Limits of Rational Choice

Several policy outcomes are now familiar. The war in Iraq is widely viewed as brinkmanship that backfired, 'a flawed policy wrapped in illusion' (in the words of Representative John Murtha), 'a nightmare with no end in sight' (according to Retired Lt. Gen. Ricardo Sanchez, coalition commander in Iraq in 2003–04),[52] mismanaged in planning and execution. It isn't necessarily that Americans are against war; they are against losing war and the Iraq war appears to be a losing proposition with no end in sight. But interpreting policies as brinkmanship concerns not just the outcomes but the agendas and risk assessments underlying them.

An analysis of the savings-and-loan collapse found that poor accounting and lax regulation made it 'rational for executives to loot their companies.'[53] The executive reward system of stock options along with lax monitoring of how stocks are sold precipitated the Enron wave of corporate scandals. Can we argue along similar lines that for American policymakers brinkmanship is 'rational' even if the overall consequences spell disaster? A factor common to corporate and political brinkmanship is that executives obtain the gains but are sheltered from the losses. Different in the case of political brinkmanship is the weight of ideology and public perceptions; yet political consequences may be passed on to future administrations. Political brinkmanship produces gains for defense industries and, in operations in energy-rich areas, potentially for energy companies, which are linked to policy elites via revolving doors. Special Forces and private military contractors deal with the fallout from military interventions, in part off the record. This script is vulnerable on two points, which both materialized in Afghanistan and Iraq. The long duration of the wars stretches the armed forces beyond capacity and, as the cost increases and the prospects for victory dim, their political support drops. Even so some interpret the Iraq war, contrary to public perceptions, as a *success* for insiders and energy companies, for years down the road beckon $30 trillion in oil wealth, American geopolitical supremacy, and cheap petrol. All it takes, according to Jim Holt, is five permanent American super-bases and agreeable Iraqi politics,[54] an interpretation that holds politics constant and assumes indefinite American access.

Ideological and cultural brinkmanship are part of the equation. Many blame the neoconservatives for warmongering and the Bush administration for incompetence and deception, but their brinkmanship is the apotheosis of decades of right-wing campaigning for the 'free market' and militarism, against taxes, welfare, unions, gun control, and abortion. Thirty-five years of backlash culture and lavishly funded campaigns in defense of extreme capitalism and extreme militarism have deeply affected American public culture and set the stage for conservative overreach – even though it could not have materialized without the endorsement and support of liberals.

Neoconservatives cherish Machiavelli's counsel to the Prince that 'it is better to be feared than loved.' But ignoring soft power requires massive expenditure in hard power. Because the new wars have been driven by ideology rather than area knowledge and consider only short time frames, their risk assessments have been wishful. Policymakers underestimated the resistance in Iraq and Afghanistan and the wrath in the Islamic world. They miscalculated the price of unilateralism, which massively raises the cost of intervention, and the consequences of sidestepping international law, which leads nations to think that since international law is inoperative they can find protection only in nuclear arms.

Economic brinkmanship is rational in that low taxes and low benefits in combination with rising productivity, offshoring and outsourcing, generate superprofits for corporations, which are represented by lobbies in Washington and linked to the political elite through revolving doors. The free enterprise principle of privatizing gains and socializing losses, private wealth and public squalor applies. The downsides (job loss, no medical insurance for 47 million Americans, long working hours, two-earner households, stagnant wages) are carried by an electorate that abstains from voting in growing numbers and is socialized in 'free market values.' The idea that market forces are inherently superior to government intervention has been promoted especially during the past decades. Brinkmanship is holding on to this in the face of mounting deficits. In Stiglitz's words, 'the reason that Adam Smith's invisible hand is invisible is that it does not exist.'[55] Economic uncertainty may seem worth the long-term Republican objective of using deficits to shrink government and cut social spending. Yet faced with downsizing, stagnant wages and rising deficits, the laissez-faire consensus is coming apart at the seams. Conservatives worry about the deficit; the US imposes tariffs on imports from China; CEO remuneration is under scrutiny; communities protest against Wal-Mart; election candidates speak of 'Benedict Arnold CEOs' who outsource jobs; and plant closures, bankruptcies, and declining infrastructure are increasingly visible.

What makes political and economic brinkmanship possible is the concentration of power in the presidential system and the winner-takes-all political system. This enables the executive branch to engage in political maximalism and transfer risks to taxpayers. That resignations or firing policymakers when policies fail are rare in this system suggests power-with-impunity.

Economic brinkmanship takes on an ominous character for two other reasons, one conjunctural and the other long term. First is the intersection with political brinkmanship. While political and economic brinkmanship are each damaging their combination is fatal.

They merge in the image of 'Baghdad on the Mississippi.'[56] Baghdad and New Orleans merge in people's minds as emblems of government recklessness and ineptitude, producing national humiliation on both scores. The combination of tax cuts and war, expansion of military outlays and cutbacks in all other government programs, is gradually creating a different kind of United States. Hamid Varzi, a banker based in Tehran, offers this perspective:

> What have Americans gained from their nation's mountain of debt?
> A crumbling infrastructure, a manufacturing base that has declined
> 60 percent since World War II, a rise in the wealth gap, the lowest
> consumer-savings rate since the depths of the Great Depression, 50
> million Americans without health insurance, an educational system
> in decline and a shrinking dollar that makes foreign travel a luxury.
> The best cars, the best bridges and highways, the fastest trains and the
> tallest buildings are all to be found outside America's borders. Supply-
> siders ignore the crucial distinction between, on the one hand, debt
> employed as an investment vehicle to enhance competitiveness and,
> on the other, debt used to pay off current expenses and to create even
> more debt.[57]

Economic brinkmanship is a political platform. The question facing the US is how to become a service economy without creating a second-rate economy and a two-thirds society. First, it is not easy to split basic and high-end manufacturing. Second, by offshoring production the technical and knowledge infrastructure that sustains high value-added services shrinks too. Third, outsourcing includes white-collar jobs. Fourth, China has overtaken the US in exporting technology goods and is rapidly upgrading to high-tech production, as do other emerging economies. Fifth, a consumer economy based on borrowing from poorer countries is not sustainable. Sixth, policies of economic brinkmanship neglect inward investments in infrastructure, education, and research and development, follow short-term thinking, postpone strategic policy and leave it to corporations, which have different agendas than national well-being. Seventh, the widening shear between the American economy and the military–industrial complex and geopolitics leads to fictional politics. It is a fiction of state that the US can have guns and butter, tax cuts and war, that it is possible to do empire on the basis of a world-historic deficit. Neoconservatives have been long on power and ideology and short on economics. Combining tax cuts and war damages both the economy and hegemony.

Peter Gowan provides a lucid account of the strategic thinking underlying the new wars.[58] Yet their most striking feature is that they combine undoubted instrumental rationality with a profound irrationality of goals; they reflect a profound disjuncture between what Max Weber called instrumental rationality and value rationality. I have tried to sketch the climate that sustains this as the American bubble and I have tried to portray the grim views of security insiders and professionals. The next level should be an ethnography of the Situation Room and White House bubble. This is classified but if we read their intentions by their actions, according to the biblical saying 'by the fruits you shall know the tree,' we might be able to decode the mindset of policymakers.

I don't find comparisons between the United States and ancient Rome particularly insightful; the specifics are too different. Yet specific comparisons may be relevant. In ancient Rome, emperors, drunk with power or with the illusion of power, went mad with such frequency that it gave rise to 'imperial madness' as a trope in Roman history. A sequel theme in European history is 'the madness of kings.'[59] This may have its parallels in Washington. The idea that unipolarity has caused America to go mad has been a recurrent sentiment in reactions to the new wars worldwide. The year prior to and building up to the Iraq war was particularly tense across the world. Shortly after September 11 in a speech at the University of Turin Harold Pinter spoke of 'the nightmare of American hysteria, ignorance, arrogance, stupidity and belligerence; the most powerful nation the world has ever known effectively waging war against the rest of the world.' In January 2003 John Le Carré wrote an opinion piece in *The Times*, 'The US of America has gone mad.' 'America has entered one of its periods of historical madness, but this is the worst I can remember.... The reaction to 9/11 is beyond anything Osama bin Laden could have hoped for in his nastiest dreams.'[60] Gabriel Kolko asked, 'how long will Europe put up with a crazed America?'[61]

Madness is a crude category; there are many registers to madness, including the 'madness of reason.' Reflecting on the fall of Saddam's statue in Baghdad, Jürgen Habermas notes 'empirical objections to the possibilities of realizing the American vision.'

> Global society has become far too complex; the world is no longer accessible to a centralized control, through politics backed up by military power. In the technologically supreme and heavily armed superpower's fear of terrorism, one can sense a 'Cartesian anxiety'; the fear of a subject trying to objectify both itself and the world around it; trying to bring everything under control.

Even if the project could be implemented, he argues,

> It would generate side-effects that are undesirable according to its own normative criteria. The more that political power (understood in its role as a global civilizing force) is exercised in the dimensions of the military, secret security services and police, the more it comes into conflict with its own purposes, endangering the mission of improving the world according to the liberal vision. In the US itself, the administration of a perpetual 'wartime president' is already undermining the foundations of the rule of law.[62]

Liberals who endorse American primacy should carefully think through its political and economic consequences for the US and its real world implementation, and contemplate the price of primacy. Coercive interventions rarely bring about the aspired changes: the remedy is similar to or worse than the disease – authoritarian interventions cannot fix authoritarian polities.

SEVEN

Can the United States Correct Itself?

IS THE BALANCE OF FORCES such that, short of undergoing a major economic and political crisis, the United States can chart a significantly different course? At stake are the key problems of social inequality, hegemony, and the economy. Course corrections are in the cards, but inequality is so steep and the economy so debt-ridden that tinkering in the margins will not do. Correcting this would mean reinventing New Deal policies, and correcting foreign policy unilateralism would mean adopting genuine constructive multilateralism.

To answer the question of whether there is hope for Uncle Sam and whether the United States can correct its course, we must step back and look at American politics. In the 1960s there *was* hope for the United States and the US did correct itself by adopting civil rights legislation, ending the Vietnam War, and taking on the Great Society project. However, what happened since then has to a considerable extent been a backlash against these steps. Civil rights laws led Southern Democrats in droves to the Republican Party. Defeat in Vietnam led the Pentagon to devise methods of harnessing media, channeling public opinion, and securing congressional support. The war on poverty has turned into a war on the poor.

American policies in Iraq and Afghanistan don't work and there have been many rounds of criticism and multiple targets. Most criticism by far has been directed at the neoconservatives. The reasons for going to war were deceptive, the calculations of the architects of war failed, and the war is far more costly in lives, treasure and reputation than anticipated. Defense Secretary Rumsfeld brought insufficient boots on the ground, torpedoed diplomacy, set up alternative intelligence circuits that provided wishful intelligence, and so forth. These criticisms are operational rather than fundamental. The ire focused on the neoconservatives glosses over deeper problems. The American crisis is layered and the neoconservatives are but an outer ring, just as the Iraq war is an expression of wider problems. Entrenched behind the neoconservatives lies the far more significant power of the Southern conservatives. The neoconservatives are not in Congress; they are appointed, not elected. The Southern conservatives make up the mainstay of the GOP and have long held the power in Congress. Mainstream Democrats share the aim of primacy and have bought into the 'Reagan revolution.' Ensconced behind the conservatives lies another ring of conservative cultural militants. For decades conservatives have spent billions of dollars on think-tanks and campaigns to broadcast conservative messages. Look further beneath the culture wars and the media are corporations. Corporations are sheltered by lawmakers through intricate webs of special interest arrangements. The relations between lawmakers and corporations are embedded in the system of election campaign financing. Thus peel off layer after layer of the onion of American power and hurdle upon hurdle emerges, hurdles so deeply entrenched that – no matter the criticisms – the institutions themselves are lopsided.

In the 1980s a narrative took shape that blamed the 1960s on permissiveness. In promoting welfare dependency, government and the 'liberal elite' enabled permissiveness and stifled free enterprise.

The remedy was to impose discipline by cutting welfare and un-leashing market forces. Yet polls show that during this turn and in years hence the majority of Americans continue to hold socially progressive views, which, however, don't find expression in media or in elections. This chapter concludes with a reflection on scenarios of American decline: the main ones are crash-landing, the Phoenix and a new New Deal.

A Progressive Majority

During the Reagan years public opinion did not shift to the right: 'If anything, the voters have moved to the left since Reagan took office – there is less support for military spending; more support for domestic social programs; increased concern about arms control, hunger and poverty'; 'popular support for conservative approaches to the economy and foreign policy diminished.'[1] Reviewing public opinion polls taken between 1980 and 1984, Seymour Martin Lipset concluded that 'Americans, while voting conservative on the presidential level, are programmatically liberal.'

> Asked to choose between military and social-spending cuts, the major-ity chose to cut the Pentagon, not the poor. Even the most stigmatized programs, the right's most pernicious examples of the 'milch-cow state' – Aid to Families with Dependent Children and Food Stamps – were supported by 57 percent of people asked to choose between protecting these programs and reducing the federal deficit.[2]

Also during the 2000s the majority of Americans believe that the minimum wage should be increased by more than \$2 and think 'government should help the needy even if it means greater debt.' Two-thirds want the government to guarantee universal health care. The majority believe that 'labor unions are necessary to protect the working person' and side with labor in disputes. The majority thinks the Bush tax cuts were 'not worth it because they have in-creased the deficit and caused cuts in government programs.' Some

67 percent of Americans favor 'diplomatic and economic efforts over
military efforts in fighting terrorism.' A similar majority holds that
undocumented immigrants should be allowed 'to keep their jobs and
eventually apply for legal status,' favors tougher gun control laws,
and prefers rehabilitation over incarceration for youth offenders.[3]
Poll after poll registers that Americans hold views on taxes, redistribution, social services, health care, abortion, and gun control that
are far to the left of government, political parties, and media.

> What we find is that a whopping 86% of Americans believe that there
> need to be stricter laws and regulations to protect the environment;
> 77% think it is more important to maintain government services such
> as Medicare, Social Security and Medicaid than to cut taxes; 72% of
> Americans favor stricter laws related to the control of handguns; 63%
> of Americans favor affirmative action programs designed to help blacks,
> women and other minorities get better jobs and education; 62% don't
> think Roe v. Wade should be overturned by the Supreme Court; and
> 62% would prefer a universal health insurance program run by the
> government and financed by taxpayers.[4]

Thus, as measured by countless polls, most Americans hold socially
and politically progressive views. The majority of Jewish Americans, likewise, doesn't share the neoconservatives' views and oppose
US military action in the Middle East whether in Iraq or against
Iran.[5] Again these views are not represented in media, by political
parties, or in electoral choices.

Political stagnation in America is not for want of knowledge.
Factual and critical knowledge is abundantly available and readily
accessible – on the defense industries, private military contractors,
war profiteering, corporate welfare, farm subsidies, environmental
deregulation, the labyrinthine worlds of health care, the pharmaceuticals industry, and so forth. It doesn't take much to find critical information; in a matter of minutes with Google and Google Scholar one
can find key texts on all these issues, not just in academic journals
but in readily available trade books. American crony capitalism is
not rocket science. In a matter of months one can piece together a

basic map of American crony capitalism. Analytical tools such as power structure analysis are also readily available.

But the available knowledge doesn't reach the public. The tendency in media is to equate politics with elections and elections with numbers. This horse-race trivialization of politics marginalizes politics as a public conversation about national goals. Such conversations that take place are mostly confined to the elite. Questions of national goals and strategy are discussed in think-tanks, journals, and venues such as the National Defense University, the armed forces graduate school. By its nature this is not a reflexive or critical conversation; participants share the objective of primacy while they differ on how it is to be achieved. What trickles down from this elite conversation are media soundbites that focus on *how* rather than what. Questions of values and ethics are not explored because 'American values' is a showstopper.

The media are closed to critical information, with the partial exception of public broadcasting, most of which is so dry that it only appeals to a professional audience and the criticism is inane. Thus Americans are left alone in their dismay, alone in their growing awareness that their society is dysfunctional and corrupt. This leads to the conclusion that the United States is in effect a colonized country, a country colonized by corporations and corporate media. The public sphere is colonized by 24/7 commercial media, progressive views can't find a platform, and a corporate plutocracy rules the land of the free.

An operational twist is that 'Conservatives offer inferior policies, but dominate through superior marketing.' Strategic communications in naming and framing, promotion and placement, and managing the distribution channels, add to the structural advantage of corporations. As Laurie Spivak notes, 'They name legislation "No Child Left Behind," "Healthy Forests," "Clear Skies" and "Patriot Act," essentially forcing legislators to support their bills, lest they be accused of leaving children behind, favoring polluted forests and skies, or being branded as unpatriotic.'[6] Marketing language as everyday currency creates an upside-down world. Tax cuts for the wealthy are cast as the 'jobs and economic growth package.' Pollster and electoral strategist Frank Luntz is credited with coining the term 'Healthy Forests Initiative' for Bush administration policies that favor expanded logging by the timber industry. Bogus marketing language has become routine in media and politics and is somehow presented as extraordinarily smart.[7] Republican framing and agenda-setting, the Republican noise machine and its media echo, marginalize progressive views, which barely get airtime except on comedy shows and arts pages.

Progressives recognize that 'The rise of the machinery of ideas on the right has been impressive' and have begun counter-organizing in earnest with funding from donors such as George Soros, alternative media such as Air America, progressive framing via the Internet and blogs, media campaigns by Move On, websites such as Daily Kos, AlterNet, Counterpunch, liberal think-tanks such as the Center for American Progress, and vocal figures such as Michael Moore and Al Franken. The Center for American Progress seeks to emulate the conservative institutions: 'A message oriented war room will send out a daily briefing to refute the positions and arguments of the right. An aggressive media department will book liberal thinkers on cable TV. There will be an "edgy" web site and a policy shop to formulate strong positions on foreign and domestic issues.'[8]

As new generations – Gen X (born between 1961 and 1976) and the 'Millennials' (the 18- to 30-year olds in 2008) – enter politics they do so in a well-honed institutional setting. New technologies make an impact – direct mail has yielded to the Internet, blogs, YouTube, Facebook, and indie media. Their political influence is growing, yet broadcasting technologies continue to carry the day. 'If a story isn't on TV in America, it doesn't exist in our culture.'[9] But when it comes to elections,

> social networks like Facebook, Blackplanet, blogs and SMS, as well as basic email, can be layered onto the clean new databases to reach voters wherever they are, for much less money than TV advertising. We are in

the middle of a massive wave of campaign innovation, led by organizers who will eventually spread outward to every nook and cranny of progressive politics. The larger significance of this architectural revolution in progressive politics isn't clear, but it is the first sustained challenge to the dominance of television and direct mail in the political system since those media displaced the urban machines in the 1960s.[10]

The new media and technologies are subject to the same pressures of ownership and commercialization as the old ones. Internet neutrality may not last. Relying on new information technologies for the renewal of democracy is a flawed premiss.

Although Americans have repeatedly voted in conservative presidents (Nixon, Reagan, Bush 41 and 43) and re-elected two of them, the majority by and large holds progressive views. This suggests that the discussion should shift from *policies* to *politics*, while the trivialization of politics and elections suggests that the focus should shift from *politics* to *institutions*, and beyond institutions the focus should also be on *political culture*, including the American bubble. Conservative campaigns cloud the airwaves but political outcomes aren't just a matter of conservative chicanery. Joan Didion observes her home state California carrying 'the idea of individual rights to dizzying and often punitive lengths.'[11] In an angry speech the mayor of Salt Lake City, Ross Anderson, urges,

> We must avoid the trap of focusing the blame solely upon President Bush and Vice-President Cheney.... They were enabled by members of both parties in Congress, they were enabled by the pathetic mainstream news media, and, ultimately, they have been enabled by the American people – 40% of whom are so ill-informed they still think Iraq was behind the 9/11 attacks – a people who know and care more about baseball statistics and which drunken starlets are wearing underwear than they know and care about the atrocities being committed every single day in our name by a government for which we need to take responsibility.[12]

While experiencing several generations of economic success and prosperity Americans have turned their backs on politics and focused on individual pursuits or identity politics, allowing the institutions to become elite playgrounds. Populist sentiment critiquing Washington goes back to the nineteenth century, but 'revolutionary elections' have gone out of style. As mentioned before, since the 1980s commentators refer to government and Congress as 'Permanent Washington' and to the relationship between Congress, lobbyists, and media as an 'iron triangle.'[13] The relationship between legislators–lobbyists–corporations underlies the innumerable ways in which the US is dominated by vested interests. Business-friendly government, parties and legislation occur throughout the world but the US is in a different league – Washington is the capital of a world power; no fundamental ideological differences divide its political parties; judicial supremacy is deeply entrenched; and corporate media dominate the public sphere. Washington is the capital of a world power comparable to the capital cities of past imperial and hegemonic powers such as Rome, Madrid, Amsterdam, The Hague, and London. With these it shares cycles of rise, high power, and decline; but unlike these it is also the capital of a continental power with large resources and a large domestic market. The system of parties reflecting the class interests of labor and farmers doesn't apply in the US; no major ideological differences separate the two parties. The two parties go back to the mid-nineteenth century and are the oldest of any party structure among advanced countries – Britain's Labour Party developed in the 1890s; leading parties of European countries and Japan emerged after the Second World War. The iron triangle is well entrenched.

Scenarios of Decline

Comparative studies of imperialism and comparisons of British and American hegemonic careers produce diverse perspectives on hegemonic decline.[14] Revisiting the thesis of imperial overstretch after September 11, Paul Kennedy makes various suggestions for recovering American hegemony but ends by asking 'the ultimate political question,' namely 'is the striving for the maintenance of America's present place in the world actually desirable?' and notes that 'the U.S. becoming a "normal" country' is unavoidable sooner or later.[15]

Political and corporate unaccountability are structurally entrenched and public forums to address them barely exist. Social inequality in the US has grown steadily and markedly since the 1970s (with a brief upward blip during the 1990s). Empowerment for Americans would mean reinventing a New Deal kind of economic regulation. The New Deal took shape in response to crisis, and short of crisis a New Deal politics is unlikely. The US has been marked all along by a greater preponderance of business over labor than any advanced country. 'What is good for GM is good for America' made sense when business was national, but since large corporations have become transnational and capitalism has gone global, pro-business policies have different consequences.

At issue are long-term shifts in the global balance of forces. The frailties of the American economy are structurally embedded so the capacity for self-correction is limited. It follows from free-enterprise ideology that there is no government industrial policy, and it follows from accelerated globalization that there is no commitment on the part of US transnationals to the national economy beyond shareholders and the quarterly bottom line. In social market capitalism, government policies seek to balance the interests of employers, labor, and stakeholders such as communities and consumers; in free enterprise capitalism government policy primarily serves corporations and becomes corporatist. The lack of balanced government policy and the weakness of social organization make this a high-risk form of capitalism, capable of high growth but vulnerable, as many point out.[16] Deregulation has gradually removed more safeguards, and social forces that represent different interests have been eroded. American companies earn superprofits that, courtesy of deregulation, don't feed back into the American economy. Because belief in free enterprise is deeply entrenched, there is no provision for the American economy as such. Corporate social responsibility is much less influential than in Europe. 'Taxes are for suckers.' The cascade of corporate scandals from Enron to the subprime mortgage crisis displays a market with inadequate regulation. Now Uncle Sam is at another threshold with unsustainable deficits and a sinking dollar. Many view the new wars as part of the twilight of American hegemony. There are different strands to what is considered unsustainable:

- an economic policy – the military–industrial complex, tax cuts and war, deficit financing;
- an economic model – neoliberalism in its downturn phase with reduced manufacturing, high imports, high debt;
- an American way of life – high consumption, low savings ('affluenza') plus deindustrialization;
- unilateralism and reliance on military power and empire of bases rather than soft power, legitimacy and cooperative security.

The judgment about what is declining and why follows from assumptions that lie beyond these judgments. Neoconservatives believe that power is a creative agent that solves problems along the way; they believe in the ability of power to change circumstances and create 'facts on the ground.' Neoliberals believe that the free market unleashes such entrepreneurial creativity and innovation that it will solve the problems that are worth solving. Liberal hawks believe that a dangerous world requires order and there is a lasting demand for American power. Historians of different stripes revisiting the British Empire in the kaleidoscope of present times see different patterns. Orthodox Marxists believe that the tendency for the rate of profit to decline spells the end of American capitalism as its capacity to incorporate outlying areas runs out. Neo-Marxists believe that capitalism can prolong its career by using military force to effect 'accumulation by dispossession' and in the process turns into fascism. Adherents of world-system theory hold that American administrations have been trying to slow the decline of hegemony since the 1970s and view the new wars as installments in this process.

Each of these predictions selects a different set of variables as decisive and marginalizes others; each holds different assumptions about what matters. We cannot see the processes that we cannot observe except through the lens of our paradigms, our grid of assumptions. One's investment in a paradigm is also an investment in a future, as if each paradigm is a universe unto itself. An example is the White House official who distinguished between the faith-based and the reality-based community and argued that the faith-based community acts to 'make reality.'[17]

There is no consensus on the state of American corporations. According to Robert Brenner, corporate profits have been down and the rate of profit is declining. I don't share Brenner's thesis that American economic problems stem from overproduction; his argument of overcapacity in American industries since the 1960s is in my view untenable. According to government estimates the profits of companies operating in the US rose at an average annual rate of 7 percent in 1997–2007, whereas profits of American companies from their overseas operations increased by 13.7 percent.[18] The share of profits coming from overseas operations increased from 7 percent in the 1960s to 29 percent in 2007. This suggests that profitability in the US is steady but that a growing share of profits derives from overseas operations. What explains this disparity in part is financial engineering, so in some sectors profits are high, short of indicating a sound economy.

Many indicators have been down for some time. The question now is not whether the US is declining, but what form decline will take, whether it will be mild or severe, and what effects it will produce. The units are bulky, 'United States,' 'decline.' Does decline refer to the economy, the dollar and the financial system, to hegemony, or to overall decline? Decline is not necessarily negative. It is a relief for countries that have suffered the Washington Consensus and the Washington connection, though the upset of the world economy also brings hardship, certainly for countries that rely on exports to the US (Mexico, Canada, and China above all) and hold dollar assets. Decline is a relief for Americans who have felt out of place in a society under the incessant drone of marketing and a war-prone government, for two-earner households who have been working harder without seeing their prospects improve; though recession and soft fundamentals spell trouble and marketing won't stop. Decline is a source of hope, above all, because it offers the US a chance of becoming a 'normal country,' a 'country among others,' without the burden of (claiming) world leadership. But this will occur only if economic and political upset are sufficient to surrender the claim to world hegemony and to begin shrinking the defense industries and the military.

Upon reflection, decline becomes a riddle of the Sphinx, a glyph to decipher. Arguably, there are essentially three main scenarios of American decline: a crash landing, the Phoenix, and a new New Deal. Each is distinct, yet they are also in complex ways interrelated.

Crash landing   Deflation has been in motion for some time, bargain-basement America already exists, and financially the US already depends on the 'kindness of strangers.'[19] The financial press has been discussing the decoupling of the world economy from American consumers for some time. In the mild version of this script the US adjusts course, the American bubble deflates, and it is over to other centers of influence. Yet even as this unfolds significant course corrections are unlikely because Permanent Washington is well entrenched and the margins are narrow because ongoing trends mortgage future options. In financial markets there is no greater reflexivity than in 1929: new credit instruments such as derivatives are out of control, transparency is in question because the rating agencies have malfunctioned during the credit crisis. Wall Street's hope for a soft landing has yielded to the sense that the banking system is 'an accident waiting to happen' and a crash-landing is in the cards or already in motion.[20] Military budgets continue to balloon even aside from war. With the accumulation of executive privilege there is less restraint on the White House.

A dramatic script that may be too catastrophist is the *Titanic*, a favorite trope in relation to the world economy in Davos circles. According to Clyde Prestowitz, 'In many respects it resembles the *Titanic*, a magnificent machine with serious and largely unrecognized internal flaws heading at full speed for icebergs, armed with knowledge and assumptions significantly at odds with reality.'[21] The *Titanic* in this passage refers to the global economy, but according to the gist of the book it applies mainly to the US.

Yet, endings are also beginnings. As a crash-landing unsettles elites and closes paths, it opens new ones; so Uncle Sam's journey may take several directions. First, it may simply be decline, rapid or gradual. This doesn't mean total breakdown but a climb down from the top – the dollar losing its role as world money, foreigners less keen to hold dollar assets, hence the need to raise interest rates, slowing down the economy. Yet even after a recession or two the US remains a substantial economy, if no longer number one. Considering that the US suffers from spleen deficit, a crash-landing may generate the requisite spleen – greater thoughtfulness would remedy many American ailments. Public recognition of a trend break might curb Pentagon expansion and Wall Street excesses and restore fiscal sanity. Thus decline, whether mild or catastrophic, may lead into two possible scripts of decline-as-hope, the Phoenix scenario and New Deal 2 scenario.

The Phoenix Joachim Rennstich argues that Britain carried the day during *two* accumulation cycles, the commercial-maritime cycle at the turn of the eighteenth century ('Britannia rules the waves') and the nineteenth-century industrial cycle ('workshop of the world'). British hegemony declined and then rose again and the same may happen to the US. The US rose on the basis of industrial mass production at the turn of the nineteenth century, underwent deindustrialization during the late twentieth century and may climb back in the twenty-first century riding the wave of new-economy technologies.[22]

There are several intertwined pros and cons regarding this script. In brief, the US economy is large and diverse, but also import-dependent. The US higher education system is the envy of much of the world, yet the cost of education is rising. The infrastructure is good but old-fashioned and the transportation system involves inefficient energy use. Because the US is in extreme climate zones it is more energy intensive. On the plus side are a lead in services from the Internet to Hollywood, and attractiveness to and social mobility for immigrants. Yet it has also an aging population, a dysfunctional health care system, and is headed for impending fiscal catastrophe. It has great cultural diversity but low social solidarity. Pleading against American resurrection also are unsustainable consumption patterns, a dysfunctional political system, an oversized military, self-seeking elites, and corporatist welfare with low investments in product improvement. Prima donna narcissism and laissez-faire don't help sorting out and rising from the ashes.

Thus a Phoenix scenario is possible, but not in the short run. During the Clinton–Gore years this could have been an option – America's smart way forward on the information superhighway with innovation, research and development, smart solutions, ecological sustainability. Yet, already then innovation also meant financial engineering, the deregulation of telecoms and energy, opening a wide road to Wall Street profit-taking and Enron creative accounting, along with triangulation, welfare reform, Nafta and WTO, and humanitarian militarism. With the Bush administration the smart Phoenix option was definitively off the program; the America of conservatives and neoconservatives is authoritarian, militarist, brawn over brain. The Project for a New American Century is the opposite of the smart way forward – another American century built on war and fear, 'Americans are from Mars,' channeling innovation into future weapons systems, Star Wars, Total Information

Awareness and surveillance, e-espionage rather than e-clever, a fear economy rather than a smart economy. Merge and mix the propensity to war with the ideology of small government and tax cuts and the outcome is a $1.6 trillion credit card bill. War and tax cuts, deindustrialization and imports, consumption and deficits mortgage American futures and reinforce outsourcing and offshoring, so for years smart America has been leaving America. Smart America has not even been betting on the dollar. The key problem of the US, by comparison to Europe and Japan, is decades of underinvestment in productive assets. Instead of innovating and bringing out new products American companies have tapped and tweaked old value streams, bilked cheap labor offshore, and a sheltered home market – quite different from Siemens, Nokia, BMW, Toyota. Thus the foundation and resilience of a Phoenix approach is lacking.

Britain's commercial and maritime hegemony laid the foundation for and sustained and sheltered the workshop of the world; triangular trade marshaled manpower and resources in overseas colonies that fed the Manchester cotton mills and Birmingham industries; colonial trade and tariff policies fostered Britain's industrial rise. There is no such continuity – a lead in one accumulation strategy laying the foundation for the next – in the US case, or what there is, is too thin and haphazard to serve as a platform for resurgence and is in significant respects counterproductive. American deindustrialization doesn't merely foster industrialization in emerging economies but also offshores research and development. American specialization in military power and technology (rent-a-cop) is too slim a basis for twenty-first-century resurgence. The attempts to gain control of the world's major oil and gas reserves involve such massive expenditure of political and military energies, resources and legitimacy that they endanger rather than enhance American futures. A future smart America may well hinge on corporations owned or part-owned by Chinese, Indian, and European enterprises and sovereign wealth funds, which have already started buying up American assets and futures. An American Phoenix is possible down the road but is already mortgaged and being sold off to outside interests to pay for the debts of the *Titanic* as it is heading to its rendezvous.

New Deal 2 The second scenario of decline-as-hope is rebalancing the relations between government, corporations, and society such that social stakeholders play a greater role (workers, consumers, communities, and so forth), in other words a turn to the social market, as in the New Deal. This script runs, after crisis (via Hoover), Roosevelt and the New Deal.

The laissez-faire consensus among American economists has begun to fray at the edges, and economic heterodoxy, though still marginal, has been gaining points.[23] As regards policies, many economists advocate Keynesian demand-led growth with public investments, higher wages, and stronger unions (such as Jeff Faux, Paul Krugman, Robert Kuttner, Jeff Madrick), an overall regulatory approach of 'structural Keynesianism' (Thomas Palley), full employment policies, corporate social responsibility, and smart consumerism, and progressive cities adopt various measures of economic populism.[24] A sensitive debate concerns the role of deficits. If Republicans have been running extreme budget overruns, should deficits control policy? The advocates of the free market and lean government have practiced crony capitalism, excessive military spending, and tax cuts for the wealthy. But deficit alarmism is not wise counsel at this point: 'by placing budget deficits at the center of the saving problem, it sets government up as a problem and makes a case for shrinking it.'[25] According to Robert Reich, 'fiscal balance is a false economy.' Yes budget deficits are high, 'yet as a percentage of GDP the budget deficit is now far less than in the early 1990s. If we cut corporate welfare, raised taxes on the richest Americans, and allowed the deficit to move up to 3 percent of GDP then there would be plenty of money to invest in the nation's future.' 'The nation's investment deficit [in education, health care, environment, infrastructure] is now much larger than it was in 1992.'[26] Robert

Rubin's approach of deficit cutting that worked in the 1990s is essentially a monetarist, sound-money policy. Were Rubinomics adopted now it would impair alternative policies.

Lacking are not alternatives but discussion of alternatives and the mobilization of political will around alternatives. If the key problems are not policies but politics and, beyond politics, institutions, then economics is not the place to look. According to Kevin Phillips and others the key American problems are institutional – undemocratic, aging and old-fashioned political institutions. Phillips offers drastic proposals for institutional reform, opening up institutions, yet sees little prospect of their implementation.[27] As Arnold Toynbee pointed out in his *Study of History*, declining empires tend toward the 'idolization of institutions' as people seek to restore the conditions that had made their rise possible. Reagan looked back to the 1950s and 1920s; the Project for a New American Century seeks to do the 1950s over again; the American bubble genuflects before the 'founding fathers' – and all demonstrate American institutional nostalgia.

The prospects are dim. The economy slouches from crisis to crisis – savings and loan, LTCM, the dotcom crash, Enron, Amaranth, the subprime crisis, the credit crisis. The reasons why the subprime crisis emerged are no different from the reasons why the new economy bubble popped years earlier: 'deregulation to the point of anarchy; a towering secrecy that conceals the financial world from ordinary investors; greed that distorts capitalism and the character of those who administer it; a justice system that Wall Street malefactors know they need not fear.'[28] The years pass and ailments are not fixed but deepen, and meltdown draws nearer. 'The housing bubble was a reaction from the effort to protect us from the collapse of the tech bubble. What's the next bubble going to be as a consequence of trying to protect us against this?'[29] In the words of stock market analyst Pam Martens: 'How did a 200-year old "efficient" market model that priced its securities based on regular price discovery through transparent trading morph into an opaque manufacturing and warehousing complex of products that didn't trade or rarely traded, necessitating pricing based on statistical models?' The answer is deregulation.[30]

A turn toward the interests of labor is now much less likely than it was in the 1930s. Corporations are much stronger and dispersed in their operations and headquarters, technology is more advanced, large corporations control the public sphere, trade unions are weaker and less organized, political parties are closed to substantial alternatives, the public is socialized in complacency, and the utopian imagination seems a faint and distant memory. The very meaning of 'American' has become dispersed and polycentric – American as in Halliburton's headquarters in Dubai, American as in IBM and Intel's investments in India and China, American as in tax havens in Bermuda and the Bahamas? This time around elites have learned from the Depression and can anticipate and block a social turn. Recession turning into crisis might as well bring deepening authoritarianism and extending the fear economy, deftly mobilizing disaster for yet another round of predatory enrichment – Las Vegas capitalism teaming up with disaster capitalism.

American decline is rich with opportunity and danger, which is ordinary by historical standards. A problem specific to the United States is that a mature and savvy national conversation about these dilemmas is not within reach. Which script of decline materializes depends largely on reactions to economic upset and electoral options. Economic decline follows thirty-five years of backlash politics and culture as the dominant American mood. What began as backlash against the 1960s and defeat in Vietnam has hardened in an all-round angry mood, even generating, as Thomas Frank notes, a backlash personality type.[31] Current trends are bashing globalization, free trade, China, immigrants and so on. The American bubble is not hospitable to critical reflection on corporations, Wall Street, or political institutions. A turnaround in corporate media is unlikely. Political parties remain closed to alternatives. This buffers the electoral consequences of economic upheaval. Riots in the streets are unlikely; barricades in the suburbs don't make sense and would upset the shopping season. Hence the likely trend is muddling through and deepening decline, economically, politically and institutionally.

To address Uncle Sam's problems of growing inequality and economic decline it takes not only more public investment but also private investment, which has been lagging for decades as well. 'American companies are falling behind in technology… US companies dedicate the majority of their fresh capital to fortifying older systems while companies in Europe and Asia invest in more up-to-date systems.'[32] This doesn't lend itself to an easy political fix. It requires a fundamental turnaround not just in policies but in philosophies. More is at stake and more is involved but short-hand for this U-turn is re-regulating Wall Street, just as shorthand for restraining American hegemony is cutting the Pentagon. Yet Wall Street and the Pentagon, America's luxury liners, don't easily change course. Political and corporate unaccountability are struc-turally entrenched and public forums to address them barely exist. With ample simplification, if we consider the constants of American policy – in short, support for Wall Street, the Pentagon, and Israel – there is barely variation among elites across the political spec-trum regardless of party affiliation. There are policy variations but no change in fundamentals.

So I don't think significant self-correction is in the cards in the foreseeable future. The minimum reforms that Uncle Sam should undertake are not particularly fancy or extraordinary. They are commonsensical by international standards and most Americans, were they asked, would probably agree. They include, following Chalmers Johnson, 'reversing Bush's 2001 and 2003 tax cuts for the wealthy, beginning to liquidate our global empire of over 800 military bases, cutting from the defense budget all projects that bear no relationship to national security and ceasing to use the defense budget as a Keynesian jobs program.'[33] Yet by the stan-dards of American politics these are extreme measures for which a congressional majority is far off. As long as this is the case, as long as commonsense changes are unfeasible in American politics, the US cannot self-correct. The likely course, then, is that Uncle Sam will muddle through and problems will continue to get worse, until economic decline will get so bad that elites are unseated and an overhaul finally does take place. In the meantime correction will come from outside by the actions of external forces that cease to follow the US or invest in the US, which is the theme of the closing chapter.

EIGHT

New Balance

SINCE AMERICAN HEGEMONY followed the era of British hegemony it is part of a series, part of a long stretch of Anglo-American hegemony from approximately 1820 onward, interrupted by periods of hegemonic rivalry. American decline therefore represents a system change with worldwide ripple effects. In the context of global long-term history, however, this shift, though significant, is not as earth-shattering. Through most of global history the world economy has been centered on the Orient. From about 500 CE the Middle East was the center of the world economy and the 'bridge of the world,' but by 1100 the leading edge of the world economy shifted to China and the Indian subcontinent, where it remained until well into the nineteenth century. Hence the predominance of the West dates only from the nineteenth century, the lead of Europe and then the United States refers to a relatively brief period, and with the rise of Asia and China the world economy is reverting to where it has been centered through most of world history.[1]

I will first review several questions this presents for American hegemony, for assessing the old balance is part of reading the new, and then turn to what these changes mean for the world majority. The perspective on the new balance that is most obvious – what problems it poses for the US – is also most limited; focusing on the declining hegemon is looking at future trends through the rearview mirror.

The Afterlife of Hegemony

> Above all, we cannot stop long-term shifts in the economic and strategic balances, because by our economic and social policies we ourselves are the very artificers of these futures changes; we can no more stop the rise of Asia than we can stop the winter snows and the summer heat.
>
> Paul Kennedy, 2001

American decline poses several questions: does it usher in hegemonic rivalry or a transition toward a new hegemon? As a fading hegemon can the US hold on to its financial lead, as did the United Provinces and Britain, and can it sustain its military supremacy?

Does American decline lead to a new era of hegemonic rivalry and wars of succession, as in 1870–1945, or is an altogether different configuration in the making? Complex interdependence and interweaving of economies, technologies, and polities across the world is now so extensive that retreating to national economies or regional blocs is much less viable than it was in the early twentieth century or in George Orwell's *1984* (with Oceania, Eurasia, and Eastasia). High-density globalization and hegemonic rivalry between nations or regional blocs are not compatible.

This doesn't imply that what lies ahead is, for instance, a cohesive transnational capitalist class, a global Davos elite, and a straightforward global rift between the World Economic Forum and the World Social Forum. Local, national and regional interests are deeply anchored, so more realistic are in-between patterns in which national and regional interests and policies matter, interspersed with technological interweaving, transnational corporate links and civil society networks; complex, layered patterns of competition and cooperation, and cooperation through competition.

Will the US be able to hold on to its financial lead, as did previous hegemons? The US faces major drains on its financial resources: because of rapid deindustrialization it has become an importer on a vast scale (unlike twentieth-century Britain), owes interest on a massive debt (unlike the United Provinces), and spends most of its treasure on the military (like sixteenth- and seventeenth-century Spain). The US has experienced rapid erosion of its reserves; even after a weaker dollar makes its exports more competitive it lacks the production capacity for recouping this massive drain. Although the declining dollar whittles away US debt, it is unlikely that the bulk of the debt will ever be repaid. Like twentieth-century Britain, the US has been waging war on credit and, as in Britain's case, financial vulnerability augurs decline.

Will the US be able to use its vast military resources to undertake 'accumulation by dispossession' and thus prolong its hegemony? Timothy Garton Ash notes, 'When the next recession comes along, it will be no use sending for the marines.'[2] The quagmires of Iraq and Afghanistan illustrate the limited utility of military force[3] and the limitations of American armed forces in ground warfare. In Michael Lind's words, 'The US remains the only country capable of projecting military power throughout the world. But unipolarity in the military sphere, narrowly defined, is not preventing the rapid development of multipolarity in the geopolitical and economic arenas – far from it. And the other great powers are content to let the US waste blood and treasure on its doomed attempt to recreate the post-first world war British imperium in the Middle East.'[4]

It is not straightforward whether US military might is an asset or a liability; it is both, in different arenas. American military specialization has its price, as noted before – institutionally, in tilting government and government spending toward the security apparatus; economically, by converting enterprises into military contactors; ideologically, by sustaining the superpower syndrome;

and culturally, by sustaining a brawny garrison state culture. Military force is also a temptation; if you have a hammer, every problem looks like a nail. American military specialization and deindustrialization are to an extent correlated and have precipitated the rise of other forces. Germany and Japan experienced 'economic miracles' once they let go of their military–industrial specialization – and in Japan's case were recruited as an industrial supply platform in the American cold war network, beginning with the Korean War. The US has been experiencing the reverse. American deindustrialization has been correlated with Asian industrialization. By promoting export-oriented growth and relocating garment, electronics, and high-tech plants in the Asian tigers and tiger cubs, American multi-nationals reaped super profits, acquired cheap consumer products, and boosted Asian industrialization. As a consequence American corporations neglected inward investment and the US yielded its share in global manufacturing to Asia and jacked up its trade deficit. This Pacific Rim symbiosis is now at the point that American trade and current account deficits have become unsustainable and for Asian vendors the risks of holding surplus dollars have begun to outweigh the benefits.

American decline is a byproduct of American hegemony. American geopolitics and attempts to prolong the unipolar moment have reinforced this shift. 'America's military bark is louder than its economic bite.'[5] The preoccupation with strategic primacy leaves the terrain to industrial newcomers and leaves space for industrial development in emerging economies, just as in the early twentieth century when Argentina, Brazil and other countries industrialized as the great powers were distracted by rivalry and war. Now, 'If and when the US finally lifts its gaze from the Middle East, it will find itself facing a much better placed and more formidable China.'[6] China, according to Arrighi, emerges as the beneficiary of globalization and as the real winner of the war on terrorism.[7] This makes sense if we add, beyond the Iraq war, the Asian crisis (discussed below). What is at issue in the twenty-first century turn to the east is the failure of both neoliberalism and neoconservatism – the two faces of American hegemony.

All advanced countries have been navigating the transition to a postindustrial economy and face increasing competition brought about by accelerated globalization. But only in the American case has this been combined with laissez-faire (i.e. no national economic policy), Dixie capitalism (low taxes, low services, no unions), military specialization (brawn over brain), and gargantuan debt – all factors that weaken the US's long-term position.

The picture is mixed. Some countries have an interest in continuing American hegemony of a kind; Asian exporters continue to depend on the US market and continue their vendor financing while others continue to view American military specialization as a savings on their defense budgets; yet the overall trend is away from US influence. The instability that the US has been creating is gradually producing a 'dispensable nation.'[8] The walkout by developing countries of the WTO ministerial meeting in Cancún in 2003, followed by the failure of the Free Trade Association of the Americas (FTAA) talks in 2004, illustrates the changing climate. The emergence of a new grouping of developing countries – the G22 led by Brazil, South Africa, China, and India – indicates growing clout, as if resuming the momentum of the Movement of Non-Aligned countries, at least in trade talks. At the international climate talks in Bali in December 2007, the message of delegates to the United States was blunt: provide leadership, or follow, or else get out of the way.[9]

The multipolar, multi-currency world that has been taking shape involves a shift in the global scenery in which the background becomes foreground, and vice versa. American dramas that used to be influential through the American century are becoming less salient. An economic trend report asks, 'Does it even matter if the U.S. has a cold?'[10] The decoupling scenario, cherished by the business press, in which the world economy makes up for the inevitable drop in American demand by an increase in Asian demand, is likely overdrawn. 'American consumers spent close to $9.5 trillion over the last year. Chinese consumers spent around $1 trillion and Indians spent $650 billion. It is almost mathematically impossible for China and India to offset a pullback in American consumption.'[11] Stephen Roach's point is taken; yet the bulk of demand in Asia and the Middle East is in capital goods: 'emerging markets' share of global capital spending has risen from 20 percent in the late 1990s to about 37 percent today.'[12] Thus decoupling refers to a different *kind* of demand; emerging markets' demand doesn't simply substitute consumer demand but concerns industrial inputs and commodities, which points to a parallel with the postwar boom, discussed below.

Global Realignments

> Globalization was something the rich countries did to the rest of the world – for the good of all, of course. Now it is beginning to feel like something someone else is doing to them.
>
> Philip Stephens, 2007[13]

Rather than hegemonic rivalry and transition, what is taking place are global realignments. China, India, Brazil, Russia, and South Africa emerge as alternative hubs for new combinations in trade, energy, and security. Path dependence on US hegemony is giving way to different arrangements, driven by several dynamics.[14] The world's most valuable company is PetroChina at $1 trillion, double the value of ExxonMobil. Four of the world's ten most valuable firms are now Chinese. The Industrial and Commercial Bank of China is the world's largest bank by market capitalization. China has overtaken the US as the premier location for foreign direct investment (2003) and is the world's largest exporter of technological products (2006). Japan, Korea, and Australia now export more to China than to the US. An article notes in passing 'America's mass market is second to none. Someday it will just be second.' 'In 2007 the BRICs' [Brazil Russia India China] contribution to global growth was slightly greater than that of the US for the first time. In 2007 the US will account for 20 percent of global growth, compared with about 30 percent for the BRICs.'[15] According to its 2005 report, *Mapping the Global Future*, the National Intelligence Council, the center of strategic thinking in the US intelligence community, projects the following trends:

> The likely emergence of China and India ... as new major global players similar to the advent of a united Germany in the 19th century and a powerful United States in the early 20th century will transform the geopolitical landscape with impacts potentially as dramatic as those in the previous two centuries. In this new world, a mere 15 years away, the United States will remain 'an important shaper of the international order,' probably the single most powerful country, but its 'relative power position' will have 'eroded.' The new 'arriviste powers,' not only China and India, but also Brazil, Indonesia, and perhaps others will accelerate this erosion by pursuing 'strategies designed to exclude or isolate the United States' in order to 'force or cajole' us into playing by their rules.[16]

East Asia 'is in the process of creating an economic bloc that could eventually comprise both a regional free trade area and an Asian monetary fund. Such a bloc would claim about one-fifth of the world economy, 20 percent of global trade, and $1.5 trillion in monetary (mostly dollar) reserves – about ten times those of the United States. Such an East Asian group would be a third economic superpower.'[17] The free-trade area of China and ASEAN established in 2002 is the world's largest, with a population of 1.7 billion and GDP of $2 trillion. 'While East Asia's share of global exports tripled to 19 percent between 1975 and 2001, exports within the region rose more than six fold in the same period.'[18] The re-Asianization of Asia has been ongoing for some time. A 'new silk road' has opened between East Asia and the Middle East and Eurasia, and China has expanded its role in Latin America and Africa. New trade pacts have taken shape, such as the Central Asia Economic Cooperation Organization and the Economic Cooperation Organization of Iran, Turkey, and Pakistan. 'New trade corridors show rising trade between Asia and the Middle East, Africa and Latin America. Already, Asian–European trade outstrips Asian–US trade.'[19]

These data come at us like a snowball that keeps getting larger as it approaches.[20] Until recently these changes concerned slow-moving trends, mostly in production, trade, infrastructure, and energy. But in the wake of the 2007–08 credit crisis they have gone into overdrive, unfold in international finance and, rather than being tucked away in economic trend reports and newspapers' back pages, have landed on the front pages. While the discussion whether the US subprime troubles have sparked a credit crunch, a banking crisis or a more serious solvency crisis is still ongoing, the ramifications have already spread.

With the Western banking system amid a double bubble popping – the American housing market and the easy credit bubble – emerging economies have remained largely unaffected, and headlines read: 'Emerging markets weather the financial turmoil,' 'Emerging market debt is the new safe haven.'[21] Because of cash buffers built in the wake of the Asian crisis, sovereign wealth funds from China to Singapore emerge as sources of liquidity. In the US they first met a closed door, were then eyed with suspicion, welcomed with trepidation,[22] to be finally enlisted in the rescue. 'Sovereign funds should lend support to equities,' a comment explains in the inimitable language of international finance: 'The acquisition by SWFs of strategic stakes in global companies has the potential to accelerate restructuring.'[23] Third, because of high petrol prices oil-exporting countries emerge as financial hubs. 'When financial market bubbles burst, a transfer of assets from the weak and undercapitalised to the strong and liquid invariably follows. The unprecedented scale of the credit bubble that burst last August [2007] suggests that the extent of the resulting wealth transfer will beggar belief.'[24]

China had been discreetly moving out of dollar assets and converting its reserves into energy and other assets in Africa, Latin America, Canada, and Iran. 'Chinese mining and energy companies have been investing in everything from copper in Afghanistan to tungsten in Tasmania,'[25] a pattern that drives up energy and commodity prices. The financial turbulence of 2007 has changed this pattern. The China Investment Corporation has invested $1 billion in Bear Stearns, $3 billion in Blackstone and $5 billion in a 10 percent stake in Morgan Stanley. The China Development Bank invested $3 billion in Barclays and the Industrial and Commercial Bank of China has taken a $5.5 billion share in 20 percent of Standard Bank of South Africa, a major transaction between two emerging markets institutions and the largest foreign direct investment in Africa.[26] China's State Administration of Foreign Exchange has bought shares in Australia's three largest banks at $176 million each. China's Social Security Fund is in talks with Carlyle, KKR and TPG. The overall strategy is clearly one of buying into overseas financial intermediaries.[27] According to the chairman of the China Investment Corporation, 'the fund sees a unique opportunity in the credit crisis in developed markets.'[28]

In the 'Big Red Checkbook' several trends come together: the declining dollar (down 23 percent against major currencies since 2002) depreciates Chinese dollar reserves and makes American assets relatively cheap. Combine China's massive current account surplus – its trillion-dollar question – with a turbulent financial environment, and buying into financial intermediaries and savvy becomes a necessity, on top of converting dollars into assets. Yet, as the financial crisis continues this strategy also looks problematic. The Chinese worry that they may turn into a source of 'dumb money' and 'there are rising complaints that the funds are foolish to shovel cash directly into risk-laden US banks when they could be using it in better ways, such as purchasing western commodity or manufacturing groups.'[29] In the background looms another problem.

> Wall Street's reputation, once its greatest asset, is also in jeopardy. Just as Detroit lost its reputation for high-quality cars, bankrupted dotcoms and worthless subprime debt are creating similar problems for Wall Street. You can't expect to keep your customers if you continually sell

them shoddy merchandise. Wall Street has spread hundreds of billions of dollars in losses around the world and in so doing shattered its reputation with some of its best customers.[30]

Besides Asian sovereign wealth funds, the other major investors to step into the breach are holders of petrodollars. The Abu Dhabi Investment Authority has taken a $7.5 billion share in Citigroup and the Kuwait Investment Authority invested $700 million in the Industrial and Commercial Bank of China, to pick a few out of a swath of investments by Mideast funds, again typically in financial intermediaries such as Merrill Lynch. Emerging economies seek to avoid the mistakes of Japan in the 1980s – buying cultural prestige objects that were economically vulnerable. The current trend in finance is that emerging markets are no longer targets or bystanders but become insiders. Financial markets provide liquidity, pool information, and share risk; emerging markets buying into Western financial powerhouses means that they become info insiders and market makers.

This reflects wider trends. For some time growth rates in the global South have been significantly higher than in the North and, unlike in the North, this is achieved while running current account surpluses. Initial public offerings in the BRIC represent 39 percent of the world total of IPOs in 2007 and have been to a large extent internally financed.[31] The center of finance tends to go to where the money is, and in Asia and the Middle East eleven countries have amassed nearly $4 trillion in reserves.

Niall Ferguson draws parallels between the bankruptcy of the Ottoman Empire in the 1870s, which necessitated the sale of Middle Eastern revenue streams to Europeans, and the current shift in the balance of financial power: 'Today the shift is from the US – and other western financial centres – to the autocracies of the Middle East and east Asia.... Debtor empires sooner or later have to do more than just sell shares to satisfy their creditors.'[32] The references – to satisfying eastern autocracies – are ominous.

To Ferguson this reversal of fortunes must come as a shock, for not long ago he used to advocate the expansion of American empire because, like its British predecessor, it brings the world democracy and prosperity.

The nearest parallel to the current financial crisis is what happened in the 1997–98 Asian crisis. 'The significant difference is that the debacle in Asia was followed by truly appalling losses in output and employment whereas the US is merely at risk of recession rather than slump. Not only is hypocrisy an issue here. There is folly when people in current-account glass houses throw protectionist stones.'[33] Deeper trends are also at issue. It is common for imperial and metropolitan centers to invest in emerging centers to reap profits from their value streams. As Arrighi notes, wars often played a crucial role.

> But once wars escalated, the creditor–debtor relation that linked the mature to the emerging centers was forcibly reversed and the reallocation to the emerging centers became both more substantial and permanent.... The mechanisms of the reversal varied considerably from transition to transition. In the Dutch–British reversal, the key mechanism was the plunder of India during and after the Seven Years' War, which enabled Britain to buy back its national debt from the Dutch and thus start the Napoleonic Wars nearly free from foreign debt. In the British–US reversal, the key mechanism was US wartime supply of armaments, machinery, food, and raw materials far in excess of what Britain could pay out of current incomes. But, in both cases, wars were essential ingredients in the change of the guard at the commanding heights of world capitalism.[34]

The *reversal of the creditor–debtor relation* is now unfolding between the US and Asia, especially China, and Mideast oil exporters. These developments are remarkable from several points of view. First, they unfold in international finance, the central powerhouse of Western hegemony. In emerging societies the awareness long exists that competition in production is but one phase and that the real competition with the West will unfold in finance. Second, it is through financial markets that the US has sought to penetrate and shape emerging markets. Third, it is easy to see that conservative overreach has led to imperial overstretch in wars in Afghanistan and Iraq, but the present credit bubble concerns economic and financial overreach. Wall Street was supposed to be smart. Fourth, finance is traditionally the terrain in which fading hegemons *retain* their supremacy when it has gone in economic, military, and political domains.

Structural adjustment after 1980 unleashed a series of financial crises culminating in the Asian crisis of 1997–98, which enabled US corporations to buy assets at fire-sale prices. In retrospect, this may have been the last major round of the US investing in and extracting profits from the global South. Since then the tide has begun to turn in earnest. First, the Asian crisis and IMF mismanagement signaled the *échec* of the Washington regime and financial institutions. Second, since then developing countries have taken the challenge of financial competition seriously. They scaled back their foreign debts and built financial buffers to weather storms. Third, in Asia the turn east and toward China began in earnest. Patterns of cooperation that hitherto had been simply economic became institutional, such as ASEAN+3 and the free trade agreement between ASEAN and China. These are among the signs of the new emerging balance of twenty-first century globalization. Whether they are viewed as clear indicators of change or as glyphs to decipher depends on one's perspective. Fascination with the momentum of hegemonic decline and system change may crowd out more important questions, such as what these changes portend for the world majority and the peasants and workers of the world. These are questions too large to be addressed here but I review some key variables.

First, in some respects the current period parallels the postwar boom when industrial growth in the US and Europe boosted demand for commodities. Fifty years on there is a similar boom, now centered on Asia, again boosting demand for commodities, again with an equalizing effect among countries, again with financial ramifications.

The IMF was a big factor when commodity prices were low and financial liquidity was a problem. Since 2002, however, the high commodity prices, especially for Latin American agro-mineral exports, have led to huge trade surpluses and allowed countries to pay off IMF debts and either self-finance or go to commercial private financing, avoiding IMF conditional borrowing.[35]

The twenty-first-century commodities boom reflects and contributes to the changes in global finance. 'There is a direct connection between easy credit in the United States, Wall Street irresponsibility, consumer excesses, unsustainable trade imbalances, the return of global inflation and the worldwide asset price boom,'[36] which is all true but skips the boom's main driver: industrialization and growth in emerging economies. In this setting industrialism in emerging markets combines with post-industrialism in advanced economies. Krugman's criticism that the 'Asian miracle' is a myth and a matter of new labor inputs in countries experiencing a demographic sweet spot without representing new productivity or efficiency, and Segal's question 'does China matter?',[37] are now well behind us. The rise of Asia is no fluke, and Asia represents much more than America's sweatshop. China has overtaken Japan to become the world's second largest spender on research and development. 'The IT sector in the Asia–Pacific region is set to expand nearly twice as fast as its North American counterpart in the five years to 2009, driven by explosive growth in countries such as India.'[38]

Another initial assessment was that the influx of massive new labor forces in China, India, and Eastern Europe lowers the unit cost of labor and is a boon to employers.

That long boom was made possible by the collapse of the Soviet Union and the opening of China (and to a lesser extent India) in the 1990s. The effect was to bring hundreds of millions of educated and low-waged workers into the framework of the international capitalist market – who, as the former US Federal Reserve chairman, Alan Greenspan, put it, have 'restrained the rise of unit labour costs in much of the world.' Along with the wider weakening of organised labour, the deregulated expansion of international finance and a flood of cheap imports into the rest of the world, the result has been a corporate profits bonanza and power grab which has shaped the economic and political temper of our times.[39]

Years down the road the picture looks different. Wages in China and other emerging economies have been rising, emerging markets face skills bottlenecks, and the bargaining position of skilled labor has strengthened. Thus, by another assessment, what is taking place is 'a major wealth shift from developed economies – that is, from less-skilled labor in developed economies – to emerging market workers.'[40] Now the 'China price' (based on the lowest labor cost) has become the China prize (for countries contending for Chinese investments).[41]

It is a cliché that 'The next phase of globalization will most likely have an Asian face.'[42] Yet the rise of Asia has often been viewed, by proponents and critics alike, in terms posed by the dominant Anglo-American perspectives. The usual account, from the World Bank to Thomas Friedman, is that the success of emerging markets is due to their adopting American liberalization, so the rise of Asia is an extension and assimilation of Anglo-American capitalism. The World Bank claimed the East Asian miracle as evidence that its prescriptions (liberalization, deregulation, export orientation) were valid. Alan Greenspan took the Asian crisis as testimony of the superiority of American capitalism. Thomas Friedman, likewise, views the rise of China and India as evidence of the virtues of liberalization. Robert Wade has criticized the World Bank's view as an instance of 'the art of paradigm maintenance.' Rodrik, Guthrie, Ha-Joon Chang and others argue that the Washington view overlooks the role of developmental states in establishing the conditions that make it possible to benefit from and steer liberalization.

Accounts of extreme labor exploitation in China and David Harvey's thesis of 'neoliberalism with Chinese characteristics' also apply Western yardsticks, in a different sense, and may underestimate the variety of China's developments, such as the role of small and medium-sized enterprises and the township and village enterprises (TVEs), as Rodrik, Arrighi and others argue. Criticisms of fast-lane capitalism in China and India are pertinent, yet viewing the East as an extension and variant of the West is too limiting.

It is more appropriate to view East Asia's rise in light of Asian historical dynamics and as a resurgence and comeback. According to Arrighi the twentieth-century convergence of East and West is due more to the West going East than to the East going West. A case in point is 'the displacement of vertically integrated corporations, such as General Motors, by subcontracting corporations, such as Wal-Mart, as the leading US business organization'; buyer-driven subcontracting arrangements were a distinctive feature of big business in late imperial China and remain so in Hong Kong and Taiwan.[43] Older, China-centered historical patterns are now being reproduced in East Asia. The role of the Chinese diaspora also reflects long-term trends.

The theme of the new Silk Road likewise points beyond the West. A new buzzword, 'Chime,' denotes China, India, and the Middle East. '"We want to go global by going east, not west", declared the chairman of Emaar Properties – one of the world's largest property developers, based in Dubai … "The west has got aging populations and ageing economies. The east is where the true glamour lies", according to a view echoed by top Asian and Arab business leaders.'[44]

Business studies and economic forecasting focus on emerging markets' business strategies and look at new forces in terms of business success – multinationals rising, establishing brands, whether companies can match Sony or Samsung's growth paths, and so on.[45] Merely counting aggregate growth rates and shares of world economic growth may be misleading. The term BRIC, coined by Goldman Sachs, conceals steep differences; in a phrase, 'India and China are the only real Brics in the wall.'

> The fundamental difference between China and India on the one hand and Russia and Brazil on the other is that the former are competing with the west for 'intellectual capital' by seeking to build top-notch

universities, investing in high, value-added and technologically intensive industries and utilizing successful diasporas to generate entrepreneurial activity in the mother country.... Russia and Brazil are benefitting from high commodity prices but are not attempting to invest their windfall in long-term economic development.[46]

China is building a hundred top-notch universities and India also actively competes in the race for brain power. Thus it matters to deconstruct the BRIC and the gospel of emerging markets. What matters is not just frontier capitalism and not just competition in terms of price but in terms of quality, technological upgrading and brand recognition, and ultimately what matters is what these developments entail for the rural majority and agriculture, for this is where the majority in China, India, Brazil, and South Africa are employed.[47]

American decline and growing multipolarity represent a re-organization of capitalism, not a crisis of capitalism. The crisis of capitalism, foretold since 1848, has been over 150 years in the waiting. The classic 'gospel of crisis' underestimates the ingenuity of capitalism and the ability of actors to turn crisis to advantage and underrates the heterogeneity and biodiversity of capitalism. What saves capitalism, ultimately, are *capitalisms* in the sense of different philosophies and institutions to organize the relations between markets, government, and society. 'Capitalism' in the singular is too crude a category. To understand the politics of the new globalization, capitalisms is a necessary analytical framework. The failure of the Washington Consensus, IMF mismanagement of Asian and Latin American crises and the structural weaknesses of the US economy lead countries to explore alternative policy frameworks such as the Beijing Consensus and the Latin American Bolivarian alternative. In view of the role of state forces in industrialization, trade policy and regional cooperation, and sovereign wealth funds in finance, the new globalization may involve a partial return to Keynesian economics, which also dominated during the post-war boom. Western clichés of 'command capitalism' and 'petro dictatorship' (referring to Russia, Venezuela and the Middle East) underestimate the role of the state and the lasting importance of developmental states. Also in the West the role of economic populism is growing, welfare-state liberalism is making a comeback, and the need for regulation is increasingly recognized, even in the US Congress.[48]

There are broadly three types of realignment: retrenchment, reformist, and revolutionary. Retrenchment refers to the kind of repositioning that protects national or corporate interests, such as central banks and investors reducing their dollar holdings. Reformist repositioning seeks changes that contain also future risk and enhance opportunities in finance, energy, trade, and security. The third type of realignment is revolutionary in seeking the overthrow of neoliberal capitalism and American hegemony. At present only Venezuela advocates that 'capitalism must be transcended', along with Zapatistas and activists in the World Social Forum and global justice movement. The position of groups such as al-Qaeda is reformist and defensive of positions in the Middle East and the Islamic world rather than revolutionary.

Since the global realignments are unfolding according to diverse rhythms and logics, what are emerging are complex irregular uneven moves pointing in different directions. As different centers of influence emerge the terrain shifts to other horizons, other problems, other aspirations. There is no need to romanticize alternative development paths, but there is no doubt that growing multipolarity is a step in the direction of global emancipation.

Notes

Chapter 1

1. Woodman 1990.
2. Lichtenstein 2001.
3. H. Kurtz, 'CNN Chief orders "balance" in war news,' *Washington Post*, October 31, 2001: C1.
4. Rampton and Stauber 2003: 127.
5. Bennett 2000: 213.
6. Klatch 1991.
7. E.g. Bagdikian 2004; McChesney 2004.
8. FAIR, 'In Iraq crisis, networks are megaphones for official views,' March 18, 2003, fair@fair.org.
9. Alterman 2003: 14.
10. 'Microsoft suffers stinging defeat,' *Financial Times*, September 18, 2007: 16.
11. See Angell 2004; Kassirer 2005.
12. See *Who killed the electric car?* Dir. Chris Paine, Sony Pictures Classic DVD, 2006. Thanks to Matt Youngblood for this reference.
13. H. Weitzman and F. Guerrera, 'Producers warned on insularity,' *Financial Times*, December 19, 2007: 6.
14. F. Guerrera and D. Pimlott, 'US bosses "lacking a global perspective",' *Financial Times*, December 4, 2007: 21.
15. The same author has compiled the series since 2003. David Wallechinsky, 'The world's 10 worst dictators,' *Parade*, February 22, 2004: 4–7; February 13, 2005; January 22, 2006; February 11, 2007.

16. P. Schneider, 'Across a great divide,' *New York Times*, March 13, 2004. Daniele Conversi 2007 uses the term 'liberal mono-culturalism.'

17. *New York Times*, May 18, 2004. Ali 2003.

18. *Newsweek*, June 16, 2003: 33.

19. Lazare 2007.

20. The ads appeared in June 2007 (capitals in original). In spring 2007 ads appeared in the *New York Times* sponsored by the Council for the National Interest Foundation that criticized Washington's Israel First approach.

21. June 7, 2007: A21.

22. R. Toner, 'Trust in the military heightens among baby boomers' children,' *New York Times*, May 27, 2003: A1–18.

23. Nye 2002.

24. J. Miller, 'There's a battlefield in each bedroom and backyard,' *New York Times*, March 2, 2003.

25. Der Derian 2002: 187; Orr 2004.

26. K.Q. Seelye, 'When Hollywood's big guns come right from the source,' *New York Times*, June 10, 2002: A1–19. On Hollywood and Pentagon cooperation, see van Ginneken 2007; Suid 2002.

27. Van Ginneken 2007: 166.

28. A. North Jones, 'The Navy and Marines salute America's warriors,' *New York Times*, November 26, 2002.

29. 'Spinning war, Pentagon aide chalks up wins,' *Wall Street Journal*, March 21, 2003: B1.

30. Eviatar 2003.

31. See Anderson 2004.

32. O'Brien 2004: 19.

33. Lieven 2004.

34. Lifton 2003: 11–12.

35. Seed 1999.

36. Kaplan 2005.

37. AP, 'Shooting puts spotlight on undercover marshals,' *News Gazette*, December 8, 2005.

38. Kaplan 2002: 119.

39. Scahill 2007: 6.

40. See Swofford's *Jarhead* (2003).

41. AP, 'Fallujah: Marine charges may not stick,' *News Gazette*, September 30, 2007: A7.

42. N. Podhoretz, 'World War IV: How it started, what it means, and why we have to win,' *Commentary*, September 2004; cf. John Brown, 'The return of the world warriors,' *TomPaine.com*, October 7, 2004.

43. Bolton 2007; Nederveen Pieterse 1992. Cf. Podhoretz 2003.

44. David Brooks, 'Heroes and history,' *New York Times*, July 17, 2007: A21.

45. Bennett 2000: 205.

46. See Grandin 2006.

47. Shohat and Stam 2007; Denzin 2007.

48. *Financial Times*, March 3–4, 2007: 1.

49. Sontag 2003: 13.

50. E. Bumiller, 'Keepers of Bush image lift stagecraft to new heights,' *New York Times*, May 16, 2003: A1–20; Auletta 2004.

51. 'Bush's fleurs du mal,' *New York Times*, May 27, 2007: WK11.

52. A. Ward, 'Americans shocked by Rome's rage,' *Financial Times*, June 11, 2007:3

53. Rice 2000: 49; Slater 1999: 19.

54. V. de Grazia, 'The selling of America, Bush style,' *New York Times*, August 25, 2002: WK4; cf. Steger 2005.

55. S.R. Weisman, 'On Mideast "listening tour," the question is who is hearing,' *New York Times*, September 30, 2005.

56. N. Klein, 'America is not a hamburger,' *Guardian Weekly*, March 21–27, 2002: 11.

57. S.R. Weisman and N. MacFarquhar, 'U.S. plan for Mideast reform draws ire of Arab leaders,' *New York Times*, February 27, 2004.

58. http://blogs.abcnews.com/theblotter/2007/05/us_government_g.html.

59. Schama 2003.

Chapter 2

1. Luttwak 1993: 117, 118.

2. Newfield 2003: 11.

3. Bagdikian 2003.

4. L. Browning, 'U.S. income gap widening, study says,' *New York Times*, September 25, 2003: B2; D. Gross, 'Income inequality, writ larger,' *New York Times*, June 10, 2007: 7; Frank 2007.

5. Wolff 2006, quoted in A. Stille, 'Grounded by an income gap,' *New York Times*, December 15, 2001: A15–17.

6. Krugman, 'Wages, wealth and politics,' *New York Times*, August 18, 2006: A19. 'In 2004 … households in the lowest quintile of the country were making only 2 percent more (adjusted for inflation) than they were in 1979. Those in the next quintile managed only an 11 percent rise. And the middle group was up 15 percent.… The income of families in the fourth quintile … rose by 23 percent. Only when you get to the top quintile were the gains truly big – 63 percent' (Lowenstein 2007).

7. Sklar 2003: 53; Scipes 2007.

8. Bob Herbert, 'Working harder for the man,' *New York Times*, January 8, 2007: A23.

9. Phillips 2004; Newfield 2003. According to former labor secretary Robert Reich, 'The richest 1 percent of America owns more than the bottom 90 percent put together' ('A society of owners,' *TomPaine.com*, September 7, 2004).

10. Arthur C. Brooks, 'The left's "inequality" obsession,' *Wall Street Journal*,

July 19, 2007: A15. Conservative here refers to economic pro-business conservatism.

11. Frank 2007; Phillips 1994.
12. Baker 2007.
13. Bagdikian 2003.
14. Phillips 2004.
15. Polly Toynbee, 'Inequality is the real enemy,' *Guardian Weekly*, August 19–25, 2005: 23; Wilkinson 2005.
16. E. Levin, '16% of children live in extreme poverty,' *Los Angeles Times*, May 1, 2003: A23; J. Madrick, 'Economic scene,' *New York Times*, June 13, 2002: C2.
17. Estes 2006.
18. B. Rose, 'Illinois incomes shrinking,' *Chicago Tribune*, November 17, 2005.
19. S. Roberts, 'In Manhattan, poor make 2 cents for every dollar to rich,' *New York Times*, September 4, 2005: 16.
20. See Kyle and Hansell 2005.
21. N. Munk, 'The super-rich, then and now,' *New York Times*, September 25, 2005: BU3; Bernstein and Swan 2007.
22. Phillips 2004; Ehrenreich 2003.
23. Frank 2007: xx.
24. S. Armour, 'Homelessness grows as more live check-to-check,' *USA Today*, August 12, 2003.
25. Todd Lewan, 'Please don't feed the homeless,' *News Gazette*, February 4, 2007: G1–3.
26. Wilson 2007b.
27. Lewan, 'Please don't feed the homeless.'
28. Sennett and Cobb 1972.
29. R. Pear and E. Eckholm, 'A decade after welfare overhaul, a fundamental shift in policy and perception,' *New York Times*, August 21, 2006: A12.
30. Bagdikian 2003; Kusmer 2001.
31. K. Hefling, 'Out of uniform, onto the street,' *News Gazette*, November 8, 2007: B1.
32. Schiller 2004.
33. Newitz 2003.
34. AlSayyad and Roy 2006.
35. Frank 2004: 55.
36. Tyler Cowen, 'Incomes and inequality: what the numbers don't tell us,' *New York Times*, January 25, 2007: C3; David Brooks, 'A reality-based economy,' *New York Times*, July 24, 2007: A23.
37. Cowen 'Incomes and inequality.'
38. Arthur C. Brooks, 'Happiness and inequality,' *Wall Street Journal*, October 23, 2007: 13.
39. L. Uchitelle, 'The richest of the rich, proud of a new gilded age,' *New York Times*, July 15, 2007: 1, 18–19.
40. Heckman and Krueger 2004; Lowenstein 2007.
41. Sklar 2003: 56.

42. Quoted in Alexander Stille, 'Grounded by an income gap,' *New York Times*, December 15, 2001: A15–17.
43. The superstar hypothesis refers to the winner-takes-all economy in which media reinforce celebrity rewards, from sports and entertainment to law and academia; discussed in Frank and Cook 1995.
44. Krugman 2002: 65, 66.
45. Daniel Gross, 'Income inequality, writ larger,' *New York Times*, June 10, 2007: 7.
46. Krugman 2002.
47. Phillips 2002; Beatty 2007.
48. Lowenstein 2007: 11. K. Guha et al., 'Gilded age: how a corporate elite is leaving Middle America behind,' *Financial Times*, December 21, 2006: 9. The S&P 500 is a commonly used benchmark for the overall US stock market, consisting of 500 stocks chosen for market size, liquidity, and industry grouping by a team of analysts at Standard & Poor's, one of the main rating agencies.
49. Henry M. Paulson, Jr, 'Our broken corporate tax code,' *Wall Street Journal*, July 19, 2007: A15.
50. Krugman 2002: 77; Krugman, 'Wages, wealth and politics,' *New York Times*, August 18, 2006: A19.
51. Phillips 1994: xv.
52. Reich 2007.

Chapter 3

1. Tickell and Peck 2003; cf. Harvey 2005.
2. Nederveen Pieterse 2004: ch. 1; Lind 2003; Applebome 1996, Cummings 1998.
3. 'Neoconservatism: A eulogy,' in Podhoretz 2004: 275, 282.
4. Krugman, 'Seeking Willie Horton,' *New York Times*, August 24, 2007.
5. Podhoretz 2004: 274.
6. Schneider 1988; Edsall 1988.
7. Ehrenreich 1990: 160. Mike Davis (1986) provides a political economy perspective on backlash politics.
8. Aldgate et al. 2000: xv.
9. Podhoretz 2004: 53–65.
10. Podhoretz 2004: 277.
11. Dallek 2000.
12. 'During the mid and late 1970s, lobbying groups, think-tanks and political action organizations were created; during the Reagan years, conservatives have been able to get on-the-job training in running the country.' Judis 1988: 137.
13. Lind 2003: 83–8.
14. Lind 2003: 94, 92; Judis 1988: 152–3. Nederveen Pieterse 2004: ch. 1.

15. Judis 1988: 158; Phillips 1969.
16. Bai 2003: 85; 2007.
17. Podhoretz 2004: 282.
18. *The State Journal-Register* (Springfield, IL), August 14, 2007: 5.
19. Krugman, 'Wages, wealth and politics,' *New York Times*, August 18, 2006: A19; cf. Ehrenreich 1990: 182.
20. Phillips 2006; Stiglitz 2003.
21. Phillips 2006: 268. Cf. Braudel 1984.
22. Editorial, *Financial Times*, June 25, 2007: 10.
23. Ninety-four countries experienced a severe currency crash between 1990 and 2003; R. Wade, *Financial Times*, January 5–6, 2008.
24. Phillips 2006: 293.
25. Duménil and Lévy 2004.
26. Sources include Gowan 1999; Brenner 2003; Phillips 1994, 2006.
27. T. Price, 'Greenspan has left more than a wall of worry to overcome,' *Financial Times*, July 31, 2007: 2; Roach 2005.
28. Brenner 2003.
29. Krugman, 'Bernanke and the bubble,' *New York Times*, October 28, 2005: A2.
30. Phillips 1994: 107.
31. Quoted in F. Harrop, 'The inflated Greenspan helped bankrupt America,' *Providence Journal* (RI), January 25, 2006.
32. Ibid.
33. G. Morgenson, 'Fair game,' *New York Times*, November 11, 2007: BU1.
34. In Phillips 2006: 284.
35. L. Uchitelle, 'The richest of the rich, proud of a new gilded age,' *New York Times*, July 15, 2007.
36. Petras 2007: 25–6.
37. Phillips 2006: 281. In 2005, 43 percent of US income was nonwage income; Petras 2007: 24.
38. B. Stein, 'In class warfare, guess which class is winning?' *New York Times*, November 26, 2006: BU3.
39. Dicken 2007: 384.
40. Levitt and Dubner 2005: 62.
41. Bogle 2006.
42. B. Masters and S. Scholtes, 'Payback time,' *Financial Times*, August 9, 2007.
43. Ibid.
44. W. Ferguson, 'Canada's black heart,' *New York Times*, July 18, 2007: A19.
45. Price, 'Greenspan has left more than a wall of worry to overcome.'
46. Phillips 1994: 109. Stiglitz 2003. Bogle 2006.
47. Masters and Scholtes, 'Payback time': 5.
48. L. Browning, 'The subprime loan machine,' *New York Times*, March 23, 2007: C1–4.
49. J. Dizard, 'Fed and Wall Street farther apart on the credit crunch,' *Financial Times*, August 21, 2007: 8.

50. R. Wade, *Financial Times*, January 5–6, 2008.

51. *Financial Times*, August 29, 2007.

52. Wade 2007.

53. J. Bater, *Wall Street Journal*, September 19, 2007: C8. G. Tett, *Financial Times*, November 23, 2007: 28. P. Marsh, *Financial Times*, October 29, 2007: 1.

Chapter 4

1. Lal 2004a: 37, 2. He takes this further in his book *In praise of empires* (Lal 2004b).

2. Wallerstein 1984: 38; Phillips 1994.

3. Robert Cox, quoted in Cohn 1999: 440.

4. Cohn 1999: 439; Kindleberger 1973; Keohane 1980.

5. Gilpin 1987: 90.

6. Cohn 1999: 439; Gilpin 1987.

7. Nederveen Pieterse 2001.

8. Pollack 2007.

9. Kuttner 1991: 12–13.

10. Gowan 1999; Soros 1998, 2003.

11. E. Becker and E.L. Andrews, *New York Times*, August 1, 2003.

12. Ferguson 2001: 127.

13. Nederveen Pieterse 2004: ch. 9.

14. Kennedy 1987: 436.

15. Popkin and Kobe 2003: 62; Melman 2001.

16. S. Diesenhouse, 'To save factories, owners diversify,' *New York Times*, November 30, 2003.

17. TNN, 'US Senator outsources speech to India,' *Times of India*, November 13, 2006: 11.

18. S. Rai, 'Short on priests, U.S. Catholics outsource prayers to Indian clergy,' *New York Times*, June 13, 2004: 13.

19. S. Lohr, 'Offshore jobs in technology: opportunity or threat?' *New York Times*, December 22, 2003.

20. Thacker 1999; Momani 2004.

21. Bergsten 2004.

22. Bello 2003.

23. Nederveen Pieterse 1998.

24. Kennedy 1987: 515.

25. Madrick 2003.

26. *Global Financial Stability Report 2003*, in H. Stewart, *Guardian Weekly*, April 3–9, 2003.

27. Quoted in S. Fidler and M. Husband, 'Bush foreign policy is "creating risks for US companies",' *Financial Times*, November 11, 2003. 'The important business winners in the past year have been defence companies "gratified that their equipment contributed to the successful invasion of Iraq".'

28. Borosage 2003.
29. Cf. Posen 2003.
30. Mann 2004.
31. See, e.g., Ikenberry 2001, 2002; Nye 2002; Luttwak 1998; Brutents 2000; Kagan 2004; Maynes 1997.
32. Danner 1997; Chace 1997.
33. See, e.g., Brooks and Wohlforth 2002; Odom and Dujarric 2004; see Chapter 6 below.
34. Daniels 2000; Waltz 2000; Lind 2001; Wallerstein 2003. Bellah 2002; Mandelbaum 2002.
35. Kupchan 1998; Hirsh 2003.
36. Wallerstein 1982.
37. Brenner 2003; Wallerstein 2003; Todd 2003; Reifer 2005.
38. Phillips (1994: 60–66) provides an extended and kaleidoscopic discussion of American decline. Ferguson (2004: 17) and Kolodziej and Kanet (2008) reject 'declinism.'
39. Schell 2003.
40. Moore 1972: 60.

Chapter 5

1. Nederveen Pieterse 2004: ch. 2, 'Empire as a metaphor.'
2. Bilmes and Stiglitz 2006 include opportunity cost and long-term care for the wounded. The CBO estimates $2.4 trillion for the Iraq and Afghanistan wars (per 2007), and a subsequent report brings the estimate to $3.5 trillion.
3. Extended discussion is in Nederveen Pieterse 1989 (ch. 2) and 2004.
4. Lewis 2004 provides a detailed account of donors to the Bush campaigns; Petras 2007.
5. S. Fidler and M. Husband, 'Bush foreign policy is "creating risks for US companies",' *Financial Times*, November 11, 2003; cf. Petras 2007. The Cato Institute (2004) has proposed exiting Iraq since 2004.
6. W.J. Holstein, 'Erasing the image of the Ugly American,' *New York Times*, October 23, 2005; J. Tagliabue, 'U.S. brands abroad are feeling global tension,' *New York Times*, March 15, 2003: B3.
7. Todd 2003: 134.
8. Brzezinski 1997: xiv. Cf. Meyer 2003.
9. According to President Carter's 1980 State of the Union Address, 'An attempt by any outside force to gain control of the Persian Gulf region will be regarded as an assault on the vital interests of the United States of America, and such an assault will be repelled by any means necessary, including military force.' In Robert Jensen, 'The bipartisan empire,' *TomPaine.common sense*, February 27, 2007.
10. Mitchell 2002.

11. M. Bunting, 'The age of anxiety,' *Guardian Weekly*, October 29–November 4, 2004: 5.
12. In ibid.
13. Nederveen Pieterse 2004: 45.
14. See Johnson 2004; Siddiqa 2007.
15. Bhagwat 2006.
16. E.g. Bacevich 2002; Brown 2003; Posen 2003. The war boom-arms boom connection and 'the "defense" origins of the new imperialism' is a classic theme, which in the US dates back to the 1940s; cf. Martin 1971.
17. Priest 2003.
18. Kibbe 2004; Hersh 2004.
19. Risen 2006.
20. Krauthammer 1990/91, 2002/03.
21. Fukuyama 2006.
22. Cooper 2000.
23. Nederveen Pieterse 2005.
24. Haass 1999: 38.
25. Note the earlier tradition of 'low intensity democracy'; Gills et al. 1993.
26. T. Weiner, 'A vast arms buildup, yet not enough for wars,' *New York Times*, October 1, 2004: C1–2.
27. L. Wayne, 'Pentagon spends without bids, a study finds,' *New York Times*, September 30, 2004: C1, 6.
28. Barnett 2004.
29. Lang's 2004 'Drinking the Kool-Aid' refers to Rev. Jim Jones's followers in Jonestown in 1978, who killed themselves by drinking Kool-Aid spiked with poison.
30. Gerecht 2001: 40.
31. Chalmers Johnson: 'The military adventurers of the Bush administration have much in common with corporate leaders of the defunct energy company Enron. Both groups of men thought they were the "smartest guys in the room"' (2008).
32. Todd 2004.
33. Qureshi and Sells 2003.
34. Letter, *Financial Times*, September 27–28, 2003.
35. Gowan 2006.
36. Freeman, 'Stability and chaos are just polls apart,' *Irish Independent*, September 25, 2003.
37. J. Dao, 'Warm reaction to bigger Pentagon budget,' *New York Times*, February 13, 2002.
38. Anup Shah, 'World military spending,' *Global Issues.com*, February 25, 2007.
39. Johnson 2008.
40. See Hutton 1995, 2002; Johnson 2004.
41. See Mandelbaum 2006. Emmanuel Todd's term 'arsonist–fireman' is discussed in the next chapter.

Chapter 6

1. Ignatieff 2004; Berman 2003; Smith 1994.
2. Press 2006; Farer 2008.
3. Parekh 1995: 82.
4. Mehta 1999; Semmel 1993.
5. Wallerstein 1984, 1995; Nederveen Pieterse 1989.
6. According to Judith Shklar (1984) liberal democracy is 'more a recipe for survival than a project for the perfectibility of mankind' as it seeks to protect citizens from the fear of cruelty, such as the cruelty of the Nazis (quoted in Keohane 2002: 87).
7. Ludden 2004.
8. See Berman 2008; Farer 2008; Ignatieff 2004.
9. Mamdani 2004.
10. Sestanovich 2005.
11. Brinkmanship in bargaining and corporate brinkmanship are common in the literature; but this concerns brinkmanship in economic policy.
12. O'Hanlon 1999.
13. Hersh 2004.
14. Scheuer 2004: 241–2.
15. Peters 1999; cf. Peters 2002, 2005.
16. Peters 2001: 5.
17. R. Drayton, 'Shock, awe and Hobbes,' *Guardian Weekly*, January 6–12, 2006: 5.
18. Kaplan 2002: 5, 6; 2003, 2005.
19. Barnett 2004: 305; B.K. Gagnon, 'New Pentagon vision transforms war agenda,' February 2005, http://globalresearch.ca/articles/GAG501A.html.
20. Kaplan 2005.
21. Rumsfeld 2002.
22. Boot 2003.
23. Kibbe 2004.
24. Hudson 2004.
25. Boyer 2002.
26. Todd 2004; Reifer 2005.
27. Risen 2006.
28. Stockwell 1991.
29. Johnson 2000.
30. See Mishra 2005.
31. Parker 2005; Lang 2004.
32. Todd 2003: 133, 132.
33. O'Hanlon 1999.
34. Stiglitz 2006 mentions 12 percent; by 2008 it has dwindled to less than 10 percent.
35. Klein 2007: 47.
36. Frank 2004.

37. B. Ehrenreich, 'Smashing capitalism,' *Huffington Post*, August 20, 2007.

38. Hutton 2002; L. Wayne, 'U.S. weapons, foreign flavor,' *New York Times*, September 27, 2005: C1–2.

39. Chris Giles, *Financial Times*, February 26, 2005; Warde 2005.

40. R. Hausmann and F. Sturzenegger, *Financial Times*, December 8, 2005: 13.

41. Greider 2004: 14.

42. Prestowitz 2005.

43. Paul Craig Roberts, 'The coming currency shock,' *Counterpunch*, November 16, 2004.

44. Levey and Brown 2005: 3.

45. S. Johnson, 'Indian and Chinese banks pulling out of ailing U.S. dollar,' *Financial Times*, March 7, 2005; P. Garnham et al., 'The buck stops where?' *Financial Times*, November 28, 2007: 11.

46. S. Roach, 'The rising risk of a hard landing,' *Financial Times*, November 1, 2005: 11.

47. Levey and Brown 2005: 6.

48. Setser and Roubini 2005: 195.

49. G. Magnus, 'The new reserves of economic power,' *Financial Times*, August 22, 2006: 11.

50. Maich 2005.

51. J. Grant, *Financial Times*, August 14, 2007: 2; see www.gao.gov/cghome/d071188cg.pdf.

52. CNN USA, October 13, 2007.

53. Akerlof and Romer 1993.

54. Holt 2007.

55. Stiglitz 2005: 133.

56. Trichur 2006.

57. Hamid Varzi, 'A debt culture gone awry,' *International Herald Tribune*, August 17, 2007.

58. Gowan 2006.

59. Lissner 1958; Green 1993. A comparison of the US and Rome is Murphy 2007.

60. *The Times*, January 15, 2003.

61. *Counterpunch*, February 16, 2006, www.counterpunch.org/hasso2152006.html.

62. Habermas 2003.

Chapter 7

1. Schneider 1988: 51; Judis 1988: 149.

2. Lipset quoted in Ehrenreich 1990: 189.

3. Perlstein 2007.

4. Laurie Spivak, 'How the Democrats were Betamaxed,' *AlterNet*, April 12, 2004.

5. G. Greenwald, 'New poll reveals how unrepresentative neocon Jewish groups

are,' December 12, 2007, www.salon.com/opinion/greenwald/2007/12/12/ajc_poll/.

6. Spivak, 'How the Democrats were Betamaxed.' Cf. Brock 2004.
7. Luntz 2007.
8. Bai 2003: 84.
9. Frank Rich, 'On television, torture takes a holiday,' *New York Times*, November 23, 2005: C1.
10. Stoller 2008: 23–4.
11. Didion 2003.
12. Salt Lake City, Utah, October 27, 2007, www.afterdowningstreet.org/?q=node/28179
13. Phillips 1994, 2006.
14. Frost 1992; O'Brien and Clesse 2002.
15. Kennedy 2001: 77.
16. Albert 1993; Dore 2000; Hutton 2002; Nederveen Pieterse 2004; cf. Rifkin 2004.
17. Suskind 2004.
18. Brenner 2003; Petras 2007; Madrick 2007. F. Norris, 'Bulging profits in U.S. often originate overseas,' *New York Times*, August 4, 2007.
19. 'For much of the world, the United States is now on sale at discount prices.' P.S. Goodman and L. Story, 'Foreigners buy stakes in the U.S. at a record pace,' *New York Times*, January 20, 2008: 1–14.
20. Wolf, *Financial Times*, 2007. Stephen Roach predicted a crash-landing all along (2005). Wallerstein (2003) adopted the image in the past tense, 'the eagle has crash-landed.'
21. Prestowitz 2005: 21. Cf. Lapham 1998.
22. Rennstich 2004.
23. Hayes 2007; P. Cohen, *New York Times*, July 11, 2007.
24. Madrick 2007; Krugman 2007; Kuttner 1991; Palley 1998; Blau 1999; Galbraith 2007; Derber 2003; Melman 2001.
25. Palley 2007: 22.
26. R. Reich, 'Fiscal balance is a false economy,' *Financial Times*, June 29, 2007: 9.
27. Phillips 1994: 113, 185–6; Greider 1992; Judis 2000.
28. Sherrill 2004: 57.
29. M. Darda in P.S. Goodman and F. Norris, 'No quick fix to downturn,' *New York Times*, January 13, 2008: 1, 18.
30. M. Whitney, 'The great credit unwind of 2008,' *Counterpunch*, January 29, 2008.
31. 'Today bitter self-made men – and their doppelgängers, the bitter but not quite well-to-do men – are all over the place. They have their own cable news network and their own TV personalities. They can turn to nearly any station on the AM dial to hear their views confirmed.' Frank 2004: 142.
32. B. Suh, 'American companies are falling behind in technology,' *Financial Times*, February 13, 2008: 9.
33. Johnson 2008.

Chapter 8

1. Frank 1998; Hobson 2004; Nederveen Pieterse 2006.
2. 'In the path of the storm,' *Guardian Weekly*, October 7–13, 2005: 5.
3. On the limited utility of military force, see the work by British Rtd. Gen. Rupert Smith (2005).
4. 'How the U.S. became the world's dispensable nation,' *Financial Times,* January 26, 2005. Cf. Khanna 2008.
5. H. Varzi, 'A debt culture gone awry,' *International Herald Tribune*, August 17, 2007.
6. G. Rachman, 'As America looks the other way, China's rise accelerates,' *Financial Times*, February 2, 2007: 13.
7. Arrighi 2007: 295, 301.
8. 'A new world order is indeed emerging – but its architecture is being drafted in Asia and Europe, at meetings to which Americans have not been invited…. Today the evidence of foreign co-operation to reduce American primacy is everywhere – from the increasing importance of regional trade blocs that exclude the United States to international space projects and military exercises in which the United States is conspicuous by its absence.' M. Lind, 'How the U.S. became the world's dispensable nation,' *Financial Times,* January 26, 2005.
9. T. Fuller and A.C. Revkin, *New York Times*, December 16, 2007: 1.
10. D. Gross, *New York Times*, May 6, 2007: BU4.
11. S. Roach, 'You can almost hear it pop,' *New York Times*, December 16, 2007: WK11.
12. Gross, *New York Times*, May 6, 2007.
13. P. Stephens, 'A global response is needed to the shifting world order,' *Financial Times*, November 30, 2007: 11.
14. An extended discussion of these trends is in Nederveen Pieterse 2008.
15. L. Uchitelle, 'When the Chinese consumer is king,' *New York Times*, December 14, 2003; D. Gross, 'The U.S. is losing market share, so what?' *New York Times*, January 28, 2007: BU5.
16. Fred Kaplan, '2020 vision,' *Slate*, January 26, 2005, http://slate.msn.com/id/2112697/.
17. Bergsten 2004: 91–2.
18. V. Mallet, 'Asia's impact, Part IV,' *Financial Times*, September 25, 2003: 21.
19. G. Lyons, 'The Middle East must loosen its ties to the dollar,' *Financial Times*, December 7, 2007: 11.
20. Snowballing is a metaphor used for East Asia's ascent beginning with Japan, then the Tigers, then China and India. Arrighi 2007: 2.
21. J. Chung, *Financial Times*, September 7, 2007: 22; J. Booth, *Financial Times*, August 29, 2007: 22.
22. J.F. Vail, 'A passage to the West for sovereign wealth funds,' *Financial Times*, October 31, 2007: 24.
23. G. Hoguet, *Financial Times*, December 13, 2007: 26. 'The reality [of sovereign

funds] is just another office full of harried people trying to find safe places to stick hundreds of millions or billions of dollars each month' (J. Dizard, *Financial Times*, November 27, 2007: 10).

24. J. Plender, *Financial Times*, January 3, 2008: 18.
25. G. Dyer and S. Tucker, 'China goes global, Part I,' *Financial Times*, December 4, 2007.
26. R. Gnodde, 'New actors play a vital role in the global economy,' *Financial Times*, November 12, 2007: 11.
27. 'Big US investment groups in China talks,' *Financial Times*, October 30, 2007: 1.
28. J. Anderlini, 'China's wealth fund's early coming of age,' *Financial Times*, December 21, 2007: 18.
29. G. Tett, 'Western banks face backlash as they hand out begging bowl,' *Financial Times*, February 8 2008: 22.
30. Peter D. Schiff, 'America loses another industry,' January 28, 2008, AsiaSentinel.com.
31. J. Authers, *Financial Times*, January 4, 2008: 11.
32. N. Ferguson, 'An Ottoman warning for America,' *Financial Times*, January 2, 2008: 9. Cf. ch. 4 above.
33. Plender, *Financial Times*, 2008.
34. Arrighi 2007: 234.
35. Petras 2007: 41.
36. Philip Bowring, 'Profligacy is America's problem,' *International Herald Tribune*, January 23, 2008.
37. Krugman 1994; Segal 1999.
38. 'America trails Asia's IT growth,' *Financial Times*, March 1, 2006: 13.
39. S. Milne, 'Credit crisis spells end of free market consensus,' *Guardian*, December 13, 2007; Prestowitz 2005.
40. F. Norris, 'Maybe developing nations are not emerging but have emerged,' *New York Times*, December 30, 2006: B3.
41. E.g. H. Weitzman, 'Peru takes faltering steps in bid to win China prize,' *Financial Times*, May 30, 2005.
42. P. Stephens, *Financial Times*, March 3, 2006: 13.
43. Arrighi 2007: 348. Cf. Arrighi et al., eds, 2003.
44. D. Barton and K. de Boer, 'Tread lightly along the new Silk Road,' *Financial Times*, January 30 2007: 15. Direct flights between the Gulf states and China increased from 7 a week in 2000 to 48 flights a week in 2006.
45. Agtmael 2007.
46. J. Lloyd and A. Turkeltaub, *Financial Times*, December 4, 2006: 13.
47. Cf. Amin 2006: ch. 3 on the peasant question; Nederveen Pieterse 2008.
48. M. Lind, 'The centre-ground's shift to the left,' *Financial Times*, November 28 2007: 11.

References

Agtmael, Antoine van. 2007. *The emerging markets century*. New York, Free Press.

Akerlof, G.A., and P.M. Romer. 1993. 'Looting: the economic underworld of bankruptcy for profit,' *Brookings Papers on Economic Activity* 2: 1–74.

Albert, M. 1993. *Capitalism against capitalism*. London, Whurr.

Aldgate, Anthony, James Chapman and Arthur Marwick. 2000. *Windows on the 1960s*. London, I.B. Tauris.

Ali, Tariq. 2003. *Bush in Babylon: the recolonisation of Iraq*. London, Verso.

AlSayyad, Nezar, and Ananya Roy. 2006. 'Medieval modernity: on citizenship and urbanism in a global era,' *Space and Polity* 10 (1): 1–20.

Alterman, Eric. 2003. 'How Europeans see America,' *The Nation*, February 10: 11–8.

Amin, Samir. 2006. *Beyond US hegemony?* London, Zed Books.

Anderson, Rick. 2004. *Home front: the government's war on soldiers*. Atlanta GA, Clarity Press.

Angell, Marcia. 2004. *The truth about the drug companies*. New York, Random House.

Applebome, P. 1996. *Dixie rising: how the South is shaping American values, politics, and culture*. New York, Times Books.

Arrighi, Giovanni. 2007. *Adam Smith in Beijing*. London, Verso.

Arrighi, G., T. Hamashita and M. Selden, eds. 2003. *The resurgence of East Asia: 500, 150 and 50 year perspectives*. New York, Routledge.

Auletta, Ken. 2004. 'Fortress Bush,' *New Yorker*, January 19: 53–65.

Bacevich, A.J. 2002. *American empire: the realities and consequences of US diplomacy*. Cambridge MA, Harvard University Press.

Bagdikian, Ben H. 2003. 'The secret of the permanent poor,' *San Francisco Bay Guardian*, October 22: 32.

———. 2004. *The new media monopoly*, 5th edn. Boston, Beacon Press.

Bai, Matt. 2003. 'Notion building,' *New York Times* Magazine, October 12: 82–7.

———. 2007. *The argument: billionaires, bloggers, and the battle to remake democratic politics.* New York, Penguin.

Baker, Dean. 2007. *The United States since 1980.* Cambridge, Cambridge University Press.

Baker, Kevin. 2003. 'We're in the army now: the GOP's plan to militarize our culture,' *Harper's Magazine*, October: 35–46.

Barnett, Thomas P.M. 2004. *The Pentagon's new map: war and peace in the twenty-first century.* New York, Putnam's.

Beatty, Jack. 2007. *Age of betrayal: the triumph of money in America, 1865–1900.* New York, Knopf.

Bell, Daniel. 1979. *The cultural contradictions of capitalism.* New York, Vintage.

Bellah, Robert M. 2002. 'The new American Empire: consequences of the Bush Doctrine,' *Commonweal* 129(18), October 25: 12–14.

Bello, Walden. 2003. *Deglobalization: Ideas for a new world economy.* London, Zed Books.

———. 2005. *Dilemmas of domination: the unmaking of the American empire.* New York, Metropolitan.

Bennett, Lance W. 2000. 'Media power in the United States,' in J. Curran and Myung-Jin Park, eds, *De-westernizing media studies*, 202–20. London, Routledge.

Bergsten, C. Fred. 2004. 'Foreign economic policy for the next president,' *Foreign Affairs* 83(2): 88–101.

Berman, Ari. 2008. 'The Democratic foreign policy wars,' *The Nation*, January 21: 16–22.

Berman, Paul. 2003. *Terror and liberalism.* New York, Norton.

Bernstein, P.W., and A. Swan. 2007. *All the money in the world: how the Forbes 400 make and spend their fortunes.* New York, Knopf.

Bhagwat, Niloufer. 2006. 'War in Iraq: business by other means,' *World Affairs*, 10(3): 106–27.

Bilmes, Linda, and Joseph Stiglitz. 2006. 'The economic costs of the Iraq War,' National Bureau of Economic Research, www.nber.org/papers/w12054.

Blau, Joel. 1999. *Illusions of prosperity: America's working families in an age of economic insecurity.* New York, Oxford University Press.

Blumenthal, Sydney, and T. Byrne Edsall, eds. 1988. *The Reagan legacy.* New York, Pantheon.

Bogle, John C. 2006. *The battle for the soul of capitalism.* New Haven, Yale University Press.

Bolton, John. 2007. *Surrender is not an option.* New York, Threshold.

Boot, Max. 2003. 'The new American way of war,' *Foreign Affairs* 82(4): 41–59.

Borosage, R. 2003. 'Sacrifice is for suckers,' *The Nation*, April 28: 4–5.

Bovard, James. 2006. *Attention deficit democracy.* London, Palgrave Macmillan.

Boyer, Peter J. 2002. 'A different war,' *New Yorker,* July 1: 54–67.

Braudel, Fernand. 1984. *The perspective of the world: civilization and capitalism, 15th–18th century,* vol. 3. New York, Harper & Row.

Brenner, Robert. 2003. *The boom and the bubble: the US in the world economy.* London, Verso.

———. 2004. 'New boom or new bubble?' *New Left Review* 25: 57–100.

Brock, David. 2004. *The Republican noise machine.* New York, Crown.

Brooks, S., and W. Wohlforth. 2002. 'American primacy in perspective,' *Foreign Affairs* 81(4): 20–33.

Brown, Seyom. 2003. *The illusion of control: force and foreign policy in the 21st century.* Washington DC, Brookings Institution.

Brutents, Karen. 2000. 'In search of Pax Americana (II),' *Russian Social Science Review* 41(3): 67–83.

Brzezinksi, Zbigniew K. 1997. *The grand chess game: American primacy and its geostrategic imperatives.* New York, Basic Books.

———. 2004. *The choice: global domination or global leadership.* New York, Basic Books.

Calhoun, C., P. Price and A. Timmers, eds. 2002. *Understanding September 11.* New York, New Press.

Cato Institute. 2004. *Exiting Iraq,* Report of the Special Task Force on Exiting Iraq. Washington DC.

Chace, James. 1997. 'An empty hegemony?' *World Policy Journal* 14, Summer: 97–8.

Cohn, T. 1999. 'Hegemony in the world economy,' in P.A. O'Hara, ed., *Encyclopedia of political economy,* vol. 1, 439–42. London, Routledge.

Conversi, Daniele. 2007. 'Democracy, nationalism and culture: the limits of liberal mono-culturalism,' *Sociology Compass* 1(3).

Cooper, R. 2000. *The postmodern state and the world order.* London, Foreign Policy Centre.

Cummings, Stephen D. 1998. *The Dixiefication of America: the American odyssey into the conservative economic trap.* Westport CT, Praeger.

Dallek, M. 2000. *The right moment: Ronald Reagan's first victory and the decisive turning point in American politics.* New York, Free Press.

Daniels, Robert V. 2000. 'Home alone: can America play the superpower role?' *Dissent* 47(4): 53–8.

Danner, Mark. 1997. 'Marooned in the cold war: America, the alliance, and the quest for a vanished world,' *World Policy Journal* 14: 1–23.

Dasgupta, Samir, and J. Nederveen Pieterse, eds. 2008. *Politics of globalization.* New Delhi and London, Sage.

Davis, Mike. 1986. *Prisoners of the American dream.* London, Verso.

Denzin, Norman. 2007. *Flags in the windows: dispatches from the American war zone.* New York, Peter Lang.

Derber, Charles. 2003. *People before profit.* New York, Picador.

Der Derian, James. 2002. '9/11: before, after, and in between', in C. Calhoun, P.

Price, and A. Timmers, eds, *Understanding September 11*, 177–90. New York, New Press.

Dicken, Peter. 2006. *Global shift: reshaping the global economic map in the 21st century*, 5th edn. New York: Guilford.

———. 2007. *Global shift: mapping the changing contours of the world economy*. New York, Guilford.

Didion, Joan. 2003. *Where I was from*. New York, Knopf.

Dore, Liz. 1996. 'The changing faces of imperialism,' *NACLA Report on the Americas* 30: 10–13.

Dore, Ronald P. 2000. *Stock market capitalism/welfare capitalism: Japan and Germany versus the Anglo-Saxons*. Oxford, Oxford University Press.

Duménil, Gérard, and Dominique Lévy. 2004. 'The economics of US imperialism at the turn of the 21st century,' *Review of International Political Economy* 11(4): 657–76.

Edsall, T. Byrne. 1988. 'The Reagan legacy,' in S. Blumenthal and T. Byrne Edsall, *The Reagan legacy*, 3–50. New York, Pantheon.

Ehrenreich, Barbara. 1990. *Fear of falling: the inner life of the middle class*. New York, Harper Perennial.

———. 2003. 'Class struggle 101,' *The Progressive*, November: 12–13.

Eichengreen, Barry. 2002. 'The United States and the world economy after September 11th,' in C. Calhoun, P. Price, and A. Timmers, eds, *Understanding September 11*, 121–35. New York, New Press.

Estes, Richard. 2006. *At the crossroads: development challenges of the new century*. Dordrecht, Kluwer Academic.

Eviatar, Daphne. 2003. 'The press and Private Lynch,' *The Nation*, July 7: 18–20.

Farer, Tom. 2008. *Confronting global terrorism and American neoconservatism: the framework of a liberal grand strategy*. New York, Oxford University Press.

Ferguson, Niall. 2001. 'Clashing civilizations or mad mullahs: the United States between informal and formal empire,' in S. Talbott and N. Chanda, eds, *The age of terror: America and the world after September 11*, 115–41. New York, Basic Books.

———. 2003. 'Hegemony or Empire?' *Foreign Affairs* 82(5): 154–61.

———. 2004. *Colossus: the price of American empire*. New York, Penguin.

———. 2006. 'Are empires past their prime?' *Foreign Policy* 156: 46–54.

Frank, A.G. 1998. *ReOrient: global economy in the Asian age*. Berkeley, University of California Press.

Frank, Robert H. 1999. *Luxury fever*. New York, Free Press.

———. 2006. *Richistan: a journey through the American wealth boom and the lives of the new rich*. New York, Crown.

———. 2007. *Falling behind: how rising inequality harms the middle class*. Berkeley, University of California Press.

Frank, Robert H., and P. J. Cook. 1995. *The winner-take-all society*. New York, Free Press.

Frank, Thomas. 2000. *One market under god: extreme capitalism, market populism and the end of economic democracy*. New York, Doubleday.

———. 2004. *What's the matter with Kansas?* New York, Henry Holt.

Friedman, Thomas L. 2005. *The world is flat.* New York, Farrar Straus & Giroux.

Frost, Raymond M. 1992. 'Losing economic hegemony: U.K. 1850–91 and U.S. 1950–90,' *Challenge* 35(4): 30–35.

Frum, David, and Richard Perle. 2004. *An end to evil: how to win the war on terror.* New York, Random House.

Fukuyama, Francis. 2006. *America at the crossroads: democracy, power, and the neoconservative legacy.* New Haven, Yale University Press.

Galbraith, James K. 2007. 'What kind of economy?', *Nation*, March 5: 15–18.

Gerecht, Reul Mark. 2001. 'The counterterrorist myth,' *Atlantic Monthly* 288(1), July–August: 38–42.

Gibson, J. William. 1991. 'The return of Rambo: war and culture in the post-Vietnam era,' in Alan Wolf, ed., *America at century's end*, 376–95. Berkeley, University of California Press.

Gills, B., J. Rocamora, and R. Wilson, eds. 1993. *Low intensity democracy.* London, Pluto.

Gilpin, Robert. 1987. *The political economy of international relations.* Princeton NJ, Princeton University Press.

Gowan, Peter. 1999. *The global gamble: Washington's Faustian bid for world dominance.* London, Verso.

———. 2006. 'The Bush turn and the drive for primacy,' in A. Colás and R. Saull, eds, *The war on terror and the American Empire after the Cold War*, 131–54. London, Routledge.

Grandin, Greg. 2006. *Empire's workshop: Latin America, the United States and the rise of new imperialism.* New York, Metropolitan.

Green, Vivian. 1993. *The madness of kings: personal trauma and the fate of nations.* New York, St Martin's Press.

Greider, William. 1992. *Who will tell the people? The betrayal of American democracy.* New York, Simon & Schuster.

———. 2004. 'The serpent that ate America's lunch,' *The Nation*, May 10: 11–18.

Haass, Richard N. 1999. 'What to do with American primacy?' *Foreign Affairs*, September–October: 37–49.

Habermas, Jürgen 2003. 'Understanding the fall of a Monument,' *Constellations*, 10(3).

———. 2006. *Time of transitions.* Cambridge, Polity.

Harvey, David. 2004. *The new imperialism.* New York, Oxford University Press.

———. 2005. *A brief history of neoliberalism.* New York, Oxford University Press.

Hayes, Christopher. 2007. 'Hip heterodoxy,' *Nation*, June 11: 18–24.

Heckman, James, and Alan Krueger. 2004. *Inequality in America.* Cambridge MA, MIT Press.

Helmus, Todd C. 2007. *Enlisting Madison Avenue: the marketing approach to earning popular support in theaters of operation.* Santa Monica CA, Rand.

Hersh, Seymour. 2004. *Chain of command: from 9/11 to Abu Ghraib.* New York, HarperCollins.

Hirsh, Michael. 2003. *At war with ourselves: why America is squandering its chance to build a better world.* New York, Oxford University Press.

Hobson, John M. 2004. *The Eastern origins of Western civilisation.* Cambridge, Cambridge University Press.

Holt, Jim. 2007. 'It's the oil,' *London Review of Books,* October 18.

Howard, Michael. 1981. *War and the liberal conscience.* Oxford, Oxford University Press.

Hudson, Leila. 2004. 'Lessons from Wal-Mart and the Wehrmacht: Team Wolfowitz on administration in the information age,' *Middle East Policy* 11(2): 25–38.

Hutton, Will. 1995. *The state we're in.* London, Jonathan Cape.

———. 2002. *The world we're in.* London, Little, Brown.

Ignatieff, Michael. 2003. 'The burden,' *New York Times* Magazine, January 5: 22–7 ff.

———. 2004. *The lesser evil: political ethics in an age of terror.* Princeton NJ, Princeton University Press.

Ikenberry, G. John. 2001. 'Getting hegemony right,' *National Interest* 63: 17–24.

——— ed. 2002. *America unrivaled: the future of the balance of power.* Ithaca NY, Cornell University Press.

Johnson, Chalmers. 2000. *Blowback: the costs and consequences of American empire.* New York, Henry Holt.

———. 2002. 'American militarism and blowback: the costs of letting the Pentagon dominate foreign policy,' *New Political Science* 24(1): 21–38.

———. 2003. 'The war business: squeezing a profit from the wreckage in Iraq,' *Harper's* Magazine, November: 53–8.

———. 2004. *The sorrows of empire: militarism, secrecy, and the end of the Republic.* New York, Metropolitan.

———. 2008. 'The economic disaster that is military Keynesianism,' *Le Monde diplomatique,* February.

Judis, John B. 1988. 'Conservatism and the price of success,' in S. Blumenthal and T. Byrne Edsall, eds, *The Reagan legacy,* 135–72. New York, Pantheon.

———. 2000. *The paradox of American democracy: elites, special interests, and the betrayal of public interest.* New York, Pantheon.

Kagan, Robert. 2004. 'America's crisis of legitimacy,' *Foreign Affairs* 83(2): 65–87.

Kaplan, Robert D. 2002. *Warrior politics: why leadership demands a pagan ethos.* New York, Random House.

———. 2003. 'Supremacy by stealth: ten rules for managing the world,' *Atlantic Monthly,* July/August: 66–83.

———. 2005. *Imperial grunts: the American military on the ground.* New York, Random House.

Kassirer, Jerome D. 2005. *On the take: how medicine's complicity with big business can endanger your health.* New York, Oxford University Press.

Kennedy, Paul. 1987. *The rise and fall of the great powers: economic change and military conflict from 1500 to 2000.* New York, Random House.

———. 2001. 'Maintaining American power: from injury to recovery,' in S.

Talbott and N. Chanda, eds, *The age of terror: America and the world after September 11*, 53–80. New York, Basic Books.

Keohane, R.O. 1980. 'The theory of hegemonic stability and changes in international economic regimes, 1967–1977,' in O.R. Holsti, R.M. Silverson, and A.L. George, eds, *Change in the international system*, 131–62. Boulder CO, Westview.

———. 2002. 'The globalization of informal violence, theories of world politics and the "liberalism of fear",' in C. Calhoun, P. Price and A. Timmers, eds, *Understanding September 11*, 77–91. New York, New Press.

Khanna, Parag. 2008. 'Waving goodbye to hegemony,' *New York Times* Magazine, January 27: 34–41.

Kibbe, Jennifer D. 2004. 'The rise of the shadow warriors,' *Foreign Affairs* 83(2): 102–15.

Kindleberger, Charles. 1973. *The world in depression*. Berkeley, University of California Press.

Klare, Michael T. 2003. 'Blood for oil: the Bush–Cheney energy strategy,' in *The New imperial challenge: Socialist Register 2004*, ed. Leo Panitch and Colin Leys, 166–85. New York: Monthly Review Press.

Klatch, Rebecca. 1991. 'Complexities of conservatism: how conservatives understand the world,' in Alan Wolf, ed., *America at century's end*, 361–75. Berkeley, University of California Press.

Klein, Naomi. 2007, *The shock doctrine: the rise of disaster capitalism*. New York, Penguin.

Kolodziej, Edward A., and Roger E. Kanet, eds. 2008. *From superpower to besieged global power: restoring world order after the failure of the Bush Doctrine*. Athens, University of Georgia Press.

Koval, J.P., L. Bennett, M.L.I. Bennett, F. Demissie, R. Garner, and K. Kim, eds. 2006. *The new Chicago: a social and cultural analysis*. Philadelphia, Temple University Press.

Krauthammer, Charles. 1990/91. 'The unipolar moment,' *Foreign Affairs* 70(1): 23–33.

———. 2002/03. 'The unipolar moment revisited,' *National Interest*, Winter: 5–17.

Krugman, Paul. 1994. 'The myth of Asia's miracle,' *Foreign Affairs* 73(6): 62–79.

———. 2002. 'How the permissive capitalism of the boom destroyed American equality,' *New York Times* Magazine, October 20: 62–7, 76–7, 141–2.

———. 2003. 'Strictly business,' *New York Review of Books*, November 20: 4–5.

———. 2003. *The great unraveling*. New York, Norton.

———. 2007. *The conscience of a liberal*. New York, Norton.

Kupchan, Charles A. 1998. 'After Pax Americana: benign power, regional integration, and the sources of a stable multipolarity,' *International Security* 23(2): 40–79.

Kusmer, K.L. 2001 *Down and out, on the road: the homeless in American history*. New York, Oxford University Press.

Kuttner, Robert. 1988. 'Reaganism, liberalism, and the Democrats,' in S.

Blumenthal and T. Byrne Edsall, eds, *The Reagan legacy*, 99–134. New York, Pantheon.

———. 1991. *The end of laissez-faire: national purpose and the global economy after the Cold War*. New York, Knopf.

———. 2007. *The squandering of America*. New York, Knopf.

Kyle, A.D., and B. Hansell. 2005. *The meth epidemic in America*. Washington DC, National Association of Counties.

Lal, Deepak. 2004a. *In defense of empires*. Washington DC, American Enterprise Institute Press.

———. 2004b. *In praise of empires*. London, Palgrave.

Lang, W. Patrick. 2004. 'Drinking the Kool-Aid,' *Middle East Policy* 11(2): 39–60.

Lapham, Lewis H. 1998. *The agony of Mammon: the imperial world economy explains itself to the membership in Davos, Switzerland*. London, Verso.

Lazare, Daniel. 2007. 'Lobbying degree zero,' *The Nation*, October 22: 23–28.

Levey, David H., and Stuart S. Brown. 2005. 'The overstretch myth,' *Foreign Affairs* 84(2): 2–7.

Levitt, S.D., and S.J. Dubner. 2005. *Freakonomics*. New York, Penguin.

Lewis, C. 2004. *The buying of the president 2004*. New York, Center for Public Integrity.

Lichtenstein, N. 2001. *State of the union: a century of American labor*. Princeton NJ, Princeton University Press.

Lieven, Anatol. 2002. 'The push for war,' *London Review of Books* 24(19), October 3.

———. 2004. *America right or wrong: an anatomy of American nationalism*. Oxford, Oxford University Press.

———. 2007. 'Relearning the art of diplomacy,' *The Nation*, November 19: 32–5.

Lifton, Robert Jay. 2003. 'American apocalypse,' *The Nation*, December 22: 11–17.

Lind, Michael. 2001. 'The not-so-super U.S. power,' *New Leader* 84(2): 18–20.

———. 2003. *Made in Texas: George W. Bush and the Southern takeover of American politics*. New York, Basic Books.

———. 2006. *The American way of strategy*. New York, Oxford University Press.

Lissner, Ivar. 1958. *The Caesars: might and madness*. New York, Putnam.

Lowenstein, Roger. 2007. 'The inequality conundrum,' *New York Times* Magazine, June 10: 11–14.

Ludden, David. 2004. 'America's invisible empire,' *Economic and Political Weekly*, October 30.

Luntz, Frank. 2007. *Words that work*. New York, Hyperion.

Luttwak, Edward N. 1993. *The endangered American dream*. New York, Touchstone.

———. 1998. 'Why we need an incoherent foreign policy,' *Washington Quarterly* 21(1): 21–31.

McChesney, Robert W. 2004. *The problem of the media*. New York, Monthly Review Press.

Madrick, Jeff. 2003. 'The Iraqi time bomb,' *New York Times* Magazine, April 6: 48–51.

———. 2007. 'How to fix our broken economy,' *The Nation*, October 22: 19–22.

Maich, Steve. 2005. 'Is America going broke?' *Macleans*, March 2.

Mamdani, Mahmood. 2004. *Good Muslim, bad Muslim: America, the cold war and the roots of terror.* New York, Pantheon.

Mandelbaum, Michael. 2002. 'The inadequacy of American power,' *Foreign Affairs* 81(5): 61–73.

———. 2006. *The case for Goliath: how America acts as the world's government in the 21st century.* New York, Public Affairs.

Martin, James J. 1971. *Revisionist viewpoints.* New York, Ralph Myles.

Maynes, Charles W. 1997. '"Principled" hegemony,' *World Policy Journal* 14: 31–6.

Mearsheimer, John J., and Stephen M. Walt. 2006. 'The Israel lobby,' *London Review of Books*, March 23: 3–12.

———. 2007. *The Israel lobby and U.S. foreign policy.* New York, Farrar Straus & Giroux.

Mehta, Uday Singh. 1999. *Liberalism and empire: a study in nineteenth-century British thought.* Chicago, University of Chicago Press.

Melman, Seymour. 2001. *After capitalism: from managerialism to workplace democracy.* New York, Random House.

Meyer, Karl E. 2003. *The dust of empire: the race for mastery in the Asian heartland.* New York, Public Affairs.

Mishra, Pankaj. 2005. 'The real Afghanistan,' *New York Review of Books*, March 10: 44–8.

Mitchell, Timothy. 2002. 'McJihad: Islam in the US global order,' *Social Text* 20(4): 1–18.

Momani, Bessma. 2004. 'American politicization of the International Monetary Fund,' *Review of International Political Economy* 11(5): 880–904.

Moore Jr, Barrington. 1972. *Reflections on the causes of human misery and upon certain proposals to eliminate them.* Boston, Beacon Press.

Murphy, Cullen. 2007. *Are we Rome? The fall of an empire and the fate of America.* Boston, Houghton Mifflin.

Nederveen Pieterse, Jan. 1989. *Empire and emancipation.* New York, Praeger.

———. 1992. 'The history of a metaphor: Christian Zionism and the politics of apocalypse,' in J. Nederveen Pieterse, ed., *Christianity and hegemony*, 191–233. Oxford, Berg.

———. 2001. *Development theory: deconstructions/reconstructions.* London, Sage.

———. 2004. *Globalization or empire?* New York, Routledge.

———. 2005. 'Tough liberalism: the Human Development Report and cultural liberty,' *Development and Change* 36(6): 1267–73.

———. 2006. 'Oriental globalization: past and present,' in Gerard Delanty, ed., *Europe and Asia Beyond East and West: towards a new cosmopolitanism*, 61–73. London, Routledge.

———. 2008. 'New globalization: towards the twenty-first-century international division of labor,' in S. Dasgupta and J. Nederveen Pieterse, eds, *Politics of globalization.* New Delhi and London, Sage.

——— ed. 1998. *Humanitarian intervention and beyond: world orders in the making.* London and New York, Macmillan and St Martin's.

Newfield, J. 2003. 'How the other half still lives: in the shadow of wealth, New York's poor increase,' *The Nation*, March 17: 11–18.

Newitz, Annalee. 2003. 'The poor are fat: five myths about the poor that are poisoning public policy,' *San Francisco Bay Guardian*, October 22: 28–9.

Nichols, John. 2005. 'Progressive cities in a conservative sea,' *The Nation*, June 20: 13–16.

Nye, Joseph S., Jr. 2002. *The paradox of American power: why the world's only superpower can't go it alone.* New York, Oxford University Press.

———. 2003. 'U.S. power and strategy after Iraq,' *Foreign Affairs* 82 (4): 60–73.

O'Brien, Geoffrey. 2004. 'Is it all just a dream?' *New York Review of Books*, August 12: 17–19.

O'Brien, P.K., and A. Clesse, eds. 2002. *Two hegemonies: Britain 1846–1914 and the United States 1941–2001.* Burlington VT, Ashgate.

Odom, William E., and R. Dujarric. 2004. *America's inadvertent empire.* New Haven, Yale University Press.

O'Hanlon, Michael. 1999. 'Defense and foreign policy: time to end the budget cuts,' in H.J. Aaron and R.D. Reischauer, eds, *Setting national priorities: the 2000 election and beyond*, 37–72. Washington DC, Brookings Institution Press.

Orr, Jackie. 2004. 'The militarization of inner space,' *Critical Sociology* 30 (2): 451–82.

Packer, George. 2005. *The assassin's gate: America in Iraq.* New York, Farrar Strauss & Giroux.

Palley, Thomas I. 1998. *Plenty of nothing: the downsizing of the American Dream and the case for structural Keynesianism.* Princeton NJ, Princeton University Press.

———. 2007. 'The flaws in Rubinomics,' *Nation*, May 21: 21–3.

Parekh, Bhikhu. 1995. 'Liberalism and colonialism: a critique of Locke and Mill,' in J. Nederveen Pieterse and B. Parekh, eds, *The decolonization of imagination*, 81–98. London, Zed Books.

Parenti, Christian. 2004. *The freedom: shadows and hallucinations in occupied Iraq.* New York, New Press.

Paris, Michael. 2002. *Warrior nation: images of war in British popular culture, 1850–2000.* London, Reaktion Books.

Perlstein, Rick. 2007. 'Will the progressive majority emerge?' *The Nation*, July 9: 11–16.

Peters, Ralph. 1999. *Fighting for the Future: will America triumph?* Mechanicsburg PA, Stackpole Books.

———. 2001. 'Stability, America's enemy,' *Parameters*, Winter: 5–20.

———. 2002. *Fighting for the future: will America triumph?* Mechanicsburg PA, Stackpole Books.

———. 2003. 'Constant conflict,' *Parameters* 97, http://carlisle-www.army.mil/usawc/Parameters/97summer/peters.htm.

———. 2005. *New Glory: expanding America's supremacy.* New York, Sentinel HC.

Peterson, Peter G. 2004. *Running on empty.* New York, Farrar Straus & Giroux.

Petras, James. 2006. *The power of Israel in the United States.* Atlanta GA, Clarity Press.

———. 2007. *Rulers and ruled in the US empire.* Atlanta GA, Clarity Press.

Phillips, Kevin. 1969. *The emerging Republican majority.* New Rochelle NY, Arlington House.

———. 1994. *Arrogant capital.* Boston, Little, Brown.

———. 2002. *Wealth and democracy: a political history of the American rich.* New York, Broadway.

———. 2004. *American dynasty.* New York, Viking.

———. 2006. *American theocracy.* New York, Viking.

Podhoretz, Norman. 2003. *The prophets: who they were, what they are.* New York, Free Press.

———. 2004. *The Norman Podhoretz reader,* ed. T.L. Jeffers. New York, Free Press.

Pollack, J.D. 2007. 'US strategies in northeast Asia: a revisionist hegemon,' in B.-K. Kim and A. Jones, eds, *Power and security in Northeast Asia: shifting strategies,* 55–95. Boulder CO, Lynne Rienner.

Popkin, J., and K. Kobe. 2003. 'Securing America's future,' *Challenge* 46(6): 62–109.

Posen, Barry R. 2003. 'Command of the commons: the military foundation of U.S. hegemony,' *International Security* 28(1): 5–46.

Press, Eyal. 2006. 'The left gets real: the promise – and pitfalls – of an alliance with foreign policy realists,' *Nation,* August 14–21, 2006: 28–32.

Prestowitz, Clyde. 2005. *Three billion new capitalists: the great shift of wealth and power to the East.* New York, Basic Books.

Priest, Dana. 2003. *The mission.* New York, Norton.

Qureshi, Emran, and Michael A. Sells, eds. 2003. *The new Crusades: constructing the Muslim enemy.* New York, Columbia University Press.

Rai, Ajai K. 2000. 'Media at war: issues and limitations,' *Strategic Analysis* 24(9).

Rampton, S., and J. Stauber. 2003 *Weapons of mass deception: the uses of propaganda in Bush's War on Iraq.* Los Angeles, Tarcher.

Reich, Robert B. 2007. *Supercapitalism.* New York, Knopf.

Reifer, Thomas E. 2005. 'Globalization, democratization, and global elite formation in hegemonic cycles: a geopolitical economy,' in J. Friedman and C. Chase-Dunn, eds, *Hegemonic declines: past and present,* 183–203. Boulder CO, Paradigm.

——— ed. 2004. *Globalization, hegemony and power: antisystemic movements and the global system.* Boulder CO, Paradigm.

Rennstich, Joachim Karl. 2004. 'The Phoenix cycle: global leadership transition in a long-wave perspective,' in Thomas E. Reifer, ed., *Globalization, hegemony and power: antisystemic movements and the global system.* Boulder CO, Paradigm.

Rice, Condoleezza. 2000. 'Campaign. 2000: promoting the national interest,' *Foreign Affairs* 79(1): 45–6.

Rieff, David. 2005. *At the point of a gun: democratic dreams and armed intervention.* New York, Simon & Schuster.

Rifkin, Jeremy. 2004. *The European dream.* New York, Tarcher Putnam.

Risen, James. 2006. *State of war: the secret history of the CIA and the Bush administration.* New York, Free Press.

Roach, Stephen S. 2005. 'Alan Greenspan,' *Foreign Policy*, January–February: 18–24.

Rumsfeld, Donald H. 2002. 'Transforming the military,' *Foreign Affairs* 81(3): 20–32.

Savage, Michael. 2005. *Liberalism is a mental disorder.* New York, Nelson Current.

Scahill, Jeremy. 2007. 'Blackwater's business,' *The Nation*, December 24: 6–7.

Schama, Simon. 2003. 'The unloved American,' *New Yorker*, March 10: 34–9.

Schell, Jonathan. 2003. *The unconquerable world.* New York, Penguin.

Scheuer, Michael. 2004. *Imperial hubris: why the West is losing the war on terror.* New York, Brassey.

Schiller, Bradley R. 2004. *The economics of poverty and discrimination*, 9th edn. Upper Saddle River NJ, Prentice Hall.

Schneider, William. 1988. 'The political legacy of the Reagan years', in Sydney Blumenthal and T. Byrne Edsall, eds, *The Reagan legacy*, 51–98. New York, Pantheon.

Schwenninger, Sherle R. 2007. 'Undebated challenges,' *The Nation*, November 19: 17–20.

Scipes, Kim. 2007. 'Neo-liberal economic policies in the United States: the impact on American workers,' *ZNet*, February 2.

Seed, David. 1999. *American science fiction and the Cold War.* Edinburgh, Edinburgh University Press.

Segal, Gerald. 1999. 'Does China matter?' *Foreign Affairs* 78(5): 24–36.

Semmel, Bernard. 1993. *The liberal ideal and the demons of empire: theories of imperialism from Adam Smith to Lenin.* Baltimore, Johns Hopkins University Press.

Sennett, Richard. 2006. *The culture of the new capitalism.* New Haven, Yale University Press.

Sennett, Richard, and Jonathan Cobb. 1972. *The hidden injuries of class.* New York, Knopf.

Sestanovich, Stephen. 2005. '"Maximalism" in U.S. foreign policy,' *National Interest* 79: 13–25.

Setser, Brad, and Nouriel Roubini. 2005. 'Our money, our debt, our problem,' *Foreign Affairs* 84(4): 194–8.

Sherrill, Robert. 2004. 'Why the bubble popped,' *The Nation*, May 3: 57–61.

Siddiqa, Ayesha. 2007. *Military Inc.* London, Pluto.

Shklar, Judith. 1984. *Ordinary vices.* Cambridge MA, Harvard University Press.

Sklar, Holly. 2003. 'Life in the new millennium,' *Z Magazine*, May: 53–9.

Slater, David. 1999. 'Locating the American Century: themes for a post-colonial perspective,' in D. Slater and P. Taylor, eds, *The American Century: consensus and coercion in the projection of American power*, 17–31. Oxford, Blackwell.

Slater, D., and P. Taylor, eds. 1999. *The American Century: consensus and coercion in the projection of American power*. Oxford, Blackwell.

Smith, Rupert. 2005. *The utility of force: the art of war in the modern world*. London, Allen Lane.

Smith, Tony. 1994. *America's mission: the US and the worldwide struggle for democracy in the twentieth century*. Princeton NJ, Princeton University Press.

Sontag, Susan. 2003. 'Courage and resistance,' *The Nation*, May 5: 11–4.

Soros, George. 1998. *The crisis of global capitalism*. New York, Public Affairs.

———. 2003. *The bubble of American supremacy*. New York, Public Affairs.

Stam, Robert, and Ella Shohat. 2007. *Flagging patriotism: crises of narcissism and anti-Americanism*. New York, Routledge.

Steger, Manfred B. 2005. 'American globalism "Madison Avenue-style": a critique of U.S. public diplomacy after 9–11,' in P. Hayden and C. el-Ojeili, eds, *Confronting globalization: humanity, justice and the renewal of politics*, 227–41. London, Palgrave.

Stiglitz, Joseph E. 2003. *The roaring nineties*. New York, Norton.

———. 2005. 'The ethical economist,' *Foreign Affairs* 84(6): 128–34.

———. 2006. *Making globalization work*. New York, Norton.

Stockwell, John. 1991. *The Praetorian guard: the US role in the new world order*. Boston, South End Press.

Stoller, Matt. 2008. 'Dems get new tools, new talent,' *The Nation*, February 11: 20–24.

Suid, Lawrence H. 2002. *Guts and glory*. Lexington, University Press of Kentucky.

Suskind, Ron. 2004. *The price of loyalty*. New York, Simon & Schuster.

Swofford, Anthony. 2003. *Jarhead: a Marine's chronicle of the Gulf and other battles*. New York, Scribner.

Thacker, S.C. 1999. 'The high politics of IMF lending,' *World Politics* 52: 38–75.

Tickell, A., and J. Peck. 2003. 'Making global rules: globalisation or neoliberalisation?' in J. Peck and H.W.-C. Cheung, eds, *Remaking the global economy: economic-geographical perspectives*. London, Sage.

Todd, Emmanuel. 2003. *After the empire: the breakdown of the American order*. New York, Columbia University Press.

Trichur, Ganesh K. 2006. 'Spectacular privatizations: perceptions and lessons from privatization of warfare and the privatization of disaster,' unpublished paper.

UNDP. 2005. *Human development report*. New York, Oxford University Press.

United Nations. 2007. *World economic situation and prospects 2007*. New York.

van Ginneken, Jaap. 2007. *Screening difference*. Lanham MD, Rowman & Littlefield.

Wade, Robert. 2007. 'Explaining US financial instability and its global implications,' *Open Democracy*, October 6.

Wallerstein, Immanuel M. 1982. 'Crisis as transition,' in S. Amin, G. Arrighi, A.G. Frank, and I. Wallerstein, *Dynamics of global crisis*. New York, Monthly Review Press.

————. 1984. *The politics of the world economy.* Cambridge, Cambridge University Press.

————. 1995. *After liberalism.* New York, New Press.

————. 2003. *The decline of American power.* New York, New Press.

————. 2004. *Alternatives: the United States confronts the world.* Boulder CO, Paradigm.

————. 2008. 'Entering global anarchy,' in S. Dasgupta and J. Nederveen Pieterse, eds, *Politics of globalization.* New Delhi and London, Sage.

Walt, Stephen M. 2005. *Taming American power.* New York, Norton.

Waltz, Kenneth N. 2000. 'Globalization and American power,' *National Interest* 59: 46–56.

Warde, Ibrahim. 2005. 'High price of the cheap dollar,' *Le Monde diplomatique*, March: 1–2.

Wilkinson, R.G. 2005. *The impact of inequality: how to make sick societies healthier.* London, Routledge.

Wilson, David. 2007. *Cities and race: America's New Black Ghetto.* London, Routledge.

————. 2007. 'City transformations and the global trope: Indianapolis and Cleveland,' *Globalizations* 4(1): 29–44.

Wolf, Alan, ed. 1991. *America at century's end.* Berkeley, University of California Press.

Wolff, Edward. 2006. *Top heavy: the increasing inequality of wealth in America and what can be done about it.* New York, New Press.

Woodman, Ross. 1990. 'Nietzsche, Blake, Keats and Shelley: the making of a metaphorical body,' *Studies in Religion* 29: 115–49.

Index